Keith Booth's life, like Caes roughly equal parts: a quartei and management training, a si ...iversity administration and finally anothe ... years in cricket scoring and writing. This is his ninth book, his seventh about a Surrey personality. His biography of Charles Alcock was shortlisted for the Cricket Society Book of the Year award in 2002, that on George Lohmann won it five years later.

Keith's wife, Jennifer, is an archivist and spent most of her career in the prestigious environment of the Tate Gallery. She now uses that expertise to identify and research sources for Keith's books and has been so heavily involved in this one that she is named as joint author.

Keith is official scorer for Surrey's 1st XI, Jennifer for the 2nd XI. Between them they have scored around 150 Test matches, ODIs and international Twenty20s. They see little of each other in the summer, meeting for the occasional breakfast to discuss who is to take responsibility for feeding the cats. In 2015 they celebrated their golden wedding anniversary.

Also by Keith Booth:

Atherton's Progress: From Kensington Oval to Kennington Oval
Knowing the Score: The Past, Present and Future of Cricket Scoring
His Own Enemy: The Rise and Fall of Edward Pooley
The Father of Modern Sport: The Life and Times of Charles W Alcock
George Lohmann, Pioneer Professional
Ernest Hayes: Brass in the Golden Age
Walter Read: A Class Act
Tom Richardson: A Bowler Pure and Simple

REBEL WITH A CAUSE

THE LIFE AND TIMES OF JACK CRAWFORD

KEITH AND JENNIFER BOOTH

First published in the UK by Chequered Flag Publishing 2016
PO Box 4669, Sheffield, S6 9ET
www.chequeredflagpublishing.co.uk

A CIP record for this book is available from the British Library

ISBN 9780993215254

To the players, staff, members and fans
of Surrey County Cricket Club;
an organisation dear to our hearts,
the native county of one and the adopted county of the other.

CONTENTS

	Foreword by Dominic Sibley	i
	Preface	iii
1	In the Beginning 1886-1900	1
2	My Boy Jack Repton 1901-05	11
3	Confidence and Ability Surrey 1904-05	21
4	Quite Exceptional South Africa 1905/06	33
5	Record Breaker Surrey 1906-07	43
6	Trip to KangarooLand Australia 1907/08	63
7	The Practical Cricketer Surrey 1908-09	81
8	Schism Surrey 1909	101
9	Return to KangarooLand South Australia 1909/10	119
10	Seasons in the Sun South Australia 1910-13	133
11	Play Ball North America 1913	151
12	Second Schism South Australia 1913/14	167
13	Frustration Otago 1914-1916	185
14	In the Army 1917-19	199
15	Back to Blighty Surrey 1919-21	209
16	Going Bananas Club and works cricket 1920-39	221
17	End of the Road 1922-63	231
	Acknowledgements	247
	Statistics	251
	Schism Correspondence	255
	Notes	262
	Bibliography	277
	Index	280

Foreword

It was the last first-class match of the 2013 season, the third of my career and my first at The Oval. I had just passed my eighteenth birthday. My performances in the previous two had been nothing out of the ordinary and I was determined to do well. There was nothing on the match: Yorkshire, our opponents, had already secured second place in the County Championship and Surrey were doomed to relegation. I opened the innings and batted time – over ten hours of it, including a partnership of 200-plus with our overseas player, Hashim Amla. It was a valuable experience and a privilege to spend time at the crease with a world-class batsman who went on to captain South Africa.

I was eventually out for 242. Although I did not realise it at the time, I had taken a number of records including becoming the youngest player to score a century and a double century for Surrey. Those records were both held by Jack Crawford and dated back to 1905 and 1908. It was quite a surprise to find out that I'd broken records that had been held for a hundred years!

At the time I knew next to nothing about Jack Crawford, but now I know a little more. He was a fast bowler and hard-hitting middle-order batsman; somebody who I now view as a role model, even though I am an opening batsman and leg-spin bowler. However, I do not recommend his off-the-field lifestyle – falling out with management and abandoning a wife!

Although he played as an amateur, his approach was nothing if not professional. What he has to say about analysing opponents, discipline and devoting hours to practice are valid and worthy of study by young cricketers a hundred years and more down the road.

I wish Keith and Jennifer every success with this book.

Dominic Sibley

PREFACE

This book might never have been written, let alone published. In 2012, I had decided that with *Tom Richardson: A Bowler Pure and Simple*, what has been called elsewhere my 'canon of Surrey biography' was as complete as it was ever going to be. It now contained half a dozen publications and seemed a balanced portfolio, containing the lives of two outstanding batsmen (Walter Read and Ernie Hayes), two world-class bowlers (George Lohmann and Tom Richardson), a wicketkeeper said to be the best in the world at the time (Ted Pooley) and a visionary administrator who changed the face of international sport (Charles Alcock).

Additionally, two of my major research resources had become less user friendly. The British Newspaper Library had upped sticks and migrated northwards to Boston Spa in Yorkshire and the excellent facility of The Oval Library had been commandeered for what in the twenty-first century is accorded a higher priority, space for corporate hospitality. The books and magazines are still there, but moved from a spacious well-lit area on the fifth floor of the pavilion (with natural daylight and an excellent view of the playing area – hence the attraction for ventures of a more commercial nature) to a smaller area on the ground floor which it shares with the club museum and trophy cabinets. Many of the books are out of reach to all but basketball players and while the seating is comfortable and ideal for an afternoon nap, the absence of natural light is a handicap to the deciphering of closely printed nineteenth-century texts. Furthermore, tables and space to spread out materials are limited. The library is no longer conducive to serious research.

Then, a couple of things happened to change my mind, one spread over a couple of days, the other a gradual discovery which took a little longer. Firstly, an emerging Surrey batsman by the name of Dominic Sibley scored 242 against Yorkshire becoming, at 18 years and 21 days, the youngest Surrey player to score a first-class century and double century, beating records which had stood for over a hundred years. Curiosity sent me off in pursuit of the previous holders. They turned out to be the same person, JN Crawford. In 1905, at the age of 18 years and 257 days, he scored 119 not out against Derbyshire at Derby, then three seasons later, at the age of 21 years and 186 days, had 232 against Somerset at The Oval.

Secondly, there was the dawning realisation that the reduction in London-based research facilities is more than counterbalanced by the increase in the resources available online. The British Newspaper Library is in the process of being digitised: its equivalents in Australia and New Zealand are further ahead (but they do have shorter newspaper histories and consequently less material). Old newspapers are not invariably correct, but are probably better than their modern counterparts which deal more in personalities and their private lives rather than facts. They provide a first draft of history, more so than family reminiscences and anecdotes distorted by time. Much material is syndicated and appears in more than one newspaper. The excellent New Zealand website, Papers Past, has proved of outstanding value.

In addition, the expanding number of genealogical websites, and the information which can be obtained from them, greatly facilitates research into family history. It is perhaps not as exciting or as satisfying as stumbling upon information after hours spent deciphering semi-legible microfilm, but in terms of the use of the scarce resource of time, it is infinitely more efficient.

Most followers of cricket with a sense of its history, especially those holding Surrey membership cards, will be aware of Crawford's prodigious performances as a schoolboy and of his rift with the club in 1909.

Not so many will know about what happened next: his time in Australia, New Zealand, Canada and the USA, his coaching, his business life, his two marriages, the weakening and rupturing of the links in a previously close-knit family and his conscious and deliberate passage into obscurity in the latter half of his life. This book attempts to fill those gaps. The super six in the canon of Surrey biography has become the magnificent seven.

Most lives are multi-faceted, but a theme can often be traced. If there is one in Jack Crawford's life it was that of rebellion against authority, of exercising his right to be different. Deference was part of the nineteenth-century social code, but with various social and left-wing movements, it was becoming less so by the twentieth. In the twenty-first century, most people would see programmes like *Downton Abbey* as good family entertainment, but also an anachronism left over from another age. Deference is now a privilege to be earned, not an automatic right, still less one bequeathed by inheritance and family wealth. Authority and its abuse are more easily challenged today. To an extent, as the son of an Anglican clergyman with the benefits of a public school education, Jack Crawford was on the fringes of the Establishment, but in so far as it was epitomised in the Surrey Committee, he was its adversary and had no hesitation in challenging it. At the time, his stance was seen by some as arrogant, foolhardy and stupid. With the benefit of hindsight it can be seen as self-confident, pioneering and courageous.

While preparing this book I was aware that Michael Burns was working on a similar project. We have neither spoken nor collaborated. He did not wish to do so. Between us we might have produced a better book than either of us has individually, but it was not to be. His effort hit his publisher's desk before this one did and he has the advantage of access to family scrapbooks, in particular those kept by Jack's father. Jennifer and I drew a blank when trying to contact Crawford's widow's relatives to elicit similar material. The scrapbooks throw light on Jack's early school cricket, and Michael's expertise as a filmmaker and access to some early newsreel footage has enabled him to analyse Crawford's bowling action in some detail. I was particularly gratified to see the contents of a cutting from *Reynold's News* in which Albert Trott shares my speculation that part of the reason for Crawford's absence at the beginning of the 1908 season was resentment at the appointment of Leveson Gower as county captain, despite his own strong claims.

However, it is where the scrapbooks run out that Burns' book, subtitled *The Chequered Life and Career of Jack Crawford*, itself becomes chequered. There are bits missing and bits that are just wrong. Burns has chosen to disregard two of the basic building blocks of biography, military records and divorce papers. It is not true that Crawford tried to 'dodge involvement in the Great War' as is suggested on the book's back cover, nor did he continue to visit his wife after joining the army. He had deserted her several months before.

It is certainly the case that, unlike many of his contemporaries, he never made the front and saw no fighting, but although his poor eyesight excluded him from the conscription lists, he volunteered on more than one occasion for the New Zealand Expeditionary Force, finally joining in July 1917 and being posted to Europe the following year. His reduction to the ranks was not because of a breach of military discipline, but rather because the exigencies of war necessitated rapid promotion to Quartermaster Sergeant, from which he was later relegated, having failed to qualify.

The split with Surrey in 1909 was pivotal in Crawford's fortunes – and in Surrey's and England's. Had a little more tact and diplomacy on either side tipped the balance the other way and Crawford's career in England continued, the history of the game and the pecking order of its greats might have been different. But life is full of 'what ifs?' and speculation. We have to deal with what is and what has been rather than what might have been. This book tries to do that.

Jennifer's enthusiasm throughout the project has been unbridled. She has been responsible for virtually all the research and literature analysis. I am delighted to name her as joint author of this book.

Keith Booth

The Crawford family in 1895: Rev JC Crawford in MCC blazer, Jack (aged 8) in front, Frank on the right, Reggie on the left.

1

In the Beginning

1886-1900

> 'The rich man in his castle,
> The poor man at his gate,
> God made them high and lowly,
> And ordered their estate.'

The third verse of Cecil Frances Alexander's children's hymn 'All Things Bright and Beautiful', published in 1848 with its endorsement of the class system, was omitted from subsequent versions, but until the First World War shattered the illusion, such simplistic, divinely ordered social classification went largely unquestioned. Class divisions were clearly delineated and those who, voluntarily or otherwise, did not fit the pattern were marginalised and recategorised as inmates of the prison, the workhouse or the lunatic asylum. It was with the latter that John Neville Crawford, known throughout his life as Jack, was most closely associated; not as an inmate, but as the sixth child (of seven) and third son of the chaplain of the Cane Hill Asylum, one of the largest institutions of its kind in the country. Crawford himself, however, though coming from a background which was the pillar of nineteenth century society, namely the Anglican Church, spent much of his life in conflict with the various authorities and institutions with which he was associated.

Jack's father had arrived at Cane Hill from Leicester where he had been curate at St Mary de Castro since 1875. He had been born in Hastings, son of Andrew Crawford, a Scottish schoolmaster who had settled in the south of England, ran his own school and after his retirement lived with the family. Rev John Charles Crawford was the first chaplain of the newly established asylum, geographically in Surrey, but built under the auspices of the London County Council. He was the successful candidate among those replying to an advertisement in *The Times* seeking a Chaplain and offering in return a package comprising a reasonable salary and a house on the premises.[1]

> SURREY. – CANE-HILL ASYLUM. – CHAPLAIN. – The Committee of Visitors of the Additional Lunatic Asylum, at Cane-hill, Coulsdon, Surrey, are about to appoint a CHAPLAIN to that Asylum. He must be in Priest's orders and not more than 35 years of age. The salary and emoluments will be £250 a year, with unfurnished house, gas, water and garden. All candidates for the appointment must send their applications and testimonials addressed to the Committee of Visitors of Cane Hill Asylum, and endorsed 'Application for the Appointment of Chaplain' to me, not later than the sixteenth day of August instant. The candidate appointed will have to be licensed to the office by the Bishop of the diocese.
>
> FREDK. HOOPER, Clerk to the Committee of Visitors. Sessions House, Newington, Surrey, SE, August 7th, 1883.

The advertisement was repeated a week later for what was clearly a responsible post, the remuneration for which compared favourably with the £150 and £100 on offer in the same column for a Senior Assistant and Junior Assistant Medical Officer.

Reverend Crawford and his wife moved to Coulsdon with their five young children, Edith, Beatrice, Vivian, Reginald and Audrey. Their sixth child, John Neville, was born in Coulsdon on 1 December 1886 and the family was completed eleven years later with a fourth daughter, Marjorie.

Mental illness is better understood today than it was in the late nineteenth century, but in any era such a post would have challenges and require a dedication above and beyond those associated with the job of a 'mainstream' clergyman.

There were relaxations, however, of which cricket was the major one. Now aged thirty-four, Rev JC Crawford had had half a dozen seasons with Kent in his twenties, an ambidextrous all-rounder with a reputation for being the quickest bowler in England, adding slow left-arm orthodox to his right-arm fast.[2] As a batsman, he was capable of switching from right to left-handed when in attacking mode, so although the nomenclature of switch-hitting may be relatively new – in cricket at least (its first known use in baseball is 1928) – the concept is not. He had played against the Australian Aboriginals in 1868, made his first-class debut for WG Grace's XI three years later and, even after his appointment at Cane Hill, continued to play for a number of teams including Surrey Club and Ground, Surrey 2nd XI and MCC. His last recorded appearance on Cricket Archive was at the age of sixty-five for Southwark Clergy against London Clergy at Lord's. Roger Packham says he played at the age of seventy-six for MCC against Whitgift Grammar School, though with what success is not mentioned.[3] A local newspaper report of his death, however, mentions a half-century for Merton at the age of seventy-five.[4] He remained a prominent member of both Surrey and MCC.

Jack's mother, Alice, was of Kentish stock, born in 1853, the daughter of Henry Gilbert and Catherine Sophia (née Brooks) and the eldest of a family of nine (six daughters and three sons). Her father was a ropemaker, employing seven men and five boys and, in addition to the family, the household included a housemaid and nurserymaid.[5] Five of the family had been born before 1861, the other four between then and 1871 by which date the ropemaking business had been relocated and reduced in size, now employing only two men and two boys and there were no longer any live-in servants.[6]

John and Alice were married at St James, Piccadilly in 1874, and began life together in Boxley where their first child, Edith, was born. That preceded the move to Leicester where John was curate at St Mary's before his appointment at Cane Hill. By 1881 one of Alice's brothers was a solicitor's clerk, one a commercial clerk and the third still at school. Her parents remained in Maidstone where her father was now a Ropemakers Foreman, graduating by 1891 to Manager of the Ropeworks.[7] So in an age of extremes of wealth and poverty, the family was somewhere in between, comfortably off, though without much to spare, but with the social standing appropriate to three sons who played their first-class cricket as amateurs.

Jack's elder brothers, Vivian (usually known by his second name of Frank) and Reginald had distinguished first-class careers. Frank followed spectacular performances at Whitgift School by playing for Surrey and then going on to the county of his birth, Leicestershire, as Secretary. Reginald, similarly qualified, played for a decade for the same county. His uncle, Major Frank (acting Lieutenant-Colonel) Crawford, the Reverend JC's younger brother, had played for Kent and later for Natal before dying in South Africa of wounds received in the Boer War. Jack's sisters were no mean performers too; Beatrice, known as Lesley, scoring a century for Woodmansterne against Caterham in 1899.

Jack's early schooling was at Glengorse Preparatory School in Eastbourne.[8] He was a contemporary of George Mallory, who was later to achieve fame as a mountaineer and lose his life attempting to conquer Everest. The school, in Chesterfield Road, had around seventy boarding pupils aged eight to fifteen under the headmastership of one Joseph Watson Willis.[9] Why Jack was sent there rather than a school nearer the parental home is not entirely clear, except the name suggests a Scottish connection and there is a family link with Sussex. The school was later to amalgamate with Hydneye School in Battle, near Hastings, Jack's father's birthplace and the location of his grandfather Andrew's school.

It may have been that the Rev Crawford had no wish for his son's early years to be over-influenced by the proximity of the lunatic asylum. Indeed when he later transferred to the local school of St Winifred's in Kenley he did so as a boarder, despite the fact that Kenley is a stone's throw from Cane Hill.[10] The connection between the Anglican church and education was a century old and a strong one: the Headmaster at

St Winifred's was Rev Isaac Wellbank Shilcock (MA Christ's College, Cambridge). In 1881 he had one Assistant Schoolmaster and one pupil boarding. By 1901 the establishment had expanded and had thirty-one boarders and a staff which now embraced an Assistant Master, Ernest Wright; a School Matron, Mary Bell; and three other teachers, James Coast, George McDonnell and a Swiss national, Hermann Fischer, a teacher of foreign languages, probably an extremely useful and economical package with the ability to instruct the boys in French, German and Italian.[11] Jack stayed here for a couple of years until 1901 when, at the age of fourteen, he began his four years at Repton.

That the Crawford family was steeped in the game is illustrated by the following in the 'Chats on the Cricket Field' series about the pivotal Rev John C Crawford who, from the stock of a cricket-loving father, played first-class cricket himself and had a brother and three sons who also did.

> The Asylum cricket ground lies just beyond the garden. At the present time the cricket ground, which has been a grass field for hundreds of years, is looking at its best, and is in surprisingly good condition for the time of year, but an afternoon's practice with the family is sufficient to convince a visitor that plenty of work can be got on the ball and that the members of the family, down to the youngest, know well enough how to take advantage of this. How on earth do a small boy of ten and a girl of thirteen learn to make a ball break quickly and to get up almost as high as themselves?
>
> The Crawfords are a standing illustration of the maxim that cricket runs in families. The grandfather, who is still living, and still takes a very keen interest in the doings of his descendants, played many years ago for the Gentlemen of Sussex, on the old Bo Peep ground at St Leonard's. His sons, the Rev JC and Major FF both played for Kent in the seventies, and have both kept well to the front ever since. The Major, who, as was announced in a recent issue of *Cricket*, is about to return to England, is invalided home after a severe attack of typhoid fever; he has done great things in army cricket in India and South Africa. Of the grandsons, VFS is well known as one of the most promising of the rising cricketers of Surrey. RT (Reggie) is now reading at home, and bids fair to make a name for himself both as a bat and a bowler – more particularly as a bowler; while JN (Jack) is certain to

> develop into a good all-round player, and already bowls a ball which has a lot of 'devil' in it.[12]

The small boy of ten is, of course, Jack, the girl of thirteen, his elder sister, Audrey.

Later, when Jack was established as a county and international cricketer, in an article about bowling technique he was able to look back and reminisce about his practices in the asylum grounds.

> To be a successful bowler implies that you must take wickets, or you cannot rank highly as a bowler. From my earliest days I have always practised a great deal. The facilities afforded me as a youngster in always having a large lawn to operate on when by myself, with the addition of the cricket ground at Cane Hill, adjoining the said lawn when my brothers were also able to practise with me, no doubt afforded me greater assistance than many another boy could possibly enjoy. The lawn tennis net for a background, and two umbrellas and grandfather's stick in the centre for a wicket, formed my materials; but as far as I can remember an old ball of full size was the assailant on the improvised wickets, for an ordinary tennis ball which youngsters used could never have smashed up the ribs in the manner they were smashed up. Often and often did my mother look out of the window when I had in imagination bowled Shrewsbury round his legs, or given Gunn a scorching hot one from 'a Richardson's' delivery, and mildly remonstrate that I must treat Father's umbrellas with a little more respect.[13]

Rev Crawford ran his own cricket team at Cane Hill, a team which often included himself and all three of his sons. Against Mr HB Sholl's XI on 20 April 1895, Frank, a few days beyond his sixteenth birthday, scored a chanceless 189 not out with two sixes, three fives and twenty-five fours. A precocious eight-year-old Jack made up the numbers. The team was strong enough to compete against the leading local club sides and had regular fixtures against Surrey Club and Ground and MCC Club and Ground.

As a family, the Crawfords made a huge impression on the local club and school scene.

> The record of the Crawford family for the season must be very satisfactory to its members. It is as follows: VFS 2913 runs and 57 wickets, RT 2330 runs and 185 wickets, young Jack Crawford 1089 runs and 210 wickets, and their father 'Parson' Crawford 1029 runs and 103 wickets.[14]

Many an inter-school match must have been ruined by the disparity between the talents of the Crawford family and the mediocrity of the other participants.

> Parson Crawford has still another boy pretty certain to make his mark in important matches presently. This is his third son 'Jack'. Playing for St Winifred's School, Kenley, at the end of last week against St Ann's, Redhill, he scored 117 and took nine of the ten wickets for no runs![15]

As the children grew up, left home, married and established their own lives and careers, family ties loosened a little, perhaps more than a little in Jack's case, but at this stage the Crawfords were a very close-knit family. 'Pa' Crawford, influential if not particularly wealthy, was a member of Surrey and MCC and Chairman of the Coulsdon Parish Council, and was closely concerned with his offspring's achievements, writing to an unidentified anorak of the time about Frank's achievements. Frank was at this time just eighteen, had played a couple of first-class matches – for Surrey against Oxford University and for the Gentlemen against the Players – and a handful of Club and Ground and 2nd XI games. In all cricket, however, his runs and wickets were of stratospheric proportions and his father, dominating the family, as he was to do throughout his life, endeavoured to discover whether Frank had established any kind of record.

The prominence of the family, both locally and further afield, can be gauged from the press report on Edith's wedding.

> The Rev JC Crawford, chaplain at the Cane Hill Asylum, is so well known and so esteemed in Coulsdon that such a happy event as the marriage of his eldest daughter, Miss Edith Margaret Crawford to Major Edward HM Elliott of Wolfilee, was certain to create an unusual amount of interest, more especially as the bride, who is the enviable possessor of a magnificent voice,

has also made herself very popular by her readiness and kindness in assisting in many efforts in the cause of charity. It is needless to say that the name of Crawford is known far beyond the bounds of this district, more than one of Mr Crawford's sons being cricketers of repute, well known in county circles. The marriage was performed in the presence of a large number of guests and friends at Coulsdon Church on Wednesday, the interior of which looked very pretty, being already decorated for the harvest thanksgiving services. The officiating clergy were the Rev JC Crawford, father of the bride, Rev Neville Dundas and Rev Granville Dickson. The bride was given away by her brother Mr RT Crawford and Major George Elliott acted as best man.

The bride was attired in a charming gown of ivory duchesse satin and wore a rope of pearls (the gift of the bridegroom) and a diamond and sapphire brooch bracelet (given by the tenants on the bridegroom's estate). Her bouquet of lilies and white roses had been sent from the bridegroom's home in Scotland. The bridesmaids were Miss Marjorie Crawford (sister of the bride) and Miss Marjorie Smith. Master John Colley acted as page. The bridesmaids were dressed in white silk and wore gold curb bracelets, the gift of the bridegroom; they also carried baskets of pink carnations and wreaths of a like flower. The bride's mother had a costume of blue and green shot silk and carried a bouquet of yellow chrysanthemums, the gift of the bridegroom. The service was fully choral. After the reception which was held at 'Glencairn' the bride and bridegroom – the former in a travelling costume of cinnamon brown – left in a motor-car for London en route to The Hague where the honeymoon will be spent.

The presents were numerous and costly.[16]

It was clearly a lavish affair, the guests including Lord Hawke and Sir Charles Dalrymple. Edith's musical talent was spread through the family. Reginald made his living from being a professional singer and Jack's baritone talents in this area were frequently called upon. On occasion, the whole family took part in fund-raising concerts.

On Wednesday a concert was held at St Andrew's Parish Hall on behalf of the Hall Furnishing Fund. The programme, varied, vivacious and most attractive, had been kindly arranged by the Rev JC Crawford and family. At the opening Mr Reginald and Miss Margaret Crawford joined in a delightfully rendered duet and was followed by a song 'A Jolly Old Cavalier' by Mr

> JN Crawford, a fine baritone, who afterwards gave 'Three for Jack' and received an encore. Miss Audrey Crawford, a pleasing soprano, gave 'Sleeping Tide' and 'A Spring Song'. The humourous [sic] part was well represented by Mr VFS Crawford in 'The tears rolled down his cheek' and 'The Sergeant of the Line'. Mr Reginald Crawford sang with much expression 'Thora' and 'I hear you calling me' and was also encored. Last but not least were the humourous and quaint stories contributed by the Rev JC Crawford. There was a large audience, the building being crowded.[17]

When Rev JC Crawford died, aged eighty-five in 1935, one son (Frank) and one daughter (Lesley) had pre-deceased him. *The Times* was able to report in its obituary notice:

> He is survived by two sons, RT and JN, and three daughters, all of whom in their younger days could bat and bowl far better than the average male club cricketer, and on more than one occasion a team of eleven Crawfords, including the grandfather, his two sons, grandsons, daughters, and nephews have taken the field.[18]

There can be few families who have had an impact on first-class cricket greater than that of the Crawfords. The Graces, Fords, Walkers, Hearnes, Lillywhites, Studds, Newhalls and Fosters spring to mind, but JN, his father, uncle and brothers (with some support from the sisters) are up there with the best of them.

courtesy of Phil Evans, oldukphotos.com

Repton School as Jack knew it, c.1906.

2

My Boy Jack

Repton 1901-1905

'The prominence of public schools in English social and political history may not be admired or even admirable, but it is inescapable', wrote Christopher Tyerman in his *History of Harrow School*. The games ethos was and remains an integral part of that style of education and it is inevitable that, while the mines and dark satanic mills of the north should produce in the main bowlers and professionals for the first-class game, the superior pitches, net facilities and professional coaching of the public schools should produce an apparently never-ending stream of amateur batsmen to grace what Neville Cardus called 'the golden age'.

Among those schools was Repton and among its products was Jack Crawford, an all-rounder whose cricket education was more than partially complete before he arrived there in the autumn term of 1901. The following summer, aged fifteen and playing with and against boys up to three years older, he had a huge impact on the school cricket team. By 1904 he was able to do what few before him or since have done; seamlessly make the transition from the school game to the first-class one. Whatever it might have done for his general character, in cricketing terms Repton was closer to his finishing school than the provider of his mainstream education, from which he emerged a fully-fledged county and international player.

Cricket was predictably and presciently optimistic about his prospects.

> The youngest of the Crawford brotherhood, John, has, I hear, gone up to Repton School. As there are good judges who regard him as likely to develop into an all-round player, even better than either VFS or RT, the Reptonians are sure to give him every possible opportunity. The present head of Repton School is the Rev LBJ Ford, one of the great cricket brotherhood of that name, which is of itself an assurance that no promising cricketer will lack a thorough trial.[1]

The late arrival – in October, when term began in September – is almost certainly explained by something that was not mentioned at the time, but emerged later in his military records when Jack joined the army in New Zealand: at the age of fourteen he had pleurisy, which does not seem to have affected his cricket, but may have restricted his opportunities for sport in the winter. He seems to have represented the school at football for one season, but not at hockey, at which he was later to prove competent at senior club level in both England and New Zealand.

CB Fry had captained a successful Repton side in 1891, but since then the school's cricket had experienced a lean decade. Writing half a century later, FRD'O Monro attributed the revival of Repton cricket in the first decade of the century to the appointment as Headmaster of cricket enthusiast and former captain, Rev Lionel Ford, who resurrected Old Reptonian cricket which, apart from the Speech Day match, had been discontinued. Two further appointments, those of Oxford Harlequins JW Stratton and KA Woodward had contributed, but success on the field was achieved in the main through Crawford's future England colleague, the also-bespectacled RA Young, and inevitably by Crawford himself.

The Headmaster, himself a Reptonian and School Captain two decades earlier, had played for Buckinghamshire and was one of a number of brothers who distinguished themselves in the game, none more so than his brother Francis, also a Reptonian, who gained a blue in all of his four years at Cambridge, played over a hundred matches for Middlesex and in all five Tests on AE Stoddart's 1894/95 tour of Australia. Cricket was back in the genes of the school.

> JN Crawford, unquestionably the greatest of Reptonian and probably of all schoolboy cricketers in the history of the game, was, even at seventeen, an all-round player of phenomenal maturity, capable of winning any school match almost by himself. He bowled medium pace with a perfect sideways, open-shouldered action and great accuracy; he could turn the ball from the off on the truest of wickets, could swing it late from leg and had a devastating fast ball. As a batsman, his power was extraordinary, whether in driving or forcing the ball off the back foot, but his attack was based on a fundamentally sound technique: he was a very fine field.
>
> Not many boy cricketers with another season to come at school have played in first-class cricket, but Crawford, who captained Repton in 1905, played for Surrey throughout August 1904, taking 44 wickets for 16 runs apiece, and with HC McDonnell, he bowled unchanged throughout a match against Gloucestershire; incidentally, his first innings in first-class cricket brought him 54 runs against the strong bowling of Kent.[2]

In his first summer at the school, 1902, still aged only fifteen and an automatic selection for a well-established and settled team, he made an immediate impact.

> Eight of the 12 who had had their colours in the previous year remained. It was in this year that J N Crawford came into the XI. He signalled his appearance by taking six wickets for 28 in the first match of the season against Wolverhampton, and followed this in the next match against the Incogniti by taking five for 10 in the first innings and four for 12 in the second; at the end of the year he headed the bowling averages with 40 wickets for 12 apiece.[3]

Jack had wickets against Repton's main rivals, Uppingham and Malvern, as well as an innings of 55 against the latter; albeit in a losing cause,

Malvern taking the match by 146 runs. Crawford's was the highest score in an innings of 140, the next highest being 26.

Old Reptonian WJ Ford, another of the Headmaster's brothers, making his last contribution to what was at this time a substantial Public Schools section in *Wisden,* wrote of the sixteen-year-old prodigy's 1903 season.

> I trust to be acquitted for my old school if I write down Crawford (Repton), brother of VFS and RT, as one of the best school bowlers I have seen for a long time. In delivery he resembles Jack Hearne very closely, with a similar open-shouldered swing, though he has not Jack's gallop up to the crease, but his varieties of pace are good, he breaks back cleverly, and bowls a good fast ball that comes with the arm... I have seen Crawford bowl excellently on a plumb pitch and shall be surprised if he does not make his mark in high-class cricket, should he get the chance, for he is quite a good batsman and an excellent field in the cover-point direction.[4]

Repton had beaten traditional rivals Uppingham for the first time for many seasons, Crawford taking nine wickets in the match. The celebrations reported in *Cricket* would now be reserved for something like winning the County Championship or an Ashes series, but at the time were not considered out of place for winning an inter-school cricket match and reflect what in retrospect was an exaggerated respect and significance given to the public school system and the place of sport within it.

> The Repton Eleven proved their excellence as an all-round side by their decisive victory over Uppingham at Uppingham. As it was the first success they had had over Uppingham for years – fifteen I have heard it stated – the victorious team had a right royal reception on their return after the match. They were drawn home in triumph from the station in a brake, and the exuberance of the admiring Reptonians went very near causing a nasty accident. As it was the pressure of those at the rear of the brake was at one time too much for the leaders, and it was fortunate, perhaps that what injuries there were were only slight, and that no great harm was done.[5]

It had been a substantial and significant victory by an innings and 27 runs. Crawford had taken six wickets in the first innings, none of his victims (numbers three and six to ten) making a single run between them. RA Young had then carried his bat for 129 in a total of 296 before Crawford had three more wickets as Uppingham were bowled out for a second time.

In the summer vacation of that year, 1903, still sixteen but only a year away from his first-class debut, he made an impact, firstly for Public Schools against MCC in a twelve-a-side match at Lord's, taking three for 22 in the first innings, all top order batsmen, then five for 27 in the second. In between, he had recorded the only double figure contribution (apart from extras) in a total of 78. The schoolboys came second by a large margin, but he had demonstrated his ability to compete – and perhaps more than that, influence an innings and a match – in men's cricket. Later, he attracted some media attention for his contribution to the Kensington Wanderers' tour of East Anglia.

> Mr JN Crawford, a younger brother of VFS and RT, and a member of this year's Repton XI, has been bowling admirably during the East Anglian tour of the Kensington Wanderers, for whom his father also plays. Right arm, medium to fast, he has a capital delivery, gets some work on the ball and with youth on his side – he is under seventeen – seems to have a bright future.[6]

Back in his own age group, he totally dominated a match on Sir Jeremiah Colman's estate at Gatton Park.

> An interesting match took place on Monday last at Gatton Park between the Young Surrey Amateurs under the leadership of Mr WT Graburn of the Oval, and a similar team selected and captained by Mr J Colman, junior, twelve playing on each side. The day was brilliantly fine and a splendid wicket had been prepared. Mr Colman's side batted first but were all out for 46 runs. The Young Surrey Amateurs, who have been making a tour in various parts of the county, were all out for 50, JN Crawford of Repton School, taking nine wickets for 18 runs. In their second innings Mr Colman's side declared when 84 for 4 wickets, Crawford carrying out his bat for 51, leaving the Young Amateurs 81 to get to win. This they eventually did, with one

wicket to go down, Crawford again securing nine wickets at the cost of 25 runs only. The teams and various visitors were entertained at lunch by Mr and Mrs Colman. The match was prolonged for a short time in order to bring it to a definite conclusion, the last man going in when three runs were required to win and which were obtained amid great excitement.[7]

By no means out of place in the first-class game, he was a colossus in schools cricket. The following year, Ford's successor, Captain WJ Seton wrote:

Crawford – now we prepare to assimilate our largest strawberry – was throughout the season superb, especially in the two school matches. Against Uppingham he took twelve wickets and against Malvern he secured the unlucky number of thirteen – unlucky indeed for Malvern. Throughout the season, he took 75 wickets, just three more than all the other bowlers of the eleven! Though undoubtedly the best public school bowler, with a strong claim to be considered the best amateur bowler of the year, as a bat he was of material assistance to put it mildly, to his school, his contribution in that department amounting to 759 runs, with an average of 54! As he is staying on at Repton another two years, there is probably trouble in store for Malvern, Uppingham and other opponents in 1905 and 1906.[8]

The following year, he wrote as follows:

During the past season one school and one player stand out above all others. To Repton and to Crawford the palm of collective and individual responsibility will be gracefully conceded by all rivals.

In all departments Crawford once again is pre-eminent, and words fail us when we attempt to estimate his superiority over all public school cricketers of the year. Whether we consider him as a lily, or as refined gold, the supply of white paint or gold leaf is utterly inadequate for the purpose of painting or gilding his reputation, according to whichever simile might be selected.[9]

Captain Seton's floral hyperbolic prose of the period reads uneasily today, but the point is clear. He goes on to say:

> His experience as an all-round schoolboy cricketer can only be challenged by two others in the last 40 years, and the names of those two occur readily to all followers of cricket. Time alone can decide whether Crawford will rival AG Steel and FS Jackson and captain a victorious English team ... in a Test match.[10]

It was not to happen. Time and other forces decided against it. Crawford was at times a successful stand-in captain for Surrey, but he never had the opportunity to captain his country. Indications are that he would have made a decent fist of it. There was a huge hole in Repton's team after he left.

> A period of comparative ill-successes was not surprising, as no school could hope to replace immediately so wonderful an all-round cricketer as JN Crawford.[11]

Writing towards the end of Crawford's first-class career in 1921, HS Altham was able to put Crawford's public school cricket into an historical context.

> THE CRAWFORD EPOCH
>
> 1904. The most sensational features of the season are centred in that group of ancient rivals – Repton, Malvern, and Uppingham. Each school possessed a pair of batsmen altogether out of the ordinary – Repton, JN Crawford and RA Young; Malvern GN Foster and AP Day; Uppingham CS Hurst and Clayton Palmer – but in bowling there was only one Crawford, and this determined the result of two out of the three matches.
>
> 1905 was Crawford's year. His side, not by any means a one-man show, played nine matches, drew one and won the other eight outright. This was my first year in the Repton XI, and, looking back to it what strikes me most was the extraordinary confidence we had in our captain. It is not too much to say that we one and all felt that, humanly speaking, it was almost impossible for us to lose a two-innings match, simply because in one innings or the other, or in both, he was bound to take charge of and dominate the game.
>
> I have no hesitation in saying that, as a bowler, Crawford was, in 1904 and 1905, better than when he bowled against S Africa in 1907, whilst as a

> batsman he was at once as sound and as powerful as any school player I can expect to see.[12]

Many years later, in an obituary tribute, Altham recalled with great affection the impact the young Crawford had on his contemporaries and in particular on the two main rival schools, Malvern and Uppingham.

> His reputation had preceded him at Repton and returning rather late for his first summer term there in 1902, he was at once summoned to the 1st XI nets where, I have always been told, he shot out his seniors as if, to quote Nyren 'they had been picked off by a rifle corps'.
>
> He was, of course, at once drafted into the XI and at the end of the term had taken 40 wickets for 12 apiece: his batting figures, though he made one 50, were very modest. The next three years are something of a fairy tale: in them he made 1929 runs and took 184 wickets, so that the overall figures for his four years at Repton read 2098 runs and 224 wickets. But even so they do not, I feel, fully reflect his dominance in inter-school cricket: to realise this, we may look at his performances in the two Repton 'Test matches' against Malvern and Uppingham, and remember that in these years, if Uppingham were of no more than average strength, Malvern were ranked, especially in batting, a formidable side. Here are the figures:
>
> - 1903 v Malvern 27, 10 wickets; v Uppingham 18, 8 wickets[13]
> - 1904 v Malvern 37 and 64, 13 wickets; v Uppingham 19 and 23, 12 wickets
> - 1905 v Malvern 139 and 12*, 9 wickets; v Uppingham 163, 10 wickets
>
> To these six matches, all of which Repton won by a very big margin, his total contribution was 512 runs and 62 wickets.[14] ... He was a magnificent fielder, to his own bowling, in the slips or, indeed, anywhere and he could throw like a catapult. As a batsman he combined in exceptional degree, orthodoxy and power. He watched the ball and played dead straight, with his head right over the line, and some of his greatest innings were played when the ball was turning enough to test any man's defence. But this was only the platform from which he could launch the truly formidable armament of his attack. I cannot believe that any schoolboy has been a better driver, alike in power and in control, along the ground or 'overhead', with one stride or 'down the track'. I was lucky enough to stay with him for some time during his 163 against Uppingham in his last school year (it took him about 2¼

hours) and can remember feeling 'a trifle apprehensive' as his drives whistled past me and the bowler to the boundary.

And how did he bowl? He had a beautiful action, with a smooth, but lively acceleration in the run-up, a pronounced lean away of the body as the 'spring was cocked' for delivery, a high full swing of the arm and a pronounced follow through. His stock ball was medium, but a medium diverted by subtle changes that Charles Fry himself found hard to detect. He could swing the ball away and when he chose a ball so fast that his slips would beg him to signal its advent. But he relied chiefly on the break back which the immense strength and elasticity of his fingers enabled him to impart. Even on the shining 'shirtfront' wickets which then prevailed in Australia he could make the ball turn; when he went there in 1907-8 with the England team he took 30 wickets in the Test matches and Clem Hill always maintained that under these conditions he was the greatest medium-paced bowler he had ever seen.

I have tried to record something of what the young Jack Crawford did and to outline a picture of the way in which he did it, but I cannot hope to convey what he meant to us who in those now distant days played with and under him. If he bestrode our cricket world like a Colossus, he remained natural and friendly with us all: he played his cricket with infinite zest and played it always as a game. Here was a Caesar: when comes another?[15]

The respect for bowling ability was not always mutual. RC Robertson-Glasgow writes that when Crawford was captain in 1905, he liked to employ Altham's lob-bowling in the nets so he could hear the tiles tumbling from the distant pavilion.[16]

Crawford retained fond memories of Repton, in later years endowing his home with the name of his former school. In 1924 Dr George Gilbert Stocks, Director of Music, set the words of John Greenleaf Whittier's 'Dear Lord and Father of Mankind' to Hubert Parry's tune from his oratorio 'Judith'. The resulting hymn tune became 'Repton' and the second line 'Forgive our Foolish Ways' is perhaps not inappropriate for the dramatis personae of this book, including at times the central character.

A rising star and his captain:
Crawford and Dalmeny on cigarette cards.

3

Confidence and Ability

Surrey 1904-05

It is a cliché but, like most clichés, more than partially true, that a state school education provides ability without confidence and a public school education provides confidence without ability. In Jack Crawford's case, he emerged from Repton with ample supplies of both, particularly as far as his cricket was concerned.

With the sense of entitlement which characterises the ex-public schoolboy, he began his Surrey cricket career fully aware of the social distinction between amateur and professional. There was already a family connection in that his elder brother Frank had preceded him at The Oval, but he left in 1903 to pursue a career as secretary and preserve his amateur status as a cricketer at Leicestershire, for which county he was qualified by birth. He did so with the good wishes of the Club and its President.

> The loss of Mr VFS Crawford was admittedly a great one, but it was quite impossible to control reasonable aspirations of a young cricketer, and they wished him every luck in his new position.[1]

Frank had replaced Walter Read as Surrey's Assistant Secretary in 1897 – as in Read's case, a part sinecure to allow him to play as an amateur. The Headmaster of Whitgift School, where Frank received his secondary education, had approached Surrey suggesting that the club might be interested in sponsoring the promising youngster through Oxford University, an education his clergyman father was clearly unable to afford. The Match Committee was predisposed to agree, but the main Committee, which held the purse strings, declined to approve the idea and Frank was diverted into stockbroking in London where he became a close friend of future Surrey captain Digby Jephson. Frank's relationship with the Committee had not had the best of starts and remained a fraught one. So Leicestershire seemed an obvious move, one which worked to mutual advantage.[2]

His younger brother had clearly made an early impression on the club: in 1903, at the age of sixteen, he was entrusted with the responsibility, along with Neville Knox who was two years his senior, of captaining one of the teams of trialists. Among them was a twenty-year-old Jack Hobbs who, with the deference appropriate to the era, referred to them as 'Mr' Crawford, for whose side he played, and 'Mr' Knox, acknowledging that they were both 'fine cricketers'.[3]

The Repton summer term over, Crawford played no 2nd XI cricket for Surrey, but did turn out regularly for the Young Amateurs at the end of August and beginning of September, playing every day from Monday to Saturday, taking the Sunday off and then playing another two. His contributions with the bat were nothing special in the first week, but with the ball he never took fewer than two wickets and had a best of seven for 25 against Teddington. In two matches the following week, however, he had a 51 not out and 45 and stepped up his bowling to have nine for 18 and nine for 26, followed by seven for 17. There were no ECB guidelines in those days to artificially curtail the number of overs which might be bowled by young cricketers. They could bowl as many as they liked, although there was no suggestion that Crawford was being overbowled or that his future prospects were being damaged.

The years of plenty of the late nineteenth century, which saw the county reap rewards from the outstanding performances of George Lohmann, Tom Richardson and Walter Read and the captaincy of John Shuter, had been followed by years of famine culminating in the chaotic year of 1904 when the club could not even find a regular captain. (It had, of course, to be an amateur one. The idea of a professional captain could not at the time be countenanced.) The situation was to change the following year with the advent of a regular captain in the form of Lord Dalmeny, a promising young professional by the name of John Berry Hobbs and, not least, the second season of the leading schoolboy cricketer of his generation, John Neville Crawford.

Towards the end of 1904 there was a hint of the stability to follow when JE Raphael became the nearest to a regular captain the county had that season. In its summing up the following year, *Wisden* recognised the contribution the new recruit had made in steadying the ship.

> At last, however, when the season was three parts over, a regular leader was found in JE Raphael ...While giving him every credit, however, for his good work both as captain and batsman, it must be said that he owed much to the presence in the eleven of an invaluable recruit in the Repton schoolboy, JN Crawford. Thanks to the bowling of that brilliant young cricketer Surrey finished up the season in far better form than they had displayed since May ... Crawford marked his first appearance for the county – against Kent at Canterbury – by getting 54 runs in irreproachable style when things were going badly for his side, but after that he was a bowler pure and simple, and an uncommonly good one. Bowling medium pace with plenty of variety he commanded, whenever the ground helped him, a really formidable off-break, and did so well as to earn golden opinions from all sorts of batsmen. Whatever the future may have in store for him it is safe to say there has been no public school bowler of equal class since CL Townsend, while still in the Clifton eleven, gained his first successes for Gloucestershire.[4]

Crawford had made his debut the previous August with a polished half century against Kent at Canterbury, making a seamless transition from schools to first class without touching club or 2nd XI cricket on the way: 'Crawford made a most promising debut making his 54 runs in an hour and three quarters in excellent style.' More than a century later he remains the youngest player to score a first-class fifty for Surrey. He came back to earth in the second innings, however: 'On Saturday, Crawford, who was not out 7 overnight, was badly run out.'[5]

Over the years public schools have had seemingly endless production lines of batsmen so, as a ready-made all-rounder, Crawford bucked that trend. In Kent's first innings, he had bowled twenty-six overs of what was called medium-pace off spin (more likely off cutters, but more of that later) and had taken three wickets for 112.

The pundits and local media were impressed by his debut and predicted a golden future.

> The success of JN Crawford in the first innings of Surrey was especially interesting and gratifying, only seventeen years of age, he is still at Repton College, and as a son of the Rev JC Crawford and brother of the famous Leicestershire players VFS and RT has special interest for local sportsmen. The critics were full of praise for he obtained top score for his side when things were going badly for them by skilful yet careful cricket. He also bowled in most promising style, and should he continue to develop his powers will rank amongst the very best players of the day. His brothers have hardly fulfilled the brilliant promise of a few years back, but Surrey men will hope that he will prove an exception and render the county the good services she stands in need of.[6]

The following week against Warwickshire at The Oval, Jack would soon have begun to appreciate that he was now bowling against *prêt-à-jouer* first-class batsmen rather than the work-in-progress *jeunesse dorée* of the upper echelons of Edwardian England. Opening the innings for Warwickshire was Tom Fishwick, himself a public school product, but now with a decade's experience of the first-class game. He was 34 short of his thousand runs for the season and played cautiously till he got there. Then:

> As soon as these runs were made he began to play his usual game, and hit JN Crawford for four fours in an over.[7]

Crawford went on to take the wickets of William Quaife and Arthur Lilley, internationals both, in a match which, after near equality on the first innings, ended in a draw. Larger hauls lay ahead. Mature for his years, he seemed to fit into the side well and in the next match, against Sussex, shared a partnership with the well-established Tom Hayward.

> When he was joined by Crawford the two men played so well that a long partnership seemed probable. But a misunderstanding, for which he could not be blamed, led to Crawford's downfall, run out when he had helped to increase the total by 43.[8]

It was the beginning of a lean spell with the bat. For six matches he failed to reach 20, but there were compensations with the ball as, beginning with a couple of four-fors against Middlesex, he turned in a number of impressive performances.

> Overnight the game had been left slightly in Surrey's favour, Middlesex being 110 runs behind with six wickets to fall, and although the pitch had dried during the night Lees and Crawford bowled so well that the home batsmen continued to experience difficulty in getting the ball away.[9]

Against Somerset at Taunton:

> When Somerset went in they could do very little with Crawford, who, bowling with excellent judgment, had all his men in difficulties from the first.[10]

The first day had been washed out and on a rain-affected pitch on day two he had six for 33 as Somerset were dismissed in their first innings for 69. Those in difficulties and losing their wickets to the precocious schoolboy included experienced cricketers Lionel Palairet, Len Braund and Sammy Woods. No such difficulties were experienced on the final day, however, as Somerset chased down 243 to achieve a seven-wicket win. Having three weeks earlier become the youngest batsman to score a half century for Surrey, Crawford now became the youngest bowler to take five wickets for the county. He was at the time aged 17 years and 266 days. No one younger was to emulate the achievement until Sam Curran, aged 17 years and 41 days, had five for 101 against Kent at The Oval in 2015.

The team moved on to Gloucestershire for Cheltenham week. No third day was required this time as the hosts failed to reach three figures in either innings and Surrey won by the comfortable margin of 119 runs.

> Their captain had a perfectly easy task in managing his bowling, for there was not the slightest necessity to change Crawford or McDonnell in either innings.
>
> Crawford and McDonnell again bowled so finely that no one except Jessop and Langdon could make any resistance against them. It is worthy of notice that McDonnell and Crawford bowled unchanged through both innings and that they each took ten wickets, seven in one innings and three in the other.[11]

Only on sixteen occasions have Surrey bowlers performed unchanged through both innings of a first-class match. This was the first of three in which Crawford was involved. George Lohmann alone, with four, has more.

So, in the first month of his first-class career, Jack Crawford had on his CV a fifty, a five-for and a ten-wicket match – until very recently the youngest to do any of these for Surrey and still unsurpassed in two of the three, Waqar Younis and Pat Pocock being well past their eighteenth birthdays when they had their first ten-wicket hauls.

In the next match, against the South Africans, Jack's first taste of international opposition, he bowled only nine overs in a match rained off after the second day with the visitors chasing a target of 461, but his partnership with John Raphael received an honourable mention in the 1 September issue of *Cricket*.

Nowadays players tend to look for days off or are 'rested' as part of a rotation policy. No such attitude at that time. If there were a day off, players tended to look for or be drafted into another match. On Saturday 3 September VFS, probably spending a weekend 'at home' before playing for Leicestershire at The Oval on the following Monday, played for

Kenley against Upper Tooting at Tooting and top-scored with 25 out of a total of 132.

His Leicestershire team then took an end-of-season drubbing in the last match of the season. It was the first time the brothers had opposed each other in a first-class fixture and the younger came out on top, he and his team emerging with the bragging rights as Surrey annihilated the midland county to the tune of an innings and 206 runs, Jack finishing his first season on a successful note with six for 28 in 11.1 overs. Among the six were his elder brother and captain, Charles de Trafford, first ball.

> JN Crawford met with great success at first, and when the total was 15 he claimed the first three wickets which had fallen ... The tail could do nothing against JN Crawford and Smith, who took the utmost advantage of their opportunities. Crawford had the satisfaction of bowling his brother VFS for two runs. By a quarter to four Surrey had gained a fine victory.[12]

In its end-of-season report, *Cricket* concluded 'It seems to be recognised that JN Crawford is the best youngster who has played for the county for many years.'[13] The local press had already formed the same opinion.

> Surrey finished their programme last week with a capital victory over Leicester, the brilliant bowling of young Crawford and Smith, following on the capital batting of Davis, Baker and Nice enabling Raphael's men to make a good finish to a disappointing season. It is, indeed, the worst season the county has experienced for twenty-three seasons. There is, however, much hope for the future in the fine way the team, as constituted for the last match with Raphael as captain, have played. If only the promise now held out is fulfilled and there is no reason why it should not be so. Surrey will not again for some years to come occupy such an ignominious position in the county championship table as she does at present. JN Crawford has proved a rare find for the county, only seventeen years of age, he concludes his first season in first-class cricket by occupying top place in the bowling averages for All England and for Surrey.[14]

Jack's success on the first-class scene did not prevent his turning out in the Young Amateurs' September fixtures. Indeed, on the day after the Leicestershire match finished, he had 62 not out and five for 26 at Guildford, then went on to improve on those figures with 115 not out against Teddington and eight for 30 against Brixton Wanderers.

The following year's Annual Report acknowledged his contribution.

> The hopeful feature of the season was the promising cricket displayed by some of the younger players in the later matches, the exceptionally fine play of Mr JN Crawford and the good form shown by Nice, Gooder, Davis and Goatly.

The following season, with Lord Dalmeny now firmly installed as captain of a more settled side, Crawford once again made the transition from almost permanent supremacy in schools cricket to more intermittent but nevertheless significant domination in county cricket.

The captain's parliamentary and other interests meant that he was unable to devote 100% of his time to cricket and was captain for only three seasons, but they were seasons which showed a marked improvement over earlier ones and at times indicated signs of resurrecting the glory years of the 1890s. Later, as Lord Rosebery, he would become a significant figure in the world of horse racing. Four years Crawford's senior, but still only in his early twenties, he forged a link with the returning Reptonian which certainly on the field and possibly off it, was a significant factor in establishing Surrey's stability.

An advantage of being an all-rounder, by which it is generally understood that competence in both batting and bowling is at a level sufficient to gain selection, is that if one discipline goes off a bit, then the other one can compensate. *Wisden* detected such a change of emphasis in Crawford's second season.

> JN Crawford bowled splendidly but on the whole his work with the ball was disappointing, and it was as a batsman that he seemed to have come on most since the previous season.[15]

Against Yorkshire at Headingley:

Lord Dalmeny and JN Crawford played a game which must have been an object lesson to the Yorkshiremen. The two batsmen showed plenty of pluck, and went for the bowling with the happiest results. For the seventh wicket they put on 62 runs in a little over three-quarters of an hour ... Crawford survived until nearly the end of the innings, being ninth out for 42, which had taken him an hour and three quarters to put together.

Crawford's was the highest score. Lord Dalmeny had 41, Rhodes 6 for 73 including Hobbs caught and bowled for a duck.

Hirst and Rhodes both played a fine game, but when Knox was put on to bowl with the total at 168, run-getting at once became a work of the greatest difficulty, and the tail could do nothing with him and Crawford.[16]

Jack finished with seven for 90 to restrict the northerners to a first-innings lead of 60, but Surrey's second innings collapse left the eventual County Champions only a handful of runs to win the match.

It was a better result at Derby the following week as:

Lord Dalmeny and JN Crawford made 69 in little over an hour by brilliant cricket. In the afternoon Crawford continued to play a fine game, and found a useful partner in Smith who helped him put on 79 in thirty-five minutes. Eventually Crawford carried his bat for 119, his first hundred in county cricket, after batting for two hours and a half.[17]

It contributed to a total of 550 and an eventual nine wicket win. His efforts gained him the award of a bat from the Cricket Committee.[18] He was 18 years and 257 days old at the time and remained the youngest player to score a first-class century for Surrey until Dominic Sibley did so at the age of 18 years and 21 days against Yorkshire at The Oval in 2013.

Against Warwickshire at Edgbaston 'Crawford and Lees also distinguished themselves with the bat.'[19] Then, back at The Oval against Northamptonshire in what *Cricket*'s report subtitled 'A remarkable match', the first day's play was restricted by the weather to an hour and a quarter, during which time Surrey advanced to 102 for 1. The second day was washed out completely after which on a rain-affected pitch:

> Wicket after wicket fell to Crawford, who was bowling at the top of his form ... Except for two overs Crawford and Smith bowled throughout both innings, the former taking eleven wickets for 44, the latter nine for 39.[20]

Northamptonshire capitulated for 55 and 32 to lose by an innings and 124 runs. Crawford's eight for 24 in the first innings were to remain his career best bowling figures. In its match report, *Wisden* added:

> Crawford, who was unchanged throughout the two innings, kept such a length and broke back so much as to be practically unplayable.[21]

A tie against Kent followed, the sixth and most recent first-class one in the county's history, then it was more outstanding batting against Leicestershire at The Oval.

> Crawford and Lord Dalmeny then came together, and by brilliant hitting scored 260 during a partnership of two hours and ten minutes. Lord Dalmeny was the first to go ... Crawford remained undefeated when the innings was declared closed at 549 for six wickets. His fine innings of 142 lasted about twenty minutes longer than that of Lord Dalmeny, and from first to last his play was most attractive; he hit twenty-two fours of which four came in one over from Gill.[22]

Wisden said, 'Crawford though going at such a pace played almost perfect cricket giving no actual chance.'[23] His innings lasted two and a half hours at a time when the length of innings was measured in time rather than balls received. Leicestershire managed to save the match, but for Crawford it marked a successful end to the Championship season in which he had averaged 45.6 with the bat and 19.5 with the ball. It was sufficient to earn him selection for Gentlemen of the South against Players of the South and the South against the Australians at the end-of-season Hastings Festival and for the Rest of England against the Champion County (Yorkshire) at The Oval. From all of these he emerged with credit.

Against the Players of the South:

> Few of the team could make anything of Crawford and Knox ... Crawford bowled unchanged through the innings ... Crawford was playing very well when heavy rain caused the game to be abandoned.[24]

His victims included Surrey colleague Tom Hayward who was to finish the season with 2,592 first-class runs at an average of 44.68.

In the match against the Australians, reduced to two days because of the weather, he had four for 69, including some distinguished opponents in the shape of Darling, Armstrong, Noble and Kelly.

Against the County Champions who were strong enough to beat the Rest of England:

> JN Crawford met with great success with the ball towards the end of the Yorkshire innings ... Crawford played a really good innings, showing plenty of confidence at a critical time ... Crawford bowled so well that the first four wickets fell for 48.[25]

In the same issue, the magazine was complimentary in its summing up of the season.

> Other young cricketers who with a limited experience of first-class cricket, greatly distinguished themselves were Lord Dalmeny, AH Hornby, JN Crawford, A Baker (Surrey) and Rothery.[26]

Jack had now finished at Repton and if he ever considered using his education to obtain gainful employment in the winter, the idea was soon eclipsed by an invitation from the MCC to spend a few months in the sunshine of South Africa along with Surrey colleagues, professionals Ernie Hayes and Walter Lees and amateur and future Surrey captain, Henry Leveson Gower.

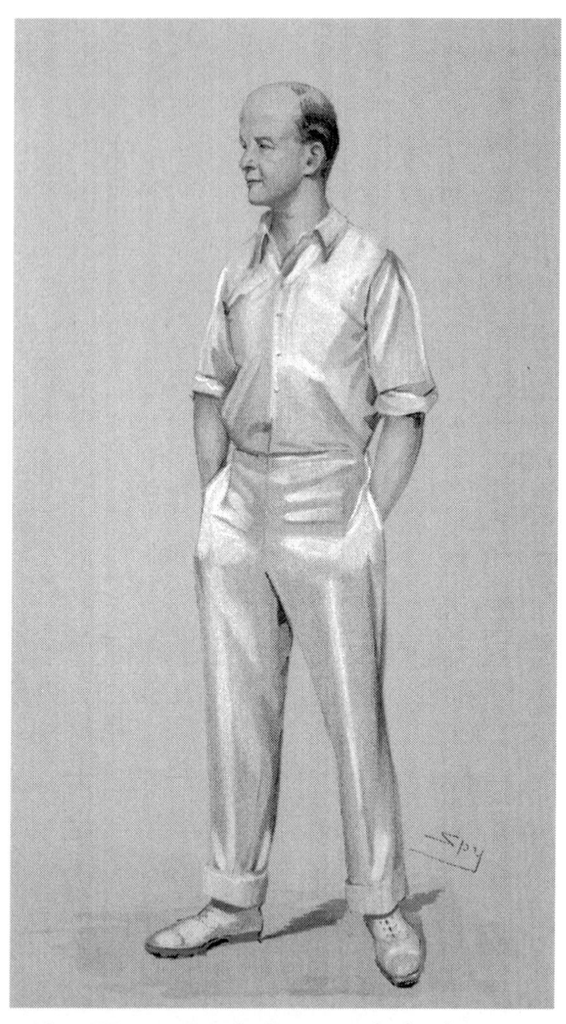

Plum Warner: Crawford's captain for his first taste of cricket abroad.

4

Quite Exceptional

South Africa 1905/06

South Africa played her first Test match in 1888/89 against CA Smith's privately funded touring side. Further matches had followed in 1891/92 against Walter Read's team and Lord Hawke's in 1895/96 and 1898/99. In all of these, the South Africans were heavily defeated. The emerging African cricketers had no answer to the bowling skills of Johnny Briggs, John Ferris, George Lohmann and Schofield Haigh and it is only tradition and convention and the reluctance of statisticians and governing bodies to unscramble what happened more than a century ago that has allowed these encounters to retain the status of Test matches. Only retrospectively were the teams called 'South Africa' and 'England'. There were no Tests in the 1901 or 1904 tours of England. The head-to-head score stood at South Africa 0 England 8.

That was all to change. Thanks in part to the efforts of English coaches, principally George Lohmann, and South African entrepreneurs such as Abe Bailey and James Logan, a new generation of cricketers was beginning to emerge spearheaded by the likes of James Sinclair, AD Nourse and the googly bowlers.

Private tours became less significant as the MCC assumed control of overseas tours in 1903, their teams playing as 'England' in Test matches and 'MCC' in other matches, both first-class and those against teams of players numbering greater than eleven. MCC took over on the condition that guarantees against financial loss were given by the local cricket authorities.

South Africa had performed better than the English public had given them credit for on the previous year's tour and justified an official tour by the MCC. Twenty-six games were to be played, which included five Test matches. A well-balanced side was chosen that was considered strong enough to uphold the honour of England but not so strong as to make the series a farce. Plum Warner, who had toured South Africa as a youngster in a previous series, was to lead the side.

Two years later Crawford was to keep a detailed record of the tour of Australia in his *Trip to KangarooLand*. On this occasion, still only eighteen and wide eyed with the novelty of it all, he was content simply to enjoy the experience at a time when it was exceptional for his countrymen to travel to foreign parts. However, Yorkshire's middle-order batsman David Denton was commissioned to write a series of articles for the *Yorkshire Post* which cast light on the non-cricket activities of the tourists at a time when it was possible to spend time between matches in places other than airports and hotels.

Almost every account of nineteenth and early twentieth century tours records rough weather at sea – in the Bay of Biscay, North Atlantic, Mediterranean or elsewhere – and this was no exception.

> The voyage out on the *Kinfauns Castle* was a particularly rough one. Windows in the smoking room and cabins were smashed by waves that broke over the ship, and the team was relieved to arrive in Cape Town on 28 November 1905.[1]

Denton reported in more detail for his newspaper, timing the earliest storms to within a few hours of leaving Southampton.

> We left Southampton at five o'clock, November 11 and in six hours' time had run into a very heavy sea. It got worse and worse as we went along, and by the time we got into the Bay it was very rough indeed. Huge waves swept

> right over the boat. The bulwarks were stove in, and the gangways carried clean away. All the windows and furniture of the smoke-room were also broken and one of the sailors had his shoulder dislocated. It was Mr Warner's eighth voyage and he told me he had never been in such a storm before.[2]

The Englishmen may have been ready for an improvement in the standard of South African cricket. It is doubtful whether they were prepared for South Africa to win her first Test match and go on from there to a 4-1 series win. There was little sign of that happening in the early provincial matches as Western Province were swept aside, first by an innings and 127 runs, then by 10 wickets.

> The innings was over before lunch on the third day, Crawford being almost irresistible ... In the return match Western Province went in first on Saturday, but could only score 81 against the bowling of Crawford, Lees and Haigh ... except for these two men (Snooke and Horwood), no one could make any effective resistance to the bowling of Crawford.[3]

In the four innings, Crawford had 0 for 12, five for 41, four for 27 and six for 79.

The tourists had been impressed by the attractiveness of the Newlands ground, by the colourful apparel of the spectators and the music of the local band. Denton draws a comparison with an occasion with which his readers, fellow Yorkshiremen, would be familiar and, on Boxing Day, perhaps envious of those able to spend time in the sun.

> On the first day of our arrival in Cape Town the afternoon found us practising at Newlands. Mr Warner describes the ground as the loveliest in the world. I must say it is very pretty indeed with its fir and pine trees all around, and Table Mountain standing in the background, its summit nestling in the clouds.
>
> Our first match began on December 2nd against the Western Province Cricket Club. A beautiful summer day, ladies with their best dresses and vari-coloured parasols, the Military band playing selections from 'The Mikado', 'Country Girl' etc. throughout the day. You might easily imagine

> yourself at Scarborough Festival, if it were not for the fact that you cannot get away from the coloured people.[4]

Nowadays the last part of that report would be edited out on the grounds of political correctness. However, this was a time when apartheid was already in place, although not formalised and legalised to the extent that it would be under the Nationalist Government of 1948 and beyond.

The team moved on to the Highveld and spent Christmas with the Mayor and Mayoress of Johannesburg ahead of the rather more serious business of the first Test at the Wanderers early in the New Year. It was a significant one in that it gave South Africa her first Test win, a result which looked highly unlikely when they were all out for 91 in their first innings in reply to England's 184. The collapse was due mainly to Crawford's fellow debutant Walter Lees who had the impressive figures of 23.1-10-34-5. Blythe had three and Crawford chipped in with a couple at the end, including that of Ernie Vogler with his first ball in Test cricket.[5] England then extended their lead to 283 and at 105 for 6, South Africa looked out of it, but the last pair of Nourse and captain Sherwell ground their way to a partnership of 48 and a one-wicket victory.

Denton described his reaction to the match and the scenes at the end. Crawford, he said, had a rare off-day (He had 0 for 49 in seventeen overs) and Haigh was ill in bed. Nevertheless:

> Across the record of this match is written large the glorious uncertainty of cricket. There was not a dull moment, the match was full of incident from start to finish and it was one of the best games I have ever taken part in ... The scene at the end of the match was indescribable. Men, women, and children went mad with delight. Hats and sticks were flying everywhere, cheers followed cheers, and both Nourse and Sherwell were carried off the field.[6]

Warner and Crawford played fine cricket, said *Cricket*, referring to the second innings.[7] The *Sportsman* had been rather more critical of the first, reporting that with the exception of Crawford and Yorkshire's Schofield Haigh, primarily a bowler but bowling only one over in the match on account of illness, the batting was 'quite unworthy of the side' – disappointing, but hardly unique in the performances of England's Test line-ups across the generations.

Crawford, with 44, had been top scorer in the first innings and only Warner's 51 exceeded his 43 in the second. There have been worse Test debuts. Until Brian Close played against New Zealand in 1949, there were none by anyone younger. For Crawford, if not for England, the future looked bright.

> Crawford did not long survive Haigh's dismissal, being out to a well-judged catch in the deep field. His innings, compared with the others, was in a class by itself. He was seldom in difficulties and never neglected an opportunity of scoring off anything like a loose ball. It was a delightful exhibition of batting on which he is to be warmly congratulated.

On the second day:

> Four wickets were down for 73 – not too good a start. At this juncture Crawford came in and for the second time in the match played superb cricket, and while he and Warner were together the bowling for the first time in the match looked easy. The feature of the rest of the innings was the batting of Crawford, who played in the most attractive manner, and was particularly severe on Sinclair, off whom in one over he made two grand strokes in succession – a big hit to leg and a cut past point. He had made 43 when Nourse clean bowled him for another great innings. The tail collapsed and the MCC were all out for 190.[8]

In days of more leisurely touring it was a couple of months before the second Test, also at the Wanderers. During that time the tourists recorded easy victories in first-class matches, by an innings and 218 runs over the Army, then by four wickets against Natal at both Durban and Pietermaritzburg and by ten wickets against Eastern Province. There were solid, if not spectacular performances by Crawford, including half centuries against The Army and Eastern Province and three for 30 and three for 25 against Natal. In that match he was used as an experimental opener with Pelham Warner – not his ideal position, as demonstrated with scores of 33, 8, 9 and 19.

In the non-first-class matches, played against teams of more than eleven players, the margins were even greater. Pretoria and District were dispatched by an innings & 80 runs, Crawford making 45 and taking five for 6 and six for 54. Against Middleburg and District it was 56 and five for 18, as MCC won by an innings and 119 runs, and four for 6 as The Border were brushed aside by an innings and 14 runs. Crawford sat out the match against Fifteen of King William's Town which MCC won by an innings and 296 runs. Then the status of these encounters as little more than exhibition matches was amply demonstrated by the approach against Eighteen of Queenstown which the tourists eventually won by an innings and 176 runs.

> At the close of the first day's play Crawford's score stood at 197. In order that he might increase his total to 200 the innings was prolonged on the following morning when the desired object was attained.[9]

He eventually finished on 212 not out from a total of 400 for eight declared.

There were draws against Midlands Districts, Grahamstown, and a win against Port Elizabeth and District, then Crawford had thirteen for 33 in a drawn match against Twenty-two of Oudtshoorn, at the time at the peak of the second ostrich feather boom. After a couple of months on the road, it was back to Johannesburg, for the second Test match, the strength of the opposition in the previous weeks having provided very little preparation for the sterner ordeal of the four back-to-back Tests, two at the Wanderers and two at Newlands, which were to occupy the last month of the tour.

In between there was time for a bit of sightseeing including the Congo Caves and some of the battlefields of the recent Boer War with names that have now passed into the history books, like Colenso, Ladysmith and Spion Kop.[10]

For the second and third Tests, Crawford moved up the order to open with Warner, displacing Frederick Fane who moved to number four. South Africa won both, by the large margins of nine wickets and 243 runs. With the series already lost before the party moved on to Cape Town for the last two Tests, Board and Relf were tried in the first innings before Warner and Crawford resumed in the second. Both went cheaply, but Fane, batting at number four, steered England to a four-wicket win, the only one of the series.

In the third:

> Denton and Crawford played well, but most of the team could make nothing of the bowling of Snooke, who took eight wickets for 70 runs.[11]

'Tip' Snooke was a fast medium bowler whose Test career continued until 1922/23. These remained his best Test figures.

After England's win in the first Newlands Test, matters reverted to what had become normal for the final match of the series, as the hosts annihilated the visitors by an innings and 16 runs. Crawford had opened and, having lost Warner and Denton with only five on the board, engineered something of a recovery. He had a little support from the middle order, but England's 187 was never going to be enough. His 74 was his highest Test score. He was one of the few successes of the tour.

> In the Test Matches only FL Fane and JN Crawford as batsmen and Lees and Blythe as bowlers earned distinction. For the most part the England batting in these all-important games was lamentable.[12]

Henry Leveson Gower, writing almost half a century later, recollected:

> Towards the end of the year the MCC team embarked in the *Kinfauns Castle*. Though perhaps not fully representative of England, we had quite a good side including Warner as Captain, Captain Wynyard, FL Fane of Essex, JN Crawford of Surrey, Denton and Haigh of Yorkshire, Blythe of Kent and Lees of Surrey. I remember we thought at the time that our team would be quite strong enough to win the Test matches, but as things turned out we were rather in the dark about the strength to which South African cricket had already attained ... Crawford, who had only just left Repton, took a

> good many wickets and made some good scores, but the rest of us did not excel.[13]

PF Warner, his MCC captain, was rather more effusive in his praise at the time than his future Surrey captain was to be.

> Mr Warner's cricket team arrived at Southampton on Saturday from South Africa in the steamship *Norman*, which made a splendid voyage. Mr Warner said he was delighted with the tour which, except from a playing standpoint, had been a great success.
>
> Questioned as to what players had been the successes of the tour, Mr Warner spoke enthusiastically of Mr Crawford, the Surrey amateur, whom he hailed as the coming Jackson.
>
> 'Indeed,' he added, 'I have never seen a player of his years with such wonderful possibilities as a batsman, bowler and fielder. He was quite exceptional.'[14]

In all matches Crawford had averaged just under forty with the bat, just over ten with the ball. And he was not yet twenty years of age.

The England cricket team in which Crawford made his home debut:
C Blythe, EG Arnold, GL Jessop, JN Crawford, LC Braund;
AFA Lilley, CB Fry, RE Foster (capt), TW Hayward;
GH Hirst, JT Tyldesley.

5

Record Breaker

Surrey 1906-07

1906 is remembered by cricket statisticians and historians as the one in which Yorkshire's George Hirst achieved the unique 'double double' of two thousand runs and two hundred wickets – an achievement unlikely to be surpassed, or even approached now that limited overs and Twenty20 cricket have increasingly marginalised the first-class game. Among a number of players to do the more modest double of one thousand runs and one hundred wickets was Jack Crawford. Hirst, however was fifteen years into a playing career which was to extend until 1929. Crawford, notwithstanding his earlier two brief post-school seasons and South African tour, was in his first full season and still only nineteen years old.

For Surrey, the stabilisation and revival which had begun the previous season under Lord Dalmeny's captaincy continued and the poor seasons of 1903 and 1904, when they had finished in the lower reaches of the Championship table, were forgotten. So much so that the county was in with a strong chance of taking the Championship until mid-August when defeats by Yorkshire and Lancashire pushed them into third place.

Cricket historians, Neville Cardus especially, have called the Edwardian period the 'golden age of cricket', starring amateur batsmen on good pitches under a sun which it was assumed would never set on the British

Empire. That may have been partially true, but Jack Crawford, unlike most of his public school contemporaries, linked bowling and fielding skills to those of his batting, and the outstanding schoolboy cricketer of his era now made a significant impact on the first-class scene.

In the season's opening first-class match against Hampshire at The Oval:

> Hobbs again proved the highest scorer … with Crawford he added 95 runs for the fifth wicket in an hour and a quarter… Hampshire were eventually set 442 to win, but fared so badly against Knox and Crawford that, by the time stumps were drawn, eight wickets were down for 83.[1]

The match was won by 337 runs, the first of three massive victories with which Surrey started the season. It was followed by a defeat of Northamptonshire by an innings and 214 runs and of Leicestershire by an innings and 270. In both Crawford played his part, albeit a relatively modest one in the Leicestershire match.

Against Northamptonshire, Hayward, who was to score 3,518 runs that season, 3,246 of them for Surrey, made 219 out of a total of 429.

> Hayward and JN Crawford made a stand, adding 53 together in forty minutes for the third wicket ... So irresistible did Crawford and Lees prove that by the time stumps were drawn, seven wickets were down for 62. Yesterday a little over half-an-hour's play proved sufficient to finish the match ... It will be seen that Crawford took six wickets for 13, and that for the whole match his record was nine for 46.[2]

An innings victory over Leicestershire followed with contributions of 43 and three for 43, before the winning sequence came to an end, Surrey being on the wrong end of a drawn match against Essex. Jack's innings of 23 may not have been statistically noteworthy. His judgment of how to bat on a sticky pitch, however, was commended.

> With an hour remaining Lord Dalmeny joined Crawford and as the pitch had become rather difficult no one could tell what would happen. Craw-

ford batted with excellent judgment, running no risks till the position was secure.[3]

Cricket acknowledged the part played by the captain, now in his second year in the job, in Surrey's revival.

The acceptance of the captaincy of the County eleven by Lord Dalmeny for last season, it is not too much to say, marked a new era in the history of Surrey cricket. For some years before, the authorities at The Oval had been unable to secure an amateur cricketer able to give the requisite time to the responsible task of managing the eleven ... There were people, and well informed people, misled by the silly rumours about the interference of the committee with the special duties of the captain, venturesome enough to suggest that in offering the captaincy to so young a player the executive had deep designs of influencing, or rather exercising a control of some sort, over the action of the captain. That their estimate was hopelessly wrong in both cases, of Lord Dalmeny in the one hand, and of the Surrey Committee on the other, it is fair to say has been shown by subsequent events.[4]

The defence of the Committee, whether justified or not, is understandable. The Surrey Secretary, Charles Alcock, was the editor of *Cricket*. The magazine tended to take a pro-establishment, pro-Surrey view and ignored anything controversial which might be seen as detrimental to Surrey's management. It is evident, however, and was to become more evident at the end of the following season when other commitments compelled him to relinquish the post, that his Lordship was unable to devote 100% of his time to the job.

During the day Lord Dalmeny motored to the Commons to record his vote in a division, but was back at the ground to see several wickets fall. During his absence the captaincy was taken over by Raphael.[5]

A wet period in the second half of May saw three matches out of four drawn in one of which at Worcester: 'Hayes, Holland, and Crawford also made useful scores ... Crawford puzzled all the batsmen, but was kept on too long, bowling at one period for two hours and ten minutes without a rest.'[6]

It was a match for which Lord Dalmeny was not available and the captaincy was probably taken over by Raphael. Bowling figures of 36.1-9-109-7 and a further 12 overs opening the bowling in the follow on before the third day was completely lost to rain suggest the criticism was not without justification. During this game, without having played a full domestic first-class season, Crawford went through 100 wickets in twenty-three Championship matches and 150 first-class in thirty-nine.

Then, after a rain-affected draw at Old Trafford when only part of the first day's play was possible, in a two-day victory over Gloucestershire at The Oval:

> Crawford and Knox shared the wickets. The former, who bowled unchanged throughout, was helped somewhat by the state of the wicket ... only Crawford who scored 29 not out in ninety minutes by very good cricket, made as many as twenty ... the feature of the play being the capital all-round display of Crawford.[7]

In early June Tom Hayward stole the limelight with four centuries in a week, two against Nottinghamshire at Trent Bridge, then two more against Leicestershire at Aylestone Road. Both matches were won, as was the next one against Sussex at The Oval when the visitors were dispatched by the margin of 289 runs. Five thousand turned up to see Hayward continue the sequence. He 'failed' with 54 and 69.

Others, however, including Crawford with 91 not out, helped post a total of 415. In one of the few innings in which he was not the dominant partner:

> Lees, however, chanced to be at his very best, and, so admirable a partner did he prove to be to Crawford that together they added 186 for the seventh wicket in two hours; the first hour of the partnership realised 110 of which number the amateur claimed but 22.[8]

Then, at Bristol:

> Crawford bowled very well indeed, his seven wickets costing a fraction over 12 runs each ... The feature of the day's cricket was a large innings by Crawford who reached 50 in sixty-five minutes, 100 in one hour and fifteen and, in all, scored 148 in one hundred and sixty minutes. He played a very bright game, but was missed when 40 and again when 102. He hit twenty fours ... Crawford, it will be seen, obtained eleven wickets in the match for 148 runs in addition to making his record score.[9]

Local newspapers are often parsimonious with the credit they give to the opposition, but that was not the case with the *Gloucester Citizen*.

> It was his highest score to date and his first innings bowling figure of 32-10-85-7 the best of the season. He had beaten Gloucestershire almost single-handed, although Hayward had a century and Hayes 4-33 in the second innings.[10]

Along with several others he was 'rested' for matches against both universities and the West Indian tourists, then came back strongly at Chesterfield where 'the wicket was good throughout, and although the light after lunch was not very satisfactory, the poor total must be attributed to Crawford's bowling, which claimed seven wickets for 86.'[11] It was Lees who did the damage in the second innings as Derbyshire crumbled for 57, Crawford supporting with three for 22.

Then, by way of light relief, Jack played for his father's XI against the Guards Depot at Caterham. The opposition played with twelve men, but it made next to no difference. They were 112 all out, Jack having seven wickets and a catch. 'Pa' Crawford's team reached the target with no difficulty, eventually reaching 409 for 6 of which Jack made 272 before being run out. All this was immediately before a Championship match against Warwickshire at The Oval in which he batted at number four and opened the bowling in both innings as the visitors followed on, more than 450 behind Surrey's massive 634. It says something for his fitness and stamina that he bowled 67 overs in the match, returning 29-9-52-2 and 38-15-85-4.

Crawford was invited to play in the Gentlemen v Players Centenary Match at Lord's, and although he failed to distinguish himself with either bat or ball, he did in the second innings share in an all Surrey scoreline of 'Crawford c Hayes b Lees'. However, in the equivalent fixture at The Oval the following week, he made a far more significant contribution. It helped that he batted at number three rather than number seven as at Lord's: 'Crawford then came in, and, giving a good display, helped to add 43 for the second wicket in thirty minutes.'[12]

In a drawn match Jack had 26 and 71 and in stamina-testing bowling, sent down over sixty overs for four for 105 in the first innings and two for 84 in the second. WG Grace, captaining the amateurs on his fifty-eighth birthday, scored 74 in the second innings.

Jack returned to competitive cricket as Surrey continued an excellent season in which they were to win eighteen out of their twenty-eight Championship matches. A high-scoring draw at Edgbaston was followed by a four-wicket win against Worcestershire at The Oval after Surrey had successfully chased down 286, thanks to unbeaten innings of 162 from Jack Hobbs and 69 from John Gordon. A tougher contest awaited at The Oval against Yorkshire, who in the late 1890s had taken over Surrey's role as the dominant county – in the decade between 1898 and 1908 they were Champions five times and never out of the top three. It was Walter Lees' native county and the professional had chosen the fixture for his benefit match. Surrey won by nine wickets to remain firmly in the driving seat for the Championship. He had shared and would share a number of match-winning batting and bowling partnerships.

This time, however, it was Crawford and Lord Dalmeny who laid the foundations.

> With Dalmeny joining Crawford a fine stand was made, the two young amateurs putting on 78 for the sixth wicket before being separated. Crawford scored 51 out of 110 in ninety-five minutes – a finely played innings.[13]

Then the wheels began to come off with the second defeat of the season at the hands of eventual champions, Kent, by 164 runs at Blackheath. It was the first season of Frank Woolley and slow left-arm Colin

Blythe was a dominant bowler, his career to be sadly curtailed eleven years later when he was killed in action at Passchendaele. In happier times, his bowling was too much for Surrey on this occasion. Having led by 83 runs on the first innings and set 245 to win in the second, they collapsed to 80 all out, thanks mainly to Blythe whose 20-12-25-5 included Crawford for three.

Surrey could only manage a draw against Nottinghamshire at The Oval, Crawford's free-flowing batting style being curtailed, at least initially.

> Crawford, upon going in, was restricted to a purely defensive game, it being quite impossible to take any liberties with the attack. During the first half hour he was in he did not score a run, but he afterwards hit so freely as to obtain 50 in fifty-five minutes. Altogether he hit ten fours and with Holland, added 128 for the fifth wicket in an hour and a half.

And then, to prove he was human, 'Iremonger was badly missed in the slips by Crawford off Lees' first delivery.'[14]

Cricket continued to enthuse about Surrey's success and team spirit:

> All round there has been a vitality and a cohesion which has done as much as anything to make them successful. The influence of such a keen captain as Lord Dalmeny has produced, as was only to be expected, the *esprit de corps* which is so essential to the best results where combination is requisite.
>
> What need to brighten the cricket with batsmen of the order of Hayward, Hayes, Holland, Mr. Crawford, Hobbs, Goatly, Lord Dalmeny and Lees – any and all of them capable of a big score? And what more useful trio of bowlers than Mr. Knox, Lees and Mr. Crawford are there to be found in the majority of county teams?[15]

Only Lees and Crawford feature in both lists. The feature appeared after the Middlesex match which Surrey won by an innings and 92 runs, but ahead of the back-to-back defeats by the two most northerly counties. In all three matches, Crawford was to the fore.

Against Middlesex at Lord's:

> The feature of the concluding portion of the innings was furnished by Crawford, who, although twice missed, played a very fine game on a wicket affected by rain. He cut in fine style and obtained his 70 out of 110 in an hour and a half ... With the score at 99 Crawford went on to bowl, and a great change came over the game, Warner, Douglas and Tarrant all being out at that figure, and Colbeck sent back two runs later.[16]

It was in this match that Jack provided one of the earliest examples of his big hitting, reaching the top balcony of the pavilion.[17]

Against Lancashire at The Oval, 'Crawford who made some fine hits ... During the innings Crawford, who had previously obtained his 1,000 runs, took his one hundredth wicket of the season.'[18]

At 19 years and 259 days he had become the youngest player at the time to achieve the double: six days later he was to reach 100 wickets for Surrey and four days after that, 1,000 runs.[19] He remains the youngest to do either. In the bowling stakes he went ahead of George Lohmann who in 1885 was fifty-two days past his twentieth birthday when he hit the target. In 1991, Waqar Younis slipped in between them. On the batting side, the previous youngest to 1,000 runs had been brother Frank in 1900 at the age of 21 years 127 days. The Crawfords retained the top two spots in the list until Graham Thorpe split them in 1989. The reduction in the first-class programme in the twenty-first century means that no challenge is envisaged in the immediate future – and probably never again.

Athletic News was prompt to recognise the achievement and paid tribute to Crawford's character, fitness and athleticism.

> Of course, the hope of Surrey lies in the return match with Yorkshire, beginning today at Bramall Lane. But there is a personal side to this popular phrase as embodied in JN Crawford who must, in conformity with fashion, be styled the old Reptonian, although this scion of a cricketing family is not twenty until December 1st, 1906. Crawford has just gained a unique distinction. When Poidevin was caught at the wicket on Saturday in the course of the Surrey and Lancashire match, Crawford obtained his hundredth wicket this season. He had previously scored 1,000 runs this summer. In this dual harvest he has this year only been preceded by George Hirst

> and John Gunn – two of the finest all-round cricketers of their time. 'Plum' Warner's prophecy in his book *The MCC in South Africa* that Crawford is going to be a very big figure in the world of cricket is being speedily realised.
>
> A thousand runs and a hundred wickets is a feat for a strongman. But JN Crawford is still in his teens – a quiet, unassuming, courteous youth who, as he peers through his spectacles, hardly suggests the cricketer he is when in ordinary attire. But he was born a player, and in flannels he presents a strong and muscular appearance. He strips like an athlete – and that is the test.
>
> Crawford is the thirty-second cricketer of modern times, that is to say since 1874 – who has fulfilled the double role of the scorer of 1,000 runs and the destroyer of 100 wickets. But no one has ever accomplished this feat at his age.[20]

Surrey came unstuck in that Bramall Lane match, taking a narrow ten-run lead in the first innings but collapsing to the bowling of George Hirst and Schofield Haigh in the second to lose by 102 runs.

> Shortly before the hundred was reached Hayes and Crawford bowled instead of Rushby and Lees and the change brought a great change over the game. At 99 Denton was bowled by Crawford, and with only one run added both Taylor and Hirst were sent back by Hayes. Shortly afterwards Crawford disposed of Rothery and Wilkinson in quick succession, the fifth wicket falling at 127 and the sixth at 129 ... Crawford bowled excellently, and well deserved his success ... An experiment was tried by sending in Crawford to open the innings with Hayward, but it was far from being a success, the amateur being caught at the wicket in the second over.[21]

It was not, in fact, much of an experiment. Crawford had already opened the innings for his country, but it remained the case that he was at his best and certainly produced his best performances in the upper-middle order.

The Championship now gone, Surrey ended the season on a high note with comfortable wins against Northamptonshire and Derbyshire and a draw against Middlesex.

Crawford continued to attract the compliments. In the Northamptonshire match, 'Crawford bowled splendidly, his analysis of five for 55 being very fine in an innings of 296.' And in the next one, against Derbyshire, 'When Lord Dalmeny and Crawford came together some free hitting was seen, the two putting on 134 for the sixth wicket in seventy minutes ... Crawford made his 74 in a hundred and twenty-five minutes.'[22]

For the final encounter of the season, Lord Dalmeny was again absent. The records do not indicate who captained the side. As one of only two amateurs (the other one was Neville Knox), it was probably Crawford. If so, it was a taste of things to come, a taste which three seasons later was to turn sour.

Wisden had no doubts about Crawford's contribution to the success of the season, still less about his place in the English cricket firmament and his future prospects.

> JN Crawford deserves a paragraph all to himself. He was the all-round man of the Surrey eleven just as Hayward, Hayes and Hobbs were the batsmen and Knox and Lees the bowlers. Confining himself to the county matches he scored 1,064 runs and took 111 wickets, and it is worthy of special notice that he is the youngest player who has ever accomplished this double feat in first-class cricket. It was most gratifying to find him in such bowling form as in 1905 there seemed some reason to fear that batting would engage all his attention. At times he bowled astonishingly well, perhaps his best work being done on the second day at Sheffield. On that afternoon he was great, combining a rare amount of spin with extreme accuracy. Only twenty on the first of December, Crawford should be an England cricketer in the immediate future. Few men, except WG Grace and AG Steel, have won a bigger position in the cricket world at the same age.[23]

Jack was one of four players to be awarded his county cap that season and, along with his Surrey colleagues Ernie Hayes and Neville Knox, he was named one of Wisden's Five Cricketers of the Year:

> That he should have done all this is the more astonishing from the fact that he invariably plays in glasses. No one handicapped in this way has ever been so consistently successful both as batsman and bowler. Few school batsmen have more readily accommodated themselves to the needs of first-class

> cricket. His hitting powers are great ... but still more remarkable is his self-control. He is more forward in style than most modern batsmen and plays perfectly straight. As a medium-pace bowler he possesses nearly every good gift. With an easy delivery he has a fine command over his pitch, and when the wicket gives him the least assistance he makes the ball come off the pitch with any amount of spin.[24]

Also included were Kent's Arthur Fielder and Ken Hutchings, described as the 'matinee idol of county cricket', with whom Jack was to strike up a friendship on the Australian tour of 1907/08 and who was one of many to lose his life in France in the global conflict of the next decade.[25]

The death in February 1907 of Charles Alcock, Surrey's Secretary for thirty-five years, more than half his lifetime, cast a shadow over the new season. It also marked a power shift in Surrey's administration. Alcock had been a huge influence on sports administration in the late nineteenth century, being responsible for the first Test match in England, the launching of the FA Cup and an enlightened approach to professionalism. Over the years his role had evolved from that of secretary and servant of the committee to that of *de facto* chief executive who ran the club and expected the committee to endorse his actions.

With his death and the appointment of William Findlay there was a swing back to management by committee and an increase in authoritarianism. For most players on the field, whether amateur or professional, it made very little difference – until perhaps they were involved in disciplinary issues or, as Crawford was to do a couple of years later, have a difference of opinion.

There was, as they say, a bit of previous. In 1897, Crawford's brother Frank had succeeded Walter Read as Assistant Secretary and, according to his close friend Digby Jephson, had an uneasy relationship with the not entirely impotent Committee.[26] For Read, of course, the position had been a virtual sinecure, the post having been created to allow the 'amateur' to play cricket full time; for Frank it would have been different: Alcock's health was no longer good and Frank, along with Acting Secretary CA Stein, would have had to work more closely with and, more significantly, at the behest of, the Committee.

On the field, it was more of the same. With Lord Dalmeny still at the helm, albeit for his last season, Surrey continued to win most of their matches, though could still finish no higher than fourth in the Championship table. Crawford played his part, achieving the double for the second consecutive year.

There were a number of outstanding performances. In the opening match of the season against Northamptonshire at The Oval:

> Crawford shared the batting honours with Hayward. The amateur timed the ball admirably, and, when he found that wickets were falling at the other end, hit out in determined fashion. He hit six fours, and made his 46 out of 81 in eighty-five minutes. On Wednesday morning Crawford and Lees finished off the innings for 102, the former altogether taking five wickets for 39 runs.[27]

Eleven wickets followed in the demolition of Essex by an innings and 162 runs.

> Crawford, keeping a good length and getting considerable break, was found to be in great form when he went on for the second time, at 75: he bowled 10 overs, 3 maidens for 17 runs and five wickets, the last seven wickets going down for 41.
>
> On Saturday morning but little resistance was made against the bowling of Crawford and Lees and before one o'clock the match was over, Surrey being left victorious by an innings and 162 runs. Crawford obtained eleven wickets in the match at a cost of six runs apiece, bowling admirably in each innings. On the last day he took five wickets in 32 balls for 17 runs.[28]

It was about this time that the feisty Queenslander Alan Marshal began to exert an influence on the Surrey scene. Recommended to Surrey by WG Grace, two years later he was to play his part in the Crawford story.

An innings victory against Hampshire followed, after which Crawford played his part with bat and ball in a seven wicket win over Derbyshire, his bowling performances of 16-9-33-3 and 24-6-64-4 being supplemented by some impressive batting.

> Crawford then came in and he played a splendid innings. With Hayes he made 73 in half an hour, and with Dalmeny 74 in similar time. He hit well all round the wicket, his chief strokes being two fives and nine fours and altogether made 82 [actually 83] out of 172 in 90 minutes.[29]

Crawford did not feature in the next match at Trent Bridge. It is not clear why, but as an almost ever-present amateur and not one of the most affluent, he had to make a living outside of the game.

> Rumour has been busy in regard to the absence of JN Crawford from the Surrey team in the match with Notts at Trent Bridge. A statement has gone round that there has been correspondence between Crawford's father, the Surrey Committee and Lord Dalmeny with reference to his inability to afford the time for cricket. The only explanation offered by Mr W Findlay, the Surrey Secretary, was that Crawford had been kept out of the team owing to business.[30]

After a rain-affected draw against Warwickshire and a ten-wicket win at home to Gloucestershire, Crawford, having made a contribution to what was until the fourth innings an evenly balanced match at Leicester, helped swing the game Surrey's way and to a victory more comfortable than had at one time seemed likely.

> The amateur, who hit a couple of sixes played a fine game, and made his 41 out of 59 in thirty-five minutes ... JN Crawford supplemented his batting with some excellent bowling, taking half the wickets for 47 runs ... Leicestershire were left with 136 to win, but against Rushby and Crawford found run getting a difficult matter and were all out for 90.[31]

Yet another outstanding all-round performance followed in a two-day innings victory against Sussex at The Oval.

> Crawford, playing admirably, helped to put on 37 in three-quarters of an hour ... Crawford, in his last eleven overs, took five wickets for 15 runs, and in the whole match obtained eleven for 63.[32]

A mid-season slump followed with draws and a defeat in the next four matches in which he played (he stood down for the match against Cambridge University at The Oval) though, despite not influencing the result, he had some reasonable performances. At Lord's, for instance:

> Upon Crawford joining Hayward some very attractive cricket was seen. The amateur was in his very best run-getting vein, and so monopolised the scoring that he completed his 50 out of 69 in sixty-five minutes, and of the 115 runs added for the fourth wicket with Hayward in an hour and a half he claimed 86; his chief hits were fourteen fours.[33]

He followed up with five for 80 in the second innings.

Along with Knox and Lees, he then missed the Warwickshire match, but had done enough to earn himself selection for the first Test match against South Africa at Lord's. He batted well enough, given the limitations of not appearing until number eight in the order: 'Crawford, playing confidently, made some good strokes and looked like staying. When he had made 22 out of 32, he was caught at the wicket.'[34]

South Africa followed on, having managed only 140 in reply to England's 428, but Crawford had a rare wicketless match, having been allowed only twelve overs across both innings by captain Reggie Foster, though it was likely that he would have bowled more on a third-day pitch, had the rain relented sufficiently to allow England to make use of it. It was South Africa's first Test appearance in England and the team showed only one change from that which had beaten England in Cape Town fourteen months previously. By contrast, Crawford and Colin Blythe were the only common elements in the English team.

Crawford returned to the county circuit, from Lord's to Derby immediately – the very next day in fact, where:

> Crawford and Hayward appeared in the Surrey eleven in place of Goatly and Hitch ... Derbyshire commenced batting on a soft and slow wicket and lost Olivierre to Crawford's second ball ... Crawford and Smith bowled unchanged, the former taking four wickets for 30 ... Crawford followed in, and remained with Hayward whilst 40 were added for the second wicket: he hit a six off Morton, out of the ground ... On a damaged wicket Smith and Crawford proved almost irresistible.[35]

Smith and Crawford, had in fact remained unchanged through both innings, bowling their team to an innings and 16 runs win and back on to the winning trail.

The momentum carried them into the match against the South Africans who were to suffer their first defeat of the tour, Surrey winning by 85 runs. Crawford made top score in the first innings and had the best bowling figures in the second. It might have been thought enough to retain his place in side for the second Test at Headingley, but the selectors were not sufficiently impressed.

Before the Test team was announced, Crawford featured in the Jubilee Gentlemen v Players match at The Oval, the fixture having been played there in 1857, though the Lord's encounter preceded it by more than half a century. The 1907 version of that had taken place a week earlier and in a rain-affected drawn match, he had made a low score and failed to take a wicket. His performance at The Oval was more convincing. The Players won by 54 runs, but Crawford had taken six for 54, 'bowling admirably' according to *Cricket* including an outstanding caught and bowled to dismiss John Gunn.[36]

Then, as Surrey beat Lancashire by 112 runs at The Oval and 'Crawford, going on at 156, took the last four wickets for one run in two overs and a ball.' In the second innings of 190, Hayward carried his bat for 114. Against Kent at Blackheath, Crawford had his hundredth first-class wicket of the season and 'bowled with such success that by the time stumps were drawn eight wickets had fallen for 138. He dismissed Mason, Blaker and Hardinge in five balls, and delivered his last nine overs and two balls for 15 runs and four wickets.'[37]

Meanwhile:

> The Selection Committee, in choosing the England team for next Monday's Test match at Leeds have picked the eleven which played at Lord's with the addition of Knox ... It is surmised that, in the event of the wicket being hard, Knox will be played in preference to Crawford.[38]

However, on the morning of the match:

> There had been rain during the previous night, and at half-past ten on the first morning a shower fell and made the wicket very soft ... The omission of Crawford, after his all-round success against the visitors in the Surrey match at the Oval, and with the wicket as it was, came as a great surprise.[39]

Crawford's absence made little difference: Knox made his debut, batted at number eleven and bowled three overs, but the match was won for England by Colin Blythe with eight for 59 and seven for 40.

There was no provision for released England players returning to their counties in those days, so Surrey had to do without their all-rounder for their match at Southend. They did well enough, beating Essex by 352 runs.

Fred Holland had chosen the home match against Yorkshire for his benefit. The visitors held out for a draw after Surrey had gained a first-innings lead.

> Wilkinson and Rhodes were both bowled by Crawford ... Lees and Crawford both bowled well, the latter certainly better than his analysis would lead one to suppose, and it was due chiefly to them that Surrey were able to claim a lead of 132 on the innings.[40]

Crawford was restored to the side for the third and final Test match at The Oval in place of Wilfred Rhodes. In another rain-affected match his contribution was minimal, two runs in each innings and no wickets. It was his second Test match in England. No one could have guessed that it would be his last. Most Test careers have not even begun at age twenty. Crawford's – in England, at least – was over.

He had, however, done enough over the season to virtually guarantee himself a place on the winter tour of Australia where he would play the last five of his twelve Test matches, bringing his Test career to an end shortly after he came of age. Before that, however, he ended the season with a flourish.

Against Kent at The Oval:

> Crawford and Holland added runs at a good pace, and during the sixty-five minutes they were in partnership put on 123 for the sixth wicket. Crawford reached 50 in sixty-five minutes and altogether scored 103 out of 172 in an hour and forty minutes. He drove with great power, hit seventeen fours but, when 5, was missed off a skier near cover-point ... Woolley was caught at mid-off and Seymour bowled off consecutive balls from Crawford.
>
> In last week's match at the Oval, JN Crawford was seen at his very best. Despite the fact that Kent are not now so difficult a side to beat as they were last season, they are still capable of playing a very close game with even the strongest of the counties. Surrey had special reasons for wanting to beat them last week, for they had not only suffered a ten-wicket defeat at their hands earlier in the season, but had not beaten them for eight years. For their success they were primarily indebted to Crawford, who, in addition to playing a superb innings of 103, took six wickets for 79 runs. The power he put into some of his strokes was remarkable. If only he can show such form in the Test matches in Australia, he should prove the most useful all-round player in the side.[41]

In its review of the county season *Cricket* looked forward to a rosy future for Crawford and a less certain one for his county.

> Mr Crawford again proved how admirable an all-round cricketer he is, and it came as no surprise when it was announced that he had been invited to go to Australia with the MCC's team. As he is still only twenty years of age, it is quite possible that he has not even yet been seen at quite his best ... When the campaign was nearly completed, it became known that Lord Dalmeny has notified the Surrey Committee of his inability to take sole charge of the Eleven in future, though he would be willing to assist the side when he could spare the time. His retirement from the captaincy will prove a distinct loss to the County, for, although now and again he might have handled his bowling

to better advantage, he has led the side very skilfully, and possesses the ideal temperament for such a position.[42]

In a light-hearted conclusion to the season before the more serious business in the Antipodes, Crawford played for an England XI on John Bamford's private ground at Oldfields, Uttoxeter.

Crawford, upon joining MacLaren, played a free game, and 50 went up at the end of half an hour. Crawford showed the brightest cricket on the side, and, before being caught in the long-field, hit two sixes – both huge drives, off Kotze and Faulkner.[43]

The big hitting had been in evidence earlier in the season in matches at The Oval where he developed a penchant for landing the ball in the dressing-rooms.

In scoring 27* v Notts, he drove a ball from John Gunn through the windows of the Surrey amateurs dressing room, and it missed by inches the illustrious head of Mr W Findlay, the Surrey Secretary. The following week he hit a ball through an open door of the same dressing room, making a neat hole in the mirror.[44]

In his much-vaunted innings against Kent Crawford produced what he himself believed to be his biggest hitting. Gerald Brodribb quotes a 1922 article by Jim Reid in *Topical Times*, who says:

A short time after his dressing room hits Crawford produced the biggest hit I have ever seen on a cricket field. He opened his shoulders to a good-length ball, met it beautifully and sent it sailing sky-high in the direction of the pavilion. For a moment I thought it was going to clear the roof and fall in the street at the back, but it descended on the tiles with a tremendous thump and brought three of them down.[45]

To put that hit into context, towards the end of the century an extra storey was added to the pavilion and Foster's, sponsors at the time, offered £10,000 to any one clearing the building. Alistair Brown came closest, but the prize went unclaimed.

The euphoria was toned down a little from the previous season, but *Wisden* remained complimentary.

> JN Crawford was essentially the all-round man of the eleven ... At one time during the summer he was rather out of form as a batsman, but he soon recovered himself and was quite at his best at the end of August, playing an astonishingly brilliant innings against Kent ... Among the young batsmen of the present day there are few who can drive so hard ... It was unfortunate for his reputation that he did not do himself justice either in the Test matches or for Gentlemen against Players. Despite these failures, however, he was one of the most interesting cricketers of the year. As a bowler for Surrey, he did a lot of splendid work ... He and Lees deserved stronger support than they received, Knox's ineffectiveness throwing an immense responsibility on them.[46]

To KangarooLand: Crawford wasn't afraid to play on a stereotype or two for his first venture into writing.

6

TRIP TO KANGAROOLAND

AUSTRALIA 1907/08

As in South Africa two years earlier, Crawford was one of the more successful members of an unsuccessful team on his first trip Down Under. Another 4-1 margin saw the Ashes return to Australia after the first two matches resulted in a narrow victory for each side.

With thirty wickets, Crawford headed the Test averages, marginally ahead of Arthur Fielder and Sydney Barnes. With Wilfred Rhodes and Colin Blythe in the team, it was a commendable effort for one so young. He celebrated his twenty-first birthday on the tour,

Even before the departure there were rumours that Crawford might settle in Australia. Eventually he did, but not until two years later, so it seems that, notwithstanding the absence of previous experience in the country, he already had partially formed ideas of an alternative to Surrey cricket before his rift with the county catalysed his decision to find one two years later.

> As the *Ophir* is due at Fremantle on October 24, the MCC team will be thirty-four days on the water. However, they will not be out of practice, as arrangements have been made for a large portion of the deck to be reserved for the players to practise on during the journey across. It is stated that JN Crawford may remain in Australia for five years or so.[1]

Similarly, Nigel Hart refers to 'unsourced comments in his scrapbooks' which mention that there was concern that 'business claims may interfere with his cricket' and that 'he might remain in Australia if opportunity presents itself'.[2] There was further speculation that Crawford had an interest in farming and might take himself off in that direction.

On arrival in Australia, Crawford denied none of this.

> It is stated in England that Mr JN Crawford, the all-round Surrey amateur member of the team is likely to settle in Australia. In answer to a question, Mr Crawford said he had not completed his plans. It was, however, probable that he would not return to England at the conclusion of the tour.[3]

So it seems a Plan B was on the back burner, though Jack does not enter into such speculative realms in his book on the tour, *Trip to KangarooLand*, which was published by the *Cricket* offices in May 1909 almost simultaneously with his other work, *The Practical Cricketer*. Illustrated by 'Rip' and containing advertisements for four competing firms of batmakers as well as for other sports good specialists, photographers and, of course, *Cricket, Trip to KangarooLand* is a well-written and well-presented work, revealing the author as a sociable young man with a sense of humour and firm friendships with his fellow players, both amateur and professional. The book is mainly a digest of what he had previously written as a columnist for the *Daily Mirror*, a sensible and practical solution to the financial difficulties which might otherwise have been faced by one of the less well-off amateur cricketers of the time. He acknowledges the *Mirror*'s permission to reuse some of the articles.

While he was away, his elder brother, Frank, kept cuttings from other newspapers which are included in the text at the appropriate places. Frank also seems to have involved himself in the general production of the book – perhaps rather too much so for his brother's liking. In his introduction Jack says:

> My brother VFS has kindly interpolated the 'cuttings,' the 'paddings,' the 'slips,' and other covering 'points', which touch upon my own doings in the

matches themselves, and which help to amplify this small volume. If I had known he was going to interfere so much, he could have done the whole lot himself.[4]

Fellow Surrey players Ernie Hayes and Jack Hobbs were in the party, as was 'brother-spectacles', Richard Young, with whom Crawford had been at Repton.

There was a large gathering to see them off at St Pancras and after a minor administrative hitch and a fairly riotous send-off, they were on the way on *Ophir*.

Unfortunately I left my passage ticket on the mantelpiece at home, and had to drive to the Shipping Agents to explain the circumstances and ask for another. There was a little demur at first, owing to my name being unknown to the official interviewed, but fortunately a junior clerk happened to recognise me as having played once or twice at The Oval, and my identity being established, I was enabled to reach St. Pancras in time to start with the others. My father and sisters and brothers were all present to see me off, the governor and sisters coming to Tilbury with me. It is reported that the former preached the next Sunday morning on Acts XX ('They accompanied him unto the ship') ... The brief proceedings, on embarking on the *Ophir* were confined to sandwiches and champagne, and a 'neat' little speech of an encouraging nature to the effect that we were an 'experimental' team, not the best that could be sent out, but still very fair, and that great things were hoped of us in spite of prognostications to the contrary. I was so struck with the 'praises' heaped on us that I forgot to say good-bye to my father, who was round the corner talking affably to the wine steward, and had to be content to wave adieu to him as the vessel moved gracefully out of the dock. However, I kissed my sisters and someone else's sisters who were with them, before they were ordered ashore (not in consequence).[5]

Jack Hobbs also recalls 'a hearty send off', as well as the adjustments to team selection caused by captain AO Jones succumbing to pneumonia.

We had a hearty send-off from a big crowd of friends and admirers when we left St Pancras station on September 20th, 1907, and many of them went on to Tilbury to see the *Ophir* sail and wish us a prosperous voyage. Our party consisted of five amateurs and nine professionals, the list being: AO Jones (captain), JN Crawford, FL Fane, KL Hutchings, RA Young, Syd Barnes, Colin Blythe, Len Braund, Arthur Fielder, Joe Hardstaff, Ernie Hayes, Joe Humphries, Rhodes and myself. As it so happened, our team in the first matches played under the captaincy of FL Fane, because AO Jones became ill. George Gunn accompanied us for the benefit of his health and was not one of the chosen team, but he played afterwards in every Test match.[6]

The voyage was monotonous and not particularly comfortable, storms in the Mediterranean, intense heat between Port Said and Colombo, the tedium broken by the usual sports and games and concerts in which Jack, having inherited some of the family's musical talent, was required to contribute with a few songs. At last they arrived in Fremantle from where a local steamer took them to Perth. After two days' practice the tour began well enough with a win by an innings and 134 against Western Australia. Crawford made 43 to go with his four for 28 and three for 31, but had only one century and three half-centuries on the tour, including one in the third Test.

Hardstaff and Crawford indulged in a useful partnership and sent the 300 up, two hundred and thirty minutes after the start. Crawford, in making 43 out of 78 in forty minutes, drove with great power, hitting a six (off Christian) and five fours and punishing W. Hogue for 22 (five fours and a two) in one over. Crawford, who had more than one catch missed off him, took four wickets for 28 runs.[7]

A local paper reported:

JN CRAWFORD'S VIGOROUS DISPLAY ... He was slow at starting, but was loudly cheered for a magnificent drive for six off Christian. At 293 Hogue took the ball from Selk. Crawford continued to hit with tremendous vigour, and punished the new bowler in one over by scoring five fours and a two.[8]

There was also a first encounter with the questionable Australian umpiring which had been a feature of earlier tours.

> Fane and I were both run out. Fane's was a very good decision, as he was halfway down the pitch at the time. My stumps were put down by the wicketkeeper when the ball was in short slip's hands: otherwise this decision was also good.[9]

The team then embarked on *Himalaya* for the voyage to Adelaide, reached after a rough crossing of the Great Australian Bight. Between the party's arrival and the second match of the tour, there was a bit of socialising to do, including a civic reception and strawberries and cream at Aldgate.

However, the weather turned bitterly cold, there was a hailstorm and opportunities for practice before the South Australia match were restricted.

Jack's one century of the tour came in that match, but it proved to be a false dawn, for he had no more hundreds on the trip. It was, however, a spectacular effort, one of four in the tourists' 660 for 8 declared and preceded some high quality bowling which enabled the MCC to win a match which was heading for a draw.

> When this match was commenced, in the presence of the Governor, Sir George Le Hunte, and suite, the temperature was 146.9 in the sun and 94.5 in the shade ... Crawford hit twenty runs (five fours) off Wright in an over, and shortly afterwards added a huge straight drive for six off Claxton. The 500 went up in four hundred minutes, and Crawford made 50 in twenty-four minutes ... When Rhodes came in, he was content to leave the run-getting to Crawford, who hit Claxton for nineteen (four fours and a three) in an over. The sixth hundred was made in thirty-five minutes, and the Surrey amateur reached three figures in fifty-three. Crawford was seventh out at 643, having made his 114 out of 171 in fifty-eight minutes by a display of hitting which was said to be unparalleled in Australia.
>
> On the last morning play commenced at 11 o'clock, but, as stumps were to be drawn at a quarter to four to enable the Englishmen to catch the train to Melbourne, it was generally thought that the home side would have

> little difficulty in effecting a draw... The chief cause of the well-won success was the fine bowling of Crawford, whose five wickets cost only 40 runs. He varied his pace very skilfully and thoroughly deserved his success.[10]

Earlier cabled reports had been even more complimentary and a month before the following had appeared in *Cricket*'s Pavilion Gossip.

> At Adelaide, Melbourne and Sydney the work of the team has been spoken of in the highest terms. In the match with South Australia, JN Crawford's innings was stated to have been 'the best hitting display ever seen at Adelaide', which, so far as it is possible to judge from the cabled reports, does not appear to be an exaggeration, notwithstanding the many vigorous innings played there by JJ Lyons. The Surrey amateur followed his fine innings by taking five wickets for 40 runs, thereby enabling England to gain a most decisive victory. It was a great personal triumph, and a noteworthy event in the annals of English cricket.[11]

By any standards it was a remarkable innings: the author of *Trip to KangarooLand* let the local media do the talking. It waxed euphoric and under the headline, 'Hurricane Hitting', reported:

> As JN Crawford, the Benjamin of the team, not yet twenty-one years old, and wearing glasses, stepped jauntily from the members' reserve … no one dreamed of what the next hour had in store. The Surrey lad is a finely moulded, square-shouldered strapping young fellow, built for a hitter, and he has the reputation of being one of the hardest straight drivers in England. But he had never quite been placed in the Jessop school. Now he is there. Hit? JJ Lyons did big things in that line on the Adelaide Oval, but never anything quite in the same category for pace as Crawford's … Crawford, however, did not look like giving a chance. Standing fast-footed he smote in all directions with wrist-power behind his strokes, and the ball seemed to have no sooner struck his bat than it rebounded from the pickets. Whack! And a fast one from McBeath went sailing away over the ropes. In twenty-four minutes Crawford had made 52! A wristy cover hit and the ball dropped on the bicycle track … Biff, bang at a fast off-theory ball and Claxton, the bowler, had it back at him. Did he hold it? No fear. It was too hot. A wonder his wrist was not broken … Crawford landed in the Commonwealth as one of

> the star attractions of the team on account of his fine all-round play at such an early age – it was said he was the best boy cricketer seen in England since AG Steel's days at Cambridge. Now he has a reputation as a cutter to live up to, and it is safe to say that wherever the team may go the people will all want to see 'Young Crawford'... The people rose to him as the hurricane ran to the dressing-room and thoroughly he deserved the ovation and the congratulations of his comrades.[12]

For the statistically minded, one newspaper listed the new records established in the match, some more significant than others.

> The victory of the English cricket team over the South Australians by an innings and 183 runs has been made even more notable owing to the number of new cricket records the Britishers established. These are as follows: record partnership for fifth wicket in international cricket in Australia – Braund and Hardstaff 270; record partnership for sixth wicket for England v South Australia – Braund and Crawford 109; record score England v South Australia 660; record number of centuries in an innings in an international game in Australia – Braund 160, Hardstaff 185, Jones 119, Crawford 114; century on first appearance against a side – Hardstaff, Crawford; record number of extras in an innings in an international match in Australia – 44 (35 byes); record number of runs hit off a bowler without obtaining a wicket – O'Connor 0-108.[13]

Crawford had obviously made a great impression on the locals. It was mutual. He admired the ground and neighbouring amenities.

> It is a magnificent ground, with great stands extending nearly halfway round it. It is said to seat about 50,000 people, and it does not belie its looks. In one of the streets we found a splendid place for iced coffee and chocolate and Hutchings (or 'dear old Hutch,' as he was termed) and I used to go there of a morning before meandering down to the ground, arriving just in time to change previous to play.[14]

It was not the kind of warm up which would impress a modern fitness instructor, nor the kind of reporting time to endear the players to a twenty-first century Director of Cricket, but for Crawford, though he himself would not realise it at the time, it signalled an embryonic affinity between ground, city and cricketer which would stand him in good stead two years later and play an important part in his subsequent career.

Against Victoria at Melbourne, he followed in the footsteps of a number of predecessors, including WG Grace and Tom Richardson, in confirming that umpiring standards in Australia were below those to which he had become accustomed in England: 'Crawford, when, 10, was out lbw – a decision which caused him some surprise.'[15]

On this occasion, however, it was Crawford's slip-fielding which caught the eye, not least that of Tom Horan who wrote under the pen-name of Felix. Under the heading 'Happy Thoughts' he wrote:

> That catch by Crawford which disposed of M'Kenzie was worth going miles to see. I was standing near the sight-board, and I shall never forget the marvellous celerity of his left-handed dive. He took the ball which was travelling at a great pace, about 6in. or 8in. from the ground. 'Hard to beat' was the comment under the tree. Afterwards he took Warne in fine style.[16]

A series of low scores followed as Jack struggled to regain the form he had exhibited in Adelaide. However, others were scoring runs and he continued his high bowling standards as MCC continued to annihilate the state sides ahead of the first Test match.

Off the field, the tedium of travelling continued. Apart from one incident, the overnight journey from Melbourne to Sydney was, Crawford says, 'dull and uninteresting'.

> At 10.45 pm the same evening we had to change trains so as to get on the narrower gauge. As luck would have it, I had the top berth of the sleeping car, and so in case of accidents, I should have the further to fall. And an accident we did have, though not a serious one, thank goodness.
>
> It was like this: We were all sleeping fairly well under the 'circs' when about 4 am I hit my poor old head such a crack against the top of the berth that I thought my last days had come. But it was only for a moment that I felt a bit dazed. I heard a lot of people shouting just outside the window, and I heard one of them say that the brakes had worked of their own accord

> and had stopped the train within about twenty yards when it was travelling at the rate of thirty miles an hour. You can imagine what a jolt there was.[17]

The team arrived in Sydney mid-morning and, despite the journey, had to find sufficient energy to attend a civic reception, practice in the afternoon and, for the super-energetic, do a bit of socialising in the evening.

> In the evening Fane and I went to the theatre, and there met some of the company which was touring in Africa when Warner's team was out there; and a right jolly meeting it was. We were all pleased to see each other again.[18]

Crawford had predicted 'the hardest match of the tour as yet', but it was an overestimate, as the tourists won by the substantial margin of 408 runs. His own contribution was not significant this time; the match-winner was Sydney Barnes with figures of six for 24 'on a perfect pitch'.

> Crawford, who was never quite comfortable, was seventh out at 232 ... Crawford who followed in commenced by hitting Johnson to square leg for six, but, after making 10, was caught at slip ... Duff, who had been missed by Braund in the slips off Barnes, was yorked by Crawford ... England, thoroughly outplaying their opponents at all points, won by the great margin of 408 runs.[19]

On the Sunday between the second and third days of the New South Wales match, the team went off for a picnic on the Government launch, but Crawford chose to spend the day with the friends he had met at the theatre 'as water and sharks do not appeal to me'. Psychologically this was probably a sensible move; it can be stultifying spending all one's spare time with the same group of people.

They moved north to Brisbane where Queensland were beaten by an innings and 44 runs and, after a bit of golf, there was an evenly balanced rain-affected draw against an Australian XI before returning to Sydney for the Test. Unlike the trip round Sydney harbour a few days earlier, the journey to Brisbane was once again no picnic.

> We had a most awful journey from Sydney to Brisbane, and got such a shaking up that we all got headaches. The springs broke in the guard's van also as we were going round a sharp curve and caused a delay of a couple of hours.[20]

It was during the Queensland visit that Crawford, whose maturity as a cricketer was ahead of his chronological age, reached his twenty-first birthday, a milestone duly and generously acknowledged by the local association.

> MR JN CRAWFORD, who celebrated his twenty-first birthday whilst in Brisbane, was presented by the Queensland Cricket Association with a handsome silver-mounted stick, suitably inscribed. The stick was made from a very rare species of palm, obtainable in only one district in Australia, and to secure which the Association had to send over a thousand miles.[21]

In his *Trip to KangarooLand*, Jack is a little more specific about the provenance of the stick and also about a present received from his friend and vice-captain, Frederick Fane.

> At my coming of age (December 1st) the Queensland Cricket Association presented me with a rare stick, made from the Black Palm, which is only found on the Daintree River, mounted with my name and date. I was told that very few people in the world possess one, so I am naturally very fond of it, and I made a good speech in return – 'Thank you very much.' It was not too long, and they did not get tired. Fane also presented me with a fountain pen and it came in most handy for writing my weekly letters and correspondence.
>
> The stick was the handiwork of Mr JN Horton, Vice-President of the Queensland Association, and the presentation was made by Mr George Morrison of the Association.[22]

Not for the first or last time, pace bowling decided the outcome of an Anglo-Australian Test match, on this occasion in the form of Albert Cotter, Australia edging the encounter by the narrow margin of two wickets.

> Crawford, although twice hit by Cotter, made 31 in fifty minutes ere being bowled off his pad; he hit six fours , three of them off Armstrong in one over.

Cotter, keeping a fine length and bowling at a great pace, took six wickets for 101 and was very well supported by the field.[23]

As well as the quality of the Australian bowling, the stifling conditions also took their toll.

Monday brought with it the hottest day we had experienced – no sun, but an awful moist heat, without a breath of air. People and critics at home have no realization of what a trial six days of it is to those who have been used only to playing cricket under England's skies.[24]

Tests were timeless in this series; the fifth day was washed out and the match was not concluded until the sixth with the result that the start of the next match, against a Victorian XI at South Melbourne, was delayed and curtailed. A result was never likely in a high-scoring draw described by Crawford as 'profoundly uninteresting' and as 'an absurd match [which] ought not to have been played at all'. As in South Africa two years earlier, he was tried as an opening batsman, joining his young Surrey colleague, Jack Hobbs.

Crawford, who went in with Hobbs began luckily, being dropped by Collins at square-leg off Armstrong before he had made a run and by McAllister in the slips off Saunders when 3. Fifty went up without loss in thirty-three minutes but thirteen runs later the first wicket fell, Crawford being caught at mid-on. He made some good hits and played confidently when set; he scored his 43 out of 63 in forty-five minutes and hit three sixes (two off Armstrong and one off Smith) and four fours ... In the entire match 901 runs were scored and 18 wickets fell.[25]

Boxing Day saw an up-country fixture in Bendigo, against eighteen of that gold-mining town. It was a hopeless mis-match which the tourists took none too seriously.

Hobbs and Crawford made 39 in twenty minutes before the latter was caught at the wickets: he hit four fours in his 25. The batting of Bendigo calls for no description as the score-sheet tells its own tale. The first four

> wickets fell at 10 and the longest partnership of the innings was 13 by Petree and Attwater for the eleventh. The only player to make any stand was the latter, a left-hander, who, going in fifth wicket down, carried out his bat for 26 – a plucky but somewhat lucky effort. Crawford and Blythe, assisted by the wicket, bowled with great effect, the innings being over in less than an hour and a half. At five o'clock rain again fell and the match had to be abandoned.[26]

England made 213, Bendigo made 55 with seven ducks and two men absent.

Neither the travelling nor weather conditions had improved: 'We had an awful time going to Bendigo. The train journey was very trying. The wind was like a blast from a furnace. In the distance bush fires were blazing. The heat was 100 degrees in the shade – a pretty thing for Christmas Eve.' Later, however, 'It rained for 27 hours, in which time five inches of rain fell. Besides this deluge a thunderstorm raged for nearly four hours, the lightning being especially vivid. The temperature fell suddenly from 100 degrees to 50 degrees – and on that account we all caught most awful colds.'[27]

The second Test, beginning on New Year's Day in Melbourne, was a more serious affair, but weather conditions were no less oppressive than in Sydney or Bendigo and the match was played against a background of disturbances among the spectators.

> Six days of heat and misery signalised the second Test match at Melbourne. Free fights took place among the crowd, and the police had to intervene very frequently. Drinks were brought out every hour, but even then each hour seemed like 360 minutes long.[28]

England eventually scraped home by the narrow margin of one wicket. It was slow, attritional cricket, predictive of what Test matches were to become over the next century. After the experiment of using Crawford as an opening batsman, he was now back to number eight, but his bowling performance continued to attract compliments: 'The cricket had been slow throughout, but the fielding and bowling, especially Crawford's and Fielder's was very good indeed ... considering the excellence of the wicket the total of 266 was by no means large. Crawford, who took five wickets for 79, was at his best and always appeared difficult.'[29]

Another report said, 'I can only describe the Australian score as very moderate, in fact, it pays a tremendous tribute to the excellence of the English bowling and fielding. Crawford bowled really finely all the time he was on, and it is quite his best performance during the tour.'[30]

Travelling and the high temperatures continued to take their toll. The pressures of back-to-back Test matches are not a recent phenomenon, but in 1908 there were not the advantages of luxury air travel.

> None of us looked forward to travelling to Adelaide by the 4.40 train. Two test matches in succession were really too much of a good thing ... when we arrived the temperature stood at 154 in the sun and 108 in the shade. We had two days' fielding in the excessive heat.[31]

The press also commented on the heat:

> Apart from the illness of the Captain, there has not been an important match in which the heat has not told adversely on some prominent English player. In the present game Crawford has suffered and news now comes from Melbourne that Humphries will there undergo a surgical operation. As Crawford's bowling has been the outstanding feature of the English effort, it is sincerely to be hoped that he will be fit to take his place in the last match.[32]

The Adelaide Test resulted in a 245-run win for the Australians, Crawford's batting attracting admiration on this occasion.

> Crawford who gave the best display on the side was then bowled for a faultless innings which contained eight fours: he hit hard whenever opportunity offered and made his 62 out of 86 in 110 minutes.[33]

Injuries and illness were, however, beginning to have their effect. Most seriously, captain AO Jones was obliged to hand over the captaincy to Frederick Fane for the first three matches and George Gunn, who had accompanied the party for his health and was not part of the original selection, found himself playing in all five Tests.

> One can ask, without being charged with making excuses for a beaten side, whether any team touring Australia has ever experienced so much misfortune as the one now there. Almost every week the cable has brought needs of some unlucky occurrence. No sooner was Jones able to resume his place in the team after his long illness, than Crawford strained his heart and Humphries found it necessary to undergo a surgical operation in Melbourne. Furthermore, Fielder sustained a strain while playing against New South Wales and was unable to take part in the last Test match in consequence. Fortune has certainly not been kind to the Englishmen throughout.[34]

The local press went into more detail about Jack's heart condition.

> Crawford was not feeling very well and consulted Dr RH Strong on Saturday. An examination revealed the fact that the right side of his heart has been strained. It was too late to prevent his playing in the Test match now going on, as he had already started; but Dr Strong advised his going on as slowly as circumstances would admit. Crawford's condition is not serious but it is imperative that he should not over-exert himself. If England wins the present match he will if possible play in the final test in Sydney but if Australia should win he will not take part in any further game during the present tour. Dr Strong has advised Crawford to consult a London specialist as soon as he returns to England.[35]

The condition did not prevent his travelling to Tasmania with the team, although he played in only the first of the two matches. In Launceston:

> Crawford, who took four wickets for 75 runs bowled most accurately and deserved a better analysis ... Crawford, who hit a five and four fours in scoring 22 out of 26 in a quarter of an hour, was bowled by the left-hander, Martin.[36]

The Tasmanian landscape around Launceston left an indelible impression, the journey from Launceston to Hobart a less favourable one.

> There is a most magnificent bit of scenery round here. The river Tamar in this part runs between two hills and on one side the path through the gorge is lit up by electricity. It has a most beautiful effect especially when the moon is at the full. We sat there for some hours and sang songs which echoed all round the hills … It took six hours to get from Launceston to Hobart, a distance of 130 miles. The track wound round the mountains something like a corkscrew, so that the front guard could nearly at times shake hands with the rear guard. They had to have a guard at each end of the train for fear they should twist round at some siding and go back again without knowing it … Fane got nearly sea-sick through turning round so much.[37]

Jack stood down for the second match against Tasmania, at Hobart, but was back for the return fixture against Victoria at Melbourne, which MCC won by 330 runs against a side weakened because the first-choice Victorian team were delayed in Sydney by an elongated match with New South Wales.[38]

> The good work was continued by Crawford, who reached 50 in forty minutes and claimed 69 of the 103 runs added for the sixth wicket in fifty minutes.[39]

It was in this match that, in days long before the Anti-Corruption Unit imposed its no-betting clauses in contracts, Crawford won a wager – a bottle of champagne – for hitting a six in his first over, from captain and medium-pacer, Frank Laver.[40]

The fourth Test at Melbourne was lost by the large margin of 308 runs, Crawford being unable to repeat his heroics in the state match, making just a single in the first innings and doing not quite as well as that in the second. He made amends with the ball however, and, as at Melbourne first time around, captured another eight wickets in the match, but could do nothing to prevent a heavy defeat.

He missed the New South Wales match at Sydney but, disregarding Dr Strong's advice, was back for the final Test and fourth defeat, though himself defiant and undefeated in what turned out to be his final Test innings.

> Barnes was bowled, leaving Crawford to carry out his bat for 24 – an innings marked by strong defence and some powerful strokes.[41]

He was less than three months past his twenty-first birthday, but incredibly his twelve-match Test career was already over. Strong defence and powerful strokes were to characterise the rest of his life, both on and off the field. In his summing up of the tour, after some acknowledgement that England had not had the best of fortune in that the captain had been sidelined with pneumonia and regretting that Hayes had not made the Test side, 'Felix' went on to say:

> Another drawback was that Crawford, through his tremendously hard work, got run down and actually played when he should have been resting. I have played a lot of cricket in my time, and I can say that in all my career I never saw any man try harder or 'graft' harder than Crawford. He lets himself go every ounce, every time.[42]

His efforts saw him top the Test bowling averages, slightly ahead of Fielder and Barnes. Furthermore, he was the leading wicket-taker in first-class matches on the tour with 66 at just over 25 each. The contribution of all three, but especially Crawford who inspired comparisons with a legendary Surrey bowler of an earlier generation, was recognised by the press.

> A Fielder, SF Barnes and JN Crawford are great bowlers, even on Australian wickets ... George Lohmann was a wonder at mixing the pace. JN Crawford who is also of Surrey, is the most proficient in this respect among the bowlers now with us. He whips in the fast ball, very cleverly, very fast and not too frequently. And it is often a yorker.[43]

Tour manager Philip Trevor said much the same, but at greater length.

> Crawford, too, holds a high place in the list of tryers and he well deserved the popularity which he gained in Australia. As a Salamander cricketer he

> certainly takes first prize. His energy was wont to rise with the thermometer; and, had the latter risen much higher, Crawford as a fast bowler would have rivalled Knox or Kortright. It was to unwearied effort that he owed much of his bowling success. He never despaired, and he never tired, and, though he did not bowl on all occasions very steadily, there was always a chance of the real Crawford ball – which is liable to defeat the best of batsmen – coming at any moment. As a batsman he hardly maintained his reputation, though his big hitting came as a revelation to many people in Australia. Still he played one absolutely first-class innings in a Test match and one very dramatic innings in a State match. No doubt the fact that Crawford did not do better as a batsman and that Young did not do well at all will be attributed by many people to the effect of Australian glare upon English spectacles. At the same time it would be difficult to name any two young cricketers who were less given to the making of excuses for personal failure than they. Indeed, they were too ready to convict themselves on slender evidence of the charge of making a mistake.[44]

The tour ended with two tame draws in Adelaide and Perth. Crawford's contributions were a half-century in the first match and four for 85 in the second from forty overs, the most he had bowled in one innings outside the Test matches. It had been an exhausting programme, stretching over almost five months extended by the team's honouring a commitment to play in a charity match in Ceylon on the return journey when some of them represented Lieut-Col Koe's XI against Mr Vanderspar's XII.

> It had been arranged on the way out that we should play a match at Colombo on our return. Some of the cricketing faculty were very anxious to see us, and the bands had been rehearsing 'See the Conquering Heroes come' up to the middle of the fourth Test match.[45]

Following a tour during which he had bowled 566 overs in first-class matches alone, mostly in hot weather, he signed off with 96 not out at number nine and five for 57 in fifteen overs, more than any other bowler. It did nothing to invalidate Felix's comments. In just over a month the first-class season in England would begin.

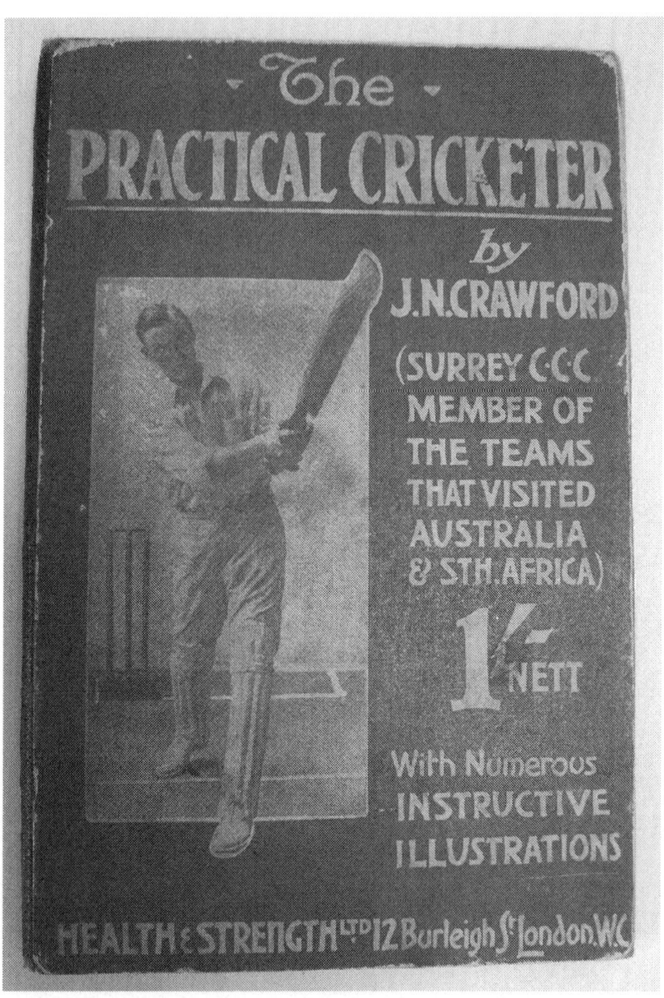

Jack's second foray into writing: a how-to book for cricketers.

7

THE PRACTICAL CRICKETER

SURREY 1908-09

Logic suggested that on the basis of his performances over the last four seasons and two overseas tours, Crawford, despite his youth – he was still only twenty-one – might be a strong candidate for the captaincy vacated by Lord Dalmeny to enable him to devote more time to his parliamentary duties.

During Crawford's absence in Australia, however, a decision had already been taken.

> It was known for some time that Lord Dalmeny, who was asked by his constituents to choose between Midlothian and mid-field, would be unable to continue the captaincy of the Surrey Eleven, although he would in all probability be able to assist the side occasionally. Much speculation was at once aroused as to who would be his successor, but it has only recently been officially announced that Mr HDG Leveson-Gower, one of the keenest of cricketers, is to undertake the duties. The choice is one upon which the County, the Committee and the player named are all to be congratulated.[1]

Leveson Gower had been offered the captaincy five years earlier when it was relinquished by Digby Jephson, but had declined because 'at my time of life, business must have the first claim on me'.[2] Now, however, he was keen to take on the role. Any speculation about alternatives which might have been aroused did not extend to the Surrey Committee where a firm decision was taken as early as January that Leveson Gower be appointed.

There is evidence of the strong bond of the old school tie (albeit Winchester and Eton) between William Findlay, the Surrey Secretary, now one year into his appointment, and Leveson Gower. When the post of Secretary became vacant on the death of Charles Alcock, Lord Harris (like Findlay, Eton and Oxford) had contacted Leveson Gower who, almost half a century later was to recall:

> No county has ever had a more far-seeing Secretary than Charles Alcock and when he had retired beyond recall, a great successor was at hand. I well remember the late Lord Harris saying to me. 'Your County will be very lucky if a great friend of mine and yours, William Findlay, could be induced to take Alcock's place. He is one in a thousand. Don't forget I told you.'[3]

There had been, at least notionally, a formal selection procedure.

> The Committee considered the list of applications for the vacant office of Secretary and from the list selected the following FH Bacon, WT Graburn, DLA Jephson, RV Ryder, RA Sawyer, GJ Weigall, FF Matthews & WE Roller.
>
> It was decided to appoint a Sub-Committee consisting of the President, Messrs Stein, S Colman, Longman, J Shuter & Lord Dalmeny to recommend three to the General Committee but any member of General Committee to have power to suggest other names ... The Sub-Committee to be held Tuesday March 19 at 4.30.[4]

The minutes are in manuscript. To the first list between Bacon and Graburn has been added the name of W Findlay; to the second between Shuter and Dalmeny, Leveson Gower. It is conceivable that the omission of one of the names was a drafting error, but it is stretching the arm of coincidence too far to conclude that both were and the strong likelihood is that both were *ex post facto* amendments.

Nonetheless, the sub-committee went through the formalities and unanimously recommended in order of merit Findlay, Ryder and Sawyer. The recommendation was accepted at the next meeting of the Committee held two days later and Findlay was appointed to the Secretaryship and elected a member, proposed by Lord Alverstone and seconded by HDG Leveson Gower.

There were hints that even the apparently doctored minutes do not tell the full story.

> As [Alcock's] successor in the post of Secretary, Mr W Findlay, the Oxford and Lancashire cricketer, was appointed. Some little soreness was felt at the committee going outside the county to find a secretary, but as Lord Alverstone explained at the Annual Meeting, a Surrey man would have been given the post if a fitting candidate had been available. According to common report two Surrey men had the refusal of the position, but for private reasons neither could accept. That in the circumstances a wise choice was made in appointing Mr Findlay there can be little doubt.[5]

Meanwhile, away from the refined heights of the Committee Room and nearer to the grass roots of the club, Jack Crawford continued to seek financial assistance. It had been agreed two years earlier at the beginning of his first full season for the club that he should receive ten shillings a day for expenses in county matches at The Oval and that a season ticket (second class) from London to Coulsdon be provided for him. The arrangement was renewed for 1907 and at the end of that season it was agreed to meet his laundry bill of £2.0s.8d. For 1908 the arrangement was amended and on Leveson Gower's proposal to the Cricket Committee, he was allowed expenses of 20/- per day for all home matches and at the same time it was agreed that amateurs be paid an extra day's allowance when a Sunday intervened between two matches.[6]

It is an illustration of the differences not between amateurs and professionals, but within the ranks of the amateurs. Meeting Lord Dalmeny's laundry bill would not have been an issue. He was the son of the former Prime Minister, succeeding to the title of the Earl of Roseberry in 1929 and adding the proceeds of horse racing to an already considerable fortune. On his death in 1974 he left a net estate of almost £10 million.[7] However comparable Crawford and Dalmeny may have been as batsmen, in terms of wealth they were leagues apart.

The benevolence of the Committee was not without limits, however, and the minutes for the following season reflect a less favourably disposed attitude. A complaint from Crawford's father is dealt with by means of a somewhat cryptic reply and a request for financial treatment similar to that enjoyed by the professionals is summarily dealt with.

> A letter from the Rev JC Crawford stating that his son Mr JN Crawford, had received no good wishes from the Committee for his success in Australia was read. The Secretary was instructed to inform Mr Crawford that his son was not allowed to leave without any expression of good wishes.[8]

> An application for 'standing down' money for Mr JN Crawford in the match Surrey v Cambridge University was not entertained.[9]

The rift between those in and those under authority was widening.

It seems likely that there was some resentment on Crawford's part over Leveson Gower's appointment which was to simmer for a season and a half and boil over in the middle of the following summer. As a cricketer, Leveson Gower had a respectable enough record at Winchester and Oxford, both of which he had captained. However, as he himself admitted in one of *Cricket*'s 'Chats on the Cricket Field', it is a step-up from there to the first-class game.[10] It was one which Crawford had made seamlessly, Leveson Gower less so. The judgment of the regulars at the Scarborough Festival with which the new captain was to be involved over a number of years might have been, with due northern forthrightness, that Leveson Gower was not fit to lace Crawford's boots.

Jack did not get away to the best of starts as Surrey opened their season at The Oval against the Gentlemen of England. The weather conditions were starkly different from what Crawford and his England colleagues had experienced in Australia.

> Although there had been a fall of snow in the early morning, it was found possible to make a start with the match at ten minutes past twelve ... Crawford and Holland added 65 by very bright cricket, the amateur, who batted an hour for 46 being responsible for the majority of the runs.
>
> Crawford, who took risks and was missed three times, made some big hits – one on to the Pavilion roof and another to the press-box ... An unfortunate and serious accident happened to Mr Leveson-Gower who, in endeavouring to stop a powerful drive off Lees, fractured the top joint of his thumb. It is not considered likely that the Surrey captain will be able to take the field again till June.
>
> Yesterday, owing to effective bowling by Crawford and Busher, there was only a short day's cricket, the Gentlemen, upon following on, collapsing for 130.[11]

Both of Crawford's brothers, Frank and Reggie, opposed Surrey in the Gentlemen of England team and played a significant part in the batting, scoring 91 and 55 of their team's first-innings total of 219. Reggie, however was part of his brother's four for 21 in the second. Ironically, it was a drive from Frank that resulted in Leveson Gower's injury, although *Cricket*'s report was over-pessimistic. He was back in harness in mid-May.

It was a significant match for another reason, being WG Grace's last in first-class cricket. Now in his sixtieth year, he captained the side, opened the batting and bowled a couple of overs.

Meanwhile, the day after the match finished:

> Mr Henry Dudley Gresham Leveson-Gower, fourth surviving son of the late Mr. Granville Leveson-Gower, of Titsey Place, Surrey, was married on Thursday last at St. George's, Hanover Square, to Enid, elder daughter of the late Mr RSB Hammond-Chambers KC, the officiating clergy being the Dean of Hereford, the Rev FAG Leveson-Gower, and the Rev F Parnell. Mr HB Chinnery acted as best man, and the Surrey County CC was represented by Mr W Findlay. As a result of his accident at The Oval two days before, the bridegroom carried his left arm in a sling. The honeymoon is being spent at the residence of the Hon Eustace and Mrs Fiennes, at Swansea.[12]

It was an establishment wedding *par excellence*. Had the bride chosen to follow the practice of appending her maiden surname to that of her husband, she could have gone through the remainder of her life on earth with a quadruple-barrelled name.

Meanwhile, Crawford had taken himself off on holiday and missed the opening three Championship matches of the season. As an amateur and not under the same contractual obligations as the professionals, he was perfectly entitled to do so and no one would begrudge him time off after an arduous tour of Australia. However, in the same way that some continental football clubs spend their winter break playing friendlies elsewhere, he enjoyed something of a busman's holiday by playing a couple of games of club cricket, one at Cane Hill and one in South Wales, having already turned out in the match against the Gentlemen of England when most would have seen the Championship fixtures as the more important.

> JN CRAWFORD had some useful practice at Coulsdon on Saturday at the expense of Middlesex Hospital. Playing for Cane Hill Asylum, he scored 56 – the only double-figure in a total of 111, which included 24 extras – and took four wickets for 32 runs and seven for 9, including the hat-trick.[13]

> JN AND RT CRAWFORD were well to the fore in the match at Newport (Mon) on Saturday last between Newport and a team raised and captained by Mr C Williams of Goytrey Hall. They had a hand in the downfall of every Newport wicket, dismissing the side for 89, and in their four innings made 102 runs, JN scoring 3 and 26 and RT 59 and 14. The latter obtained 28 runs off an over of seven balls – a six, five fours and a two – and 46 off three consecutive overs.[14]

To judge by the reaction at the Annual General Meeting, Jack was clearly being missed by the members.

> After presenting Lord Dalmeny with a silver cigar box and expressing the hope that he would play when available, President Lord Alverstone continued ... Mr Knox would become available again in July and he hoped that Mr JN Crawford (cheers) would be available for the whole summer. Lord

Dalmeny, in replying, said that no one would begrudge the last-named his holiday after all the fine work he had got through in Australia, and they all hoped he would be in the same all-round form as last season.[15]

In the meantime, Jack was devoting himself to other activities.

I understand that JN Crawford will shortly appear before the public in a new role – that of author. He is devoting his leisure time to the compilation of a booklet entitled *JN Crawford's Trip to KangarooLand*, which will be illustrated by 'Rip' and published at a shilling.[16]

Surrey had done well enough in Jack's absence. All three matches were at The Oval where a rain-affected draw against Northamptonshire was followed by comfortable wins against Hampshire and Derbyshire In the captain's continued absence, Lord Dalmeny reappeared and captained the side in the third of these before Crawford took over against Gloucestershire, also at The Oval. The first two days were washed out, but leading from the front with his own batting and bowling coupled with astute captaincy, he almost conjured a victory in the one day remaining.

Although heavy rain prevented a ball being bowled on either of the first two days so much progress was made on the third that Surrey came within an ace of winning, twenty-seven wickets going down for 378 runs and Gloucestershire, when stumps were drawn, being 102 runs behind with only four tail-end wickets in hand ... Surrey ... had a good side, including Crawford, who was captain ... Crawford joined Marshal and gave a delightful display. Of the 59 added for the fifth wicket in twenty-seven minutes, the amateur, who hit seven fours and three twos, claimed as many as 40; he made some lusty pulls and drives ... Crawford and Marshal quickly hit up 34 together and then the innings was declared closed, leaving Gloucestershire only forty-five minutes in which to obtain 143 to win. A draw appeared a certainty, but there was considerable excitement before the close.

Crawford, in addition to leading the side skilfully and giving the best display of batting on either side, bowled eleven overs for 14 runs and five wickets.[17]

In June, shortly after a 'Chat' in *Cricket* in which he rehearses how he learned and practised the game at Cane Hill and Repton and offers mature opinions on some of the Australian players he had encountered on his recent tour, Jack recorded his highest innings, 232 against Somerset, the first time Surrey had encountered the West Country side for four years.[18]

> A fortnight ago it was remarked in *Cricket* of Mr. JN Crawford: 'As a batsman his ability is great, and it is probable that, well as he has hitherto performed, he is destined to reach still greater heights as a run-getter.' Exactly a week after these words, he played by far his highest innings in first-class cricket, scoring 232 against Somerset at Kennington in just under four hours, and, in partnership with Holland (87), adding 308 runs in 210 minutes for the fifth wicket. It was a delightful example of free and vigorous cricket, which contained two fives, twenty-eight fours and eleven threes as the most remunerative strokes. He was twice missed, when 189 and 223, but at the time he offered the latter chance he had abandoned safe tactics and was hitting out with the sole idea of scoring quickly. He afterwards obtained eight wickets, and had so much to do with the easy victory secured by his side.[19]

> Crawford hit magnificently in front of the wicket, his driving being particularly powerful. His 196 not out [his score at close of play on day one] constitutes the best batting performance Crawford has ever accomplished in first-class cricket in England. The young amateur made several false hits, but so far as could be seen he only gave one real chance.[20]

308 remains the record for Surrey's fifth wicket against Somerset and was until 2005 the highest for that wicket against any opposition.[21] Until Sibley's innings in September 2013, Crawford was the club's youngest double centurion.

He bowled unchanged in the first innings and followed up with a further twenty-one overs in the second, taking four wickets in each innings. *Cricket* drew the comparison with his brothers' achievements.

> It is worthy of remark that VFS, RT, and JN, have each made over two hundred in an innings on the Surrey ground, the first-named having scored 218 for Young Amateurs v Young Professionals of Surrey in 1896, and RT 243 for Surrey Colts v Stanley CC four years later.[22]

He had two further centuries that season. Against Derbyshire he 'made some splendid hits during the 125 minutes he was in' and against Hampshire, 'he hit four sixes (all huge drives off Llewellyn) and sixteen fours and made his runs all round the wicket, excelling in driving and cutting.'[23]

In addition to the Gloucestershire match in which he had demonstrated some enterprising leadership, he captained the side on two other occasions, in the away match at Leicestershire which Surrey won by 86 runs and in the rain-ruined home match against the same county, in which his brother Frank occupied the same berth for the opposition.

Eighteen months of cricket with few breaks had taken their toll even on a fit young man in his early twenties. He was not alone in suffering the debilitating effects of the heat and travelling involved in an Australian tour and while he was far from ineffective, his bowling in particular lacked the sharpness and accuracy of earlier years.

> Up to a certain point JN Crawford was clearly the best bowler in the eleven, but as the summer advanced he became stale and as a natural consequence ineffective. Moreover, even when he was in form, he was apt to lose his pitch in the endeavour to get more spin on the ball ... When it came to serious business Hayward, JN Crawford, Marshal and Hobbs stood out by themselves ... JN Crawford was splendid up to a certain time but in batting no less than in bowling he declined as the season went on, having evidently had too much cricket.[24]

He missed a third consecutive 100 wicket and 1,000 run double by just two wickets, but had bowled fewer overs and his batting average had improved. At 40.4 for Championship matches, he was second only to Tom Hayward and had scored three of Surrey's seventeen centuries that season. Hobbs had five, Hayward and Marshal four each and Hayes one.

Even his new captain, with whom Crawford would later have an antagonistic relationship, was begrudgingly complimentary.

> JB Hobbs and JN Crawford were young players of exceptional promise and merit … among other players for Surrey in the first decade of this century were VFS Crawford, a powerful off-driver, and his brother JN who ranked as one of the best of the young all-rounders.[25]

The season over and no winter tour in 1908/09, Crawford's sporting interests switched to club hockey where he played occasionally as centre-forward for Staines and, with international HR Jordan at inside left, spearheaded some match winning performances.

> HR Jordan, the international inside left was in great form last Saturday. Playing for Staines against Ealing, he shot no less than eight goals out of twelve, the remaining quartette being notched by JN Crawford, the Surrey cricketer.[26]

> The revival of Staines is the most noteworthy topic of the week. At the beginning of the season the once prominent team failed to rise above the ordinary, which was difficult to understand with such able players as Freeman, Mansbridge, JN Crawford, Jordan and Eric Green in the ranks.
>
> For the first time since Pimm left the Staines defence got into working order, but the real explanation of the debacle was the failure of the Ealing halves against the exceptionally brilliant forward play of HP Jordan and the famous cricketer JN Crawford. The latter led the attack splendidly and showed how fine a player he would be if he turned out regularly. He scored four of the goals but it was left to Jordan to be the outstanding man of the match.[27]

Staines, formed in 1890, is one of the world's oldest hockey clubs and remains one of the country's foremost. Harry Freeman and Eric Green represented Great Britain in the gold medal winning team at the 1908 London Olympic Games, so this was clearly high standard competitive sport in which Crawford, for a short time at any rate, played a leading part. On Boxing Day, both Jack and Frank played at Horley for Mr WI Hampton's XI against Lowfield Heath. They won 11-4, Jack scoring one of the goals.

The winter must also have involved a little cricket training. Crawford had not advanced as far as he had in the first-class game without having given some thought to it, nor without sound techniques in the three disciplines of batting, bowling and fielding. He put his ideas together in a comprehensive coaching manual, *The Practical Cricketer*, published in early 1909. Parts of it are inevitably dated, but the early twentieth century was beginning to see the development of the game as we know it today and much of what he has to say has a contemporary relevance. He was certainly in no doubt about his credentials and sets them out in a self-confident preface.

> Regarding my qualifications, I do not propose to speak at any length, because obliging chroniclers have done that already, which impels me to surmise that I am already known to you ... By the ordinary method of computation, my residence on this planet has not been a lengthy one. Nevertheless, as a devotee from childhood, a variety of cricket experiences has fallen to my lot, embracing participation in Public School, Club, County, and representative cricket, with tours to Australia and South Africa respectively thrown in.

'Pace is to a great extent a gift, like red hair or a taste for collecting postage stamps,' his colleague Neville Knox had written in the *Daily Mail* two years earlier.[28] That may be partially true, for fast bowling and other aspects of the game, but even a gift has to be cultivated and *wunderkind* Jack Crawford, himself a medium-pace bowler, has sound advice for his less talented contemporaries:

> Medium, my normal pace, which in the hands of a capable bowler is a happy medium. This bowler has the privilege of being able to vary his pace in either direction, and while he can command a good deal of the slow bowler's break, he has some of the fast bowlers pace to help him.
>
> My brother RT of Leicestershire has wrought havoc on certain pitches with a ball which eludes explanation, if not description. It approaches you in a line until about a couple of yards off the pitch, then appears to be going for your leg stump, winding up by breaking from the off.[29]

The arts of spin and cut were still in their formative stages, though George Hirst and others were developing the skills of swing bowling, but we seem to have here an example of a combination of either outswing and an off-cutter or outswerve and an off-break.

> – Good length means command of length, not one length. A faulty length through ill-pitching is one thing: an over-pitched or short-pitched ball with a purpose is another.
> – A writer on cricket expressed a casual opinion some time ago that a promising opening exists for a departure from the now stereotyped off theory. His proposal was that the bowler should hammer away at the leg stump in the old round-arm style, which he suggested would have the best modern batsmen at sea. Perhaps it would, at any rate for a time. The idea has something of the novel and the reactionary. I pass it on for the benefit of bowlers with a highly experimental turn of mind.[30]

He had already gone into print with 'The Art of Bowling', a syndicated feature in which he stresses the need for constant practice, surveys the techniques of earlier and contemporary bowlers, comments on the new-fangled 'googley' bowling and mentions his own approach.

> I have always been taught to keep the ball an inch or two outside the off-stump, so that the batsman is made to play all the time.[31]

It would be a few years before this approach, still valid, would lead to the designation of 'the corridor of uncertainty'. For a number of years the received wisdom on the art of bowling had been to bowl at or outside the off stump to a packed off-side field. Walter Read had offended traditionalists by exploiting the gaps such tactics left on the leg side by developing the pull stroke, but off theory remained dominant.[32] Leg theory and bodyline were still more than twenty years in the future and off spinners bowling defensively round the wicket on to leg stump even further away. So, as Crawford says, the idea is novel and reactionary, but like other aspects of his life, is an indicator that he was a man ahead of his time.

RG Barlow lists Crawford among fifteen contemporary bowlers who adapt their bowling to the state of the pitch and 'use their heads as much as their arms'.[33] His 'off-break', says EHD Sewell, was bowled off the second finger rather than the first, suggesting that it might have been closer to an off-cutter and that he used the conventional first-finger off-break as a variation for his slower ball.[34]

Less technical, but perhaps more poetic, Cardus summed up Crawford's bowling style.

> He ran to bowl with easy swinging strides, a rhythmical and not too long line of approach, then he 'delivered' with a fling away to his left, as his arm came over, but the left shoulder and side of him were always classically forward ... He was gifted with ability so rare that I am tempted to say he possessed genius for the game.[35]

A more than competent slip fielder, though his personal preference was for cover point, he offers the following practical hints.

> The whole-hearted cricketer will regard fielding as a pleasure as well as a duty ... In catching, the hands should be adjusted to meet the angle at which the ball comes to you, so that it falls into the opening of a cup-like receptacle. A ball coming towards your person or high up should be taken with the thumbs towards each other; a dropping ball with the fingers towards each other.[36]

On batting, some of the terminology may have changed – for example, the pull has become the sweep and the hook has become the pull – but his advice on defensive technique and on driving has relevance more than a hundred years later.

> The first canon of batting is that the bat shall be held straight. This means that it shall present a straight attitude viewed from the front. Apart from the consideration of gracefulness, the advantage of this is obvious. It is a simple lesson in mathematics. The bat in that way covers a greater proportion of the wicket than any other ... Viewed at right angles, the bat should be seen to incline forward, taking an upward view of the implement, i.e. the top part

> should project. This is designed to keep the ball down. The left hand should clasp the bat so that the top of the palm just reaches the top of the handle, the right hand placed underneath almost touching.[37]

Although sound technique is the basis of all successful defensive and attacking batsmanship, Crawford's colleagues saw far more of the latter than the former. It is instructive therefore to see the hints provided by one of the foremost big-hitting batsmen of his generation.

> The on-drive is brought into play for balls pitching at the middle and leg stumps or the batsman's legs ... As with the off-drive, I favour over-pitched balls ... Take careful note of the situation of the field if you lift the ball. There is more danger with a slow bowler, because there will be more men in the out-field ... When you cannot get to the ball in the ordinary way, you may sometimes effect the stroke by the 'quick-footed' drive, going out to the ball as it pitches.[38]

There is of course nothing on switch hitting, reverse sweeps, dillscoops, doosras, reverse swing and other novelties of the late twentieth and early twenty-first centuries, but on the techniques of the game, as understood at the time, his comments are absolutely watertight.

Crawford played in spectacles, but it was no disadvantage to him, any more than it was to Percy Fender, MJK Smith, Paul Winslow, Geoffrey Boycott or Daniel Vettori. It is important to distinguish between good eyesight and a good eye. Tests on Sir Donald Bradman demonstrated that his eyesight was no better than average, slightly below in fact when compared with students at Adelaide University, but where he and others were exceptional was in the 'eye' – the ability to pick up the length of a ball from the delivery and in hand-eye co-ordination.[39] Outstanding batsmen always seem to have plenty of time and share the same attribute of seeing the ball early and playing it late. Crawford certainly had that.

Sportsmen's literary talents often lag way behind their athletic prowess and the services of a ghostwriter are required before their efforts hit the bookshops. Not so in Crawford's case, as recognised by the reviews.

> We are not aware what his academic record at Repton was, but really this book is just such a one as we should have expected from Crawford. It is written with great care – like his well-groomed hair there is not a word out of place – and it embodies in admirable English, free from a single slangy phrase, as sound and practical advice as anyone could hope to give a young cricketer. We do not remember to have seen a better definition of the various strokes – driving, cutting, leg hitting, the glance, the pull, the hook – or plainer counsel as to the best mode of acquiring perfection in them. He has also much to say as to selecting the ball to hit, jumping out, timing and power, 'carpeting' and 'ballooning', placing, adaptation of tactics, and variation of wickets. As to bowling, he tells us about accuracy of length, variation of pitch, pace and its variation, break, the 'googlie', and spin and swerve. Altogether it is an excellent shilling-worth, and we heartily commend it to the notice of every budding aspirant for honours on the cricket field.[40]

> Many excellent and sensible books have emanated from the office of 'Health and Strength', Burleigh Street, London but none of the series will be of such general and widespread interest as *The Practical Cricketer*. The author is Mr JN Crawford of Surrey and a member of the English teams visiting Australia and South Africa. Provided the ambitious young cricketer will practise on the lines laid down by Mr Crawford he will develop his cricket as highly as possible, and, incidentally, will do himself incalculable good physically. The book is not mere theory – it is fully illustrated and the text matter is so plain and concise that there is no mistaking the advice. Mr Crawford goes through the whole – the spirit of the game, batting, bowling, fielding and wicketkeeping, and speaks also of proper training and practice.[41]

That he practised what he preached is evidenced in contemporary reports and his reputation as a six-hitter is chronicled by Gerald Brodribb. Let it not be forgotten that when Crawford started playing the game (and indeed until 1910 when the Advisory Committee of the Counties resolved that all hits clearing the boundary on the full should count for six runs) a boundary six had not only to clear the boundary, but actually be hit out of the ground – easier at some venues than on others, The Oval where Crawford played his home matches being one of the larger ones with pavilion and stands beyond the normal boundary. The pavilion wall is over a hundred yards from the pitch.

The Practical Cricketer was published almost simultaneously with *Trip to KangarooLand*, both written to make him money. Unlike some of the amateurs from the aristocracy and landed gentry, he did not have a limitless supply, and though for social reasons he was keen to maintain his amateur status, he had no outside earnings and had to earn a living. The latter publication concludes with a supplementary chapter on the merits of the 1909 Australian tourists and the prospects for the forthcoming Test series. After his performances on the 1907/08 tour he could have reasonably expected to play a part in that series. The fact that he did not do so had very little to do with his ability and current form.

Crawford played no Test cricket that summer in a series in which Australia retained the Ashes, losing the first Test, winning the next two and drawing the last two. True, later in the season he suffered from an injured shoulder, but before the first Test match he had shown only a slight decline in form in 1908, and after a winter away from the game, came back strongly in the early part of the 1909 season. Additionally, he had led his county to a famous victory over the tourists at The Oval. He was in form, fit and had a better record than most of his colleagues on the 1907/08 tour of Australia. That he did not merit a place in the series seems extraordinary – but merit was not the only factor in selection.

Of those who played in the final Test in Sydney in February 1908, only three were among the fifteen invited to Edgbaston in May 1909 – Hobbs, Rhodes and AO Jones – although Archie MacLaren replaced the latter as captain. Australia, however, showed only three changes from the eleven which had represented them at the SCG. It was a similar situation to that of two years earlier when South Africa had almost the same team as had played in the previous Test and England an almost totally different one.

Losing teams inevitably attract criticism over selection and this was no exception although, at a time when the media was less critical than it has subsequently become, the accusations of cronyism and failure to select the best eleven are particularly trenchant.

On the morning of the first Test at Edgbaston, *Cricket* listed the thirteen from which the team would be chosen along with their ages. Wicketkeeper Lilley was forty-one and a half: the youngest and only player under thirty was Hobbs at twenty-six.

> It is a team of veterans, but it is very doubtful indeed if a better selection could have been made, although the inclusion of another all-round player in the side – JN Crawford or Rhodes for choice – would have strengthened the bowling.[42]

Rhodes eventually did play but bowled only one over as England, despite the media's misgivings, bowled Australia out for 74. It was a false dawn, however: there were no more Test victories for the hosts that summer during which the England selectors called on twenty-five players. Crawford was not one of them.

During the close season, the Ashes still with Australia, there was further criticism.

> Speaking at the annual dinner of the Yorkshire Cricket Council at Leeds on the 2nd inst., the Hon FS Jackson said that no one could feel that in international cricket, England had passed through a satisfactory season. No Selection Committee could have had a harder task than the England selectors were faced with. It was a mistake, especially in Test match cricket, to depend too much on reputations in selecting a team. The men with big reputations should know where to stop. He could not quite understand why England, with two or three good fast bowlers, should have entered any Test match without at least one. He hoped the mistakes committed in this direction would not occur in England again. He thought England were really beaten in their merits, but the Australian bowlers all came off at the right time, and Noble's captaincy had played a great part in the Australians' success. Hirst was feeling the effects of long years of service, though he would still prove Yorkshire's stand-by, while there was no one who should be chosen for England before Rhodes.[43]

From the other side of the globe the *New Zealand Herald* expressed not dissimilar sentiments.

> Cricket experts in the newspapers heartily congratulate the Australians on their brilliant performances in the tests and eulogise Noble's captaincy. They have generally condemned the bad management in the selection of the English team, especially in not playing a fast bowler in the final match.[44]

The selection committee comprised Lord Hawke, CB Fry and HDG Leveson Gower. In the case of the latter and one strong candidate for selection, the division between them was part of a larger picture.

Victor Trumper was diplomatic about England's failure in the Test series, but forthright enough to imply that it might have been different had the selection process and personnel been different and Crawford played.

> In answer to the question 'How did we come to beat England?' Victor Trumper said that England was just having an off season. The old men were going off, and the new men have not quite arrived. He thinks MacLaren, who is one of the finest sports he has ever met, should have been sole selector of England's team. JN Crawford, in Trumper's opinion, should have been chosen on the English side.[45]

With no England call, Crawford's only duties were with Surrey. On the field, the season had begun well, both for Surrey and for Crawford. Northamptonshire were beaten by 106 runs, Hampshire by a massive innings and 468 and Warwickshire by 171 runs. There was a setback in The Parks where, despite Crawford's six for 83 the county lost in two days. Earlier in the season he had five for 39 against Northamptonshire and scored half-centuries against that county and Hampshire.

Leveson Gower was *hors de combat* because of an injured ankle and, in his first match as captain that season, Crawford had led Surrey to victory against the Australians; a performance which had brought him considerable acclaim. In the second innings:

> The bowling was true and runs took a lot of getting. Hayward and Crawford made a good stand and caused several changes in the bowling, but it was not

> until the fourth wicket had put on 48 that Crawford was bowled for a very valuable innings of 20.
>
> Whitty, the last man joined McAllister with nineteen wanted. The latter showed fine nerve, and after making a single from each end, drove Crawford finely for four. When 200 went up a new ball was called for, but gradually the score mounted until at 207 Lees was put on for Rushby. Off the new bowler's third ball McAllister was caught at slip, Surrey winning a great game by five runs. There was a scene of much enthusiasm at the finish.[46]

> Congratulations to Surrey upon having been the first to lower the Australians' colours this tour. Hayward and Hobbs were always regarded as being bound to catch the selectors' eye for the first Test 'probables', and it is only a plethora of talent that has kept JN Crawford in the background.[47]

Jack continued to turn in decent performances but, in what turned out to be his last appearance for Surrey for a decade, was injured and unable to bowl. Perhaps that was not too great a handicap to the side as he had bowled only fourteen overs in the last four matches.

Against Essex at The Oval, 'At 268 Ducat and Leveson-Gower were bowled by successive balls, and it was largely due to Crawford, who made 63 in seventy-five minutes and hit five fours and three threes , that the total reached 336.'[48]

Immediately afterwards, against Derbyshire, 'Crawford ... reached 51 out of 119 in eighty minutes and, in all, scored 95 out of 184 in 110 minutes. His chief hits were a six (an off-drive out of the ground off Warren) and twelve fours.'[49]

Then, against Lancashire at Old Trafford, 'Crawford was unfortunate enough to run into the pavilion rails and damage the muscles of an arm.'[50]

He was about to run into an even more implacable object in the shape of the Surrey Committee.

courtesy of Surrey CCC

The Surrey side from which Crawford split acrimoniously:
here Crawford sits happily with Leveson Gower.

8

Schism

Surrey 1909

The Surrey Annual Report for 1910 states that 'The captaincy was again undertaken by Mr HDG Leveson-Gower, but owing to his unfortunate injuries, the duties devolved upon Mr JN Crawford and Mr MC Bird.'

What the report does not say is that it was not until Crawford was off the scene in mid-July that Bird became *de facto* acting captain. Bird's pedigree as a schoolboy cricketer was distinguished enough. He had captained Harrow and made a century in each innings against Eton at Lord's.

> The Eton and Harrow match at Lord's will always be remembered on account of the performance of the Harrow captain, MC Bird, in making a hundred in each innings. His play was perfect throughout and stamped him as a cricketer of most unusual attainments. In addition to scoring so well, he bowled successfully and captained the side with skill, being very happy in changing his bowling, and declaring the second innings closed at the best possible moment.[1]

Bird would himself eventually captain his county from 1911 to 1913, but at this stage was behind Crawford in the pecking order. Had Crawford stayed at Surrey and remained a good boy in the eyes of the

Committee, he may well have succeeded to the office and the history of the club and of English cricket might have been different. There is no point in hypothesising, however – Crawford was what he was, and deference to authority was not on the agenda.

In July, Crawford was asked to captain Surrey against the Australians for a second time, but with one hand tied behind his back. He was presented with a team in the selection of which he had had no say and which excluded strike bowlers Walter Lees and Tom Rushby, batsman Alan Marshal, and leg-spinning all-rounder William Davis. He declined captaining the side. It is not unusual for a captain not to be part of the selection process. England captains have not always had a vote on selection committees and it has long been the Australian practice to pick the team and then choose a captain from among them. It is unusual, however, for the captain not to be consulted at all about the team he is to lead – and that is what seems to have happened here.

Crawford had captained the Surrey side in almost half the first-class matches so far that season, his record being marginally better than the regular captain: nine matches, six wins and a draw, against Leveson Gower's ten matches, five wins and three draws.[2] It is not known whether Crawford was consulted on the composition of the team in any or all of those nine matches. If he was not, then it must be assumed he acquiesced in the team he was given, at least sufficiently so not to make an issue of it; and if he was, then the failure to consult him about the team to play Australia was a departure from established practice. Either way, it was an insult to his captaincy record. In view of what had gone on earlier, since Leveson Gower assumed the captaincy the previous season, it is difficult to avoid the conclusion that he was set up to be shot down.

The events surrounding this fixture culminated in the previous fissures between the establishment and Crawford becoming a yawning chasm. The Committee and Leveson Gower had been working towards this. On his part, so had Crawford; and he had a Plan B. He could have avoided any controversy by claiming to be injured. He was – sufficient to be unable to bowl – but still capable of batting and captaining the side. As an amateur of course, he was, unlike the professionals, not under any contractual obligation and could simply have decided not to play without having to give a reason. He chose not to take the easy way out, but to confront the Committee, the President, Secretary and Captain. It was David against Goliath, but this time there was no way David was going to win.

Lord Alverstone, the Club President, was already on record as saying that giving the amateurs a game was of at least equal priority to winning the Championship:

> I should like if possible to arrange matters in the future so that at least three places in the XI in all ordinary county matches should be filled by amateurs, and that other first class amateurs who are eligible should play two or three times in the season, so that there should be more change in the first XI. We must remember that in Surrey we have a greater choice of good amateurs than perhaps in any other county.[3]

However, it was not on this occasion a question of amateurs being played at the expense of professionals, but of professionals being disciplined for off-the-field behaviour.

Australian batsman Alan Marshal, who had qualified by residence for Surrey in 1906 and had become a close friend of Hobbs, was suspended from the team over a trivial incident during an away fixture at Derbyshire. He and some other players were walking to their hotel in Chesterfield, having arrived there from Sheffield, and were fooling around with a child's ball that they had bought in a street market. Hobbs, then at the Headingley Test, was not among them, though such a kick around was precisely the sort of innocent fun he enjoyed with his mates. But it did not seem so innocent to an officious police constable, who stopped the players and demanded Marshal's name. Feeling that no crime had been committed, Marshal refused to give it. He was then arrested and taken down to the station. In support of Marshal, the other players followed. Fortunately, when the Derbyshire Chief Constable learnt about the episode he ordered that no further action be taken.[4] The Surrey Committee, however, did not take such a broad-minded view and Marshal was given a hefty ban for 'insubordination'.

Rushby, Lees and Smith bowled Surrey to an innings victory in two days at Queen's Park before moving on to Old Trafford where all played. Then Marshal, Rushby and Davis, who had a century against Derbyshire, were omitted for the match against the Australians. With Hobbs already unavailable through injury and Crawford himself unable to bowl because of a shoulder injury, the invited acting captain dug in his heels, declining to captain the 'second eleven sort of team' he had been given and apologised to the Australians for the weakness of the side.

Marshal did not play again until August, continuing under suspension, and was to leave and return to Australia the following year. Although his attacking style of batting would have been useful, bowling was his second string. As the strength of the attack was Crawford's main concern, Marshal did not form part of the trio of Rushby, Lees and Davis that Crawford wished to have in the side.

Without being fully aware of the background, the media, both at home and overseas, could not help but notice the difference between this Surrey team and the one which had met the same opponents two months earlier.

> The remarkable feature in the composition of the Surrey team now playing the Australians is that neither the county's captain (Leveson-Gower, one of the three selectors of the All-England teams) nor the deputy-captain (JN Crawford) are in it. And there is a great change in its composition compared with the Surrey team that defeated the tourists in the first match in May last, which comprised Crawford, Hayward, Hobbs, Hayes, Marshal (an Australian), Kirwen, Spring, Hitch, Lees, Rushby and Strudwick. The personnel of the present team is MC Bird, EC Kirk (the only amateurs), Hayward, Hayes, Strudwick, Hitch, Goatly, Lees, Harrison, Ducat and WC Smith.[5]

Notwithstanding his declining to play in the match against the Australians, Crawford attended the dinner on the first evening. We know that he had apologised to the Australians and it is highly unlikely that he would not have mentioned the reasons for his not playing. It was something which Victor Trumper was to bear in mind for future reference.

As it happened, the 'second eleven sort of team' did not acquit itself too badly against an Australian side identical to that which had won the third Test at Headingley. Their pride dented by the earlier result at The Oval, they put out their strongest possible side in order to avoid a recurrence. Professional Tom Hayward took over the captaincy of Surrey, Lees did eventually play and the match was drawn.

> SURREY, at The Oval, gave a splendid account of themselves in the return match against the Australians, despite the fact they put a comparatively weak side into the field. Hobbs, Leveson-Gower and Crawford were unable to play on account of injuries, Marshal was omitted owing to temporary loss of form, and Rushby was not invited. The omission of the last-named naturally occasioned considerable comment especially as in the former match between the two sides he had taken eleven wickets for 88 runs. His inclusion in the team instead of Hitch or Kirk would have strengthened the side, and would perhaps have enabled the County to defeat the tourists for a second time.[6]

It is true that Crawford was injured, it is true that Marshal was out of form, but neither of those were the cause of their omission. There is no reason, however, to question the validity of the other observations. The following week, the half-truths in the media continued.

> At the present time Hayward, Hobbs and Leveson-Gower are unable to play, the first two owing to injuries and the latter on account of a family bereavement, whilst Crawford is showing a preference for club cricket, and Marshal has been dropped owing to temporary loss of form.[7]

The general public were largely left in the dark about the real reason for Crawford's omission from the team. At the Middlesex match at Lord's, 'there was considerable comment at JN Crawford again being an absentee.'[8]

Little were they to know that he would not play for Surrey for the next decade. The decision to sack Crawford or, in the euphemistic prose of the Committee minutes, that 'he be not invited again to play for Surrey', came at the meeting on 5 August. In a resolution and comment that have more to do with the affront to the perceived dignity of the President and captain than the future playing strength of the team:

> Correspondence with Mr JN Crawford was considered.
>
> The following resolution was passed: That in view of Mr Crawford's conduct in declining to play for Surrey on the morning of the Australian Match, after previously communicating to the Secretary his intention to play, and his subsequent letters to Lord Alverstone, the Committee resolve that he be not invited again to play for Surrey.
>
> It was proposed by Lord Midleton and seconded by Mr GH Longman that the above resolution be sent to Mr Crawford.
>
> The Committee beg to express their sympathy with Mr Leveson Gower in the trouble he has been put to in this matter, and to record their highest approval of his conduct throughout the incident.
>
> A hearty vote of thanks was passed to the President for the trouble he had taken with the Crawford correspondence.

The minutes of the meeting held two weeks later record that further correspondence with JN Crawford was considered. This would have been Crawford's reply to the Secretary's letter conveying the Committee's resolution, acknowledging receipt, suggesting that it might have been accompanied by thanks for past services and regretting the fact that he should be virtually branded a criminal for declining to captain a side which excluded three essential players. The results of the consideration are not recorded, understandably perhaps. There was no credible answer.

Football manager Brendan Rodgers, commenting on the dismissal of one of his fellow managers, referred to a decision taken by 'a business guy who knows absolutely nothing about football'. 'Absolutely nothing' (and in private conversation it may have been less euphemistic) is obviously an exaggeration for the sake of dramatic effect. While it would not be true to say that the Surrey Committee knew absolutely nothing about cricket, it is apparent, even at a distance in time of more than one hundred years and with the recognition that it was an age of deference to the establishment, that we have here a group of men, three in particular, who were more concerned with their own authority, dignity and gravitas than with the career of a prodigiously talented twenty-two year old all-rounder with a glittering future.

Of his three antagonists in the correspondence, Findlay was the agent of the Committee and Lord Alverstone remained autocratic but dignified and courteous. It is only when the captain becomes involved in the later stages that the language becomes confrontational: 'Either you or I must give up playing for Surrey'. Leveson Gower also withdrew his invitation to the Scarborough Festival in the organisation of which he was heavily involved and to the MCC's forthcoming tour of South Africa. As a member of the MCC committee, selection committee and captain designate of the party, he was fully empowered to take such a line, but the punishment of being banned from an end-of-season festival, county cricket and international cricket for a perceived offence of wishing to be involved in the selection of a team one would be captaining seems disproportionate and a draconian overreaction.

Lord Alverstone was always prepared to leave the door ajar and welcome Crawford back if he were prepared to apologise. The peremptory tone of Leveson Gower's letters suggest that this was not the case and whatever his later achievements in the administration of the game may have been, it is difficult to avoid the conclusion that on this occasion Leveson Gower's judgment was clouded by jealousy of Crawford as both a player and captain.

When selecting a party to tour South Africa in 1914 (which never happened because of the war), the Australian Board of Control asserted its right to remove any name proposed by the selection committee 'for reasons other than cricketing ability' and used the same justification for omitting Sid Barnes from the team which played West Indies in 1951/52.[9] There are parallels with the ECB's decision, over a century later that Kevin Pietersen be not invited to play for England. *Plus ça change...*

Wisden records that the Surrey Committee wanted to keep a lid on their dirty laundry:

> Surrey had trouble with some of their own professionals and, as a crowning blow, there came the unhappy quarrel with JN Crawford. In the absence

> of Leveson-Gower, Crawford was picked to captain the side in the return match with the Australians, but he refused to act, his reason being that the committee had left out essential players, among others Rushby whose bowling had done so much to win the first match. The committee were much incensed and passed a resolution that Crawford be not asked again to play for the county. At first great secrecy was preserved over the matter.[10]

Yet however much the Committee wished to keep the matter confidential, Crawford was under no obligation to do so: the letters he had written were his copyright; those he had received his own property. Crawford went public and set the record straight by forwarding to *Cricket* for publication the culmination of the exchange of correspondence which contained the Committee's resolution that he be not invited again to play for Surrey (reproduced in the appendix). It was 'to set at rest speculations concerning his absence from the County Eleven'.[11] There was no earthly way the Committee could keep the matter shrouded in secrecy. The discord was now in the open, the rift complete.

The dispute, once in the open, attracted huge public interest and was covered by most of the newspapers. *Punch*, in its typical satirical vein, published spoof correspondence, depicting Crawford as an errant schoolboy disciplined by those in authority. The piece was cut out and pasted in the personal scrapbook of Crawford's professional contemporary Ernie Hayes with an annotated marginal note: 'A skit in *Punch* on the letters between JN Crawford and Surrey representatives on his retiring.'

It is a significant entry for two reasons. Firstly, there was no suggestion that Crawford was 'retiring'. His career was to continue through a World War and beyond, characterised by brilliance on the field and more controversy off it. Secondly, and perhaps more significantly, Hayes' scrapbooks are essentially of a personal nature, recording his achievements, commenting spasmodically on politics and his sometimes fractious relations with and treatment by his employers and amateur captains. Only rarely does he stray outside those areas, so he found some amusement in the item and was probably not alone in the professionals' dressing room in identifying with the shabby treatment of his amateur colleague.

The general view was that while Crawford had erred in flouting the conventions of the time of deference to his elders and alleged betters, the punishment did not fit the crime (proportionality, it would perhaps be called in the judicial jargon of a century later) and that Surrey were cutting off their nose to spite their face and depriving not only themselves but also England of an outstanding young talent.

> There is very little doubt that Surrey have grievously missed the services of that brilliant all-round cricketer Mr JN Crawford, who at an age – he is twenty-two years old – when most men are engaged in building up a reputation, has established his claim as an international player. Much has been written in the Press concerning Mr JN Crawford and the Surrey Committee, and while a breach was undoubtedly committed, it does not appear from the facts which have been made public that the Surrey Executive displayed great wisdom in their mode of dealing with it.[12]

> I was sorry to see the difficulties known to exist between JN Crawford and the Surrey committee have not been amicably adjusted. Much as we dislike a young man saying to older men (to whom he owes official duty) 'Shan't play, then', even more, perhaps, do we dislike the decision 'Never again' applied by older men to a young one who has made a mistake. JN Crawford is only twenty-two years of age. The original error was, of course, with him. He thought the team given him to captain could and should be made stronger, and he had a perfect right to say so. But, having made the protest, he stultified his own action; for, of course, he made the team weaker still by excluding himself from it.
>
> With the subsequent correspondence I have nothing to do, but I cannot but think that the committee omitted to do the best thing by deliberately, and after due consideration, passing a resolution that this young man was never to be asked to play for Surrey again. I do not say that they were unjust; but I say that they were un-necessarily severe. Granted that Crawford was entirely in the wrong, the punishment to my mind is too severe to fit the crime.[13]

The media worldwide (or, at least the Antipodean part of it) were not slow to comment either, recognising the Committee's perfect right to act as it had, while at the same time condemning its short-sightedness and sympathising with the young amateur. One recognised the possibility that Crawford might act on an interest expressed earlier and come to Australia.

> JN CRAWFORD SUSPENDED. The Surrey Cricket Committee resolved not to invite JN Crawford to play again, because he declined to play against the Australians. Crawford was one of the amateurs who visited Australia with AO Jones's last team, and who proved a success both as a batsman and a bowler. He is one of those cricketers of the professional-amateur class, who are enabled to save out of the amounts allowed for expenses. He is one of the keenest cricketers in England, and it is just possible that, if Surrey management insist in their attitude, he will come out to Australia, where he had serious thoughts of settling when he was out with the English team.[14]

There was some sympathy for Jack among the Surrey members, but an attempt by two of them, Messrs F Abraham and A Sargent, to reduce the ban to the current season met with an instruction by the Committee to the Secretary to reply that they saw no reason for making the suggested alteration.[15]

Coincidentally and ironically, Jack's first-class career resumed the same day as the publication of the exchange of letters in the *Sporting Times*, for an England XI against the Australians at Blackpool.

> The Australians, travelling by night after their great match at The Oval, put a weak side into the field ... The feature of the play was the first wicket stand – the largest ever made in this country against Australian bowling – by Knight and Douglas ... the Crawford brothers put on 59 together in twenty-five minutes, VFS making 35 of the number by means of a six, seven fours and a single. JN Crawford batted only seventy-five minutes for 60 and hit four sixes, all big drives over the ring, and four fours in his delightful display: he was seventh out at 491.[16]

Between then and the end of the season, Jack declined merely to sulk in his tent and cashed in on lower standards than those to which he had become accustomed since his schooldays.

> JN Crawford has been having a merry time during his stay on the South coast. Playing for Teddington at the Saffrons, he secured eight of the Eastbourne wickets for 112 runs, in addition to scoring 26 and 66. For the Wanderers on the same ground he scored 59 by some brilliant hitting, and against Hastings he made 19 and 78, the latter innings helping to secure a victory on the part of the Wanderers who were put in to make 218 in ninety minutes and got them with three minutes to spare, HC Pretty making 24 off an over. On Saturday at Lewes Priory, for the South Saxons v Mr Hope's team, Crawford bowled 23 overs (eight maidens) for 23 runs and nine wickets, and scored 30 and 45 not out, the latter including six sixes. On Monday last in the match Dr Greene's XI v Bexhill the latter were all out for 32, JN's work showing eight wickets, all clean bowled, for 13 runs, including the hat-trick.[17]

He also joined his brother, Reggie, on the Wanderers tour of Kent and Sussex before concluding his disjointed season with a couple of appearances at the Hastings Festival for the Gentlemen of the South against the Players of the South where 'the only players to offer much resistance were Turner and Crawford', and for the South of England, again against the Australians.[18]

No doubt Crawford engaged the Australians in discussions about his future. New horizons beckoned in the open, sun-drenched spaces of what he had called KangarooLand.

> Mr JN Crawford has received and accepted, an offer of a resident tutorship at St Peter's College, Adelaide, and it is understood that that he will be settled in his new quarters before the end of the year. There is no need at the moment to deal with his career in detail as he should have his best years still before him, but one may recall the fact that he is the best all-round player turned out by the Public Schools since the time of AG Steel. Surrey's and England's loss will be Australia's gain and cricketers, in regretting his departure, will congratulate him on receiving such a good appointment and wish him success both on and off the field.[19]

Tom Rushby too was on his bike, although, as it turned out, only for one season.

> Next season Surrey will be obliged to take the field without Rushby, who has accepted an engagement with the Accrington Club which takes part in Lancashire League matches. That his absence is bound to be a handicap to the County team to no slight extent is evident from the fact that during the past season he took 119 wickets in first-class cricket at a cost of 16.04 runs each. It is understood that his departure from Surrey is a sequel to his omission from the return match with the Australians at the Oval in the middle of July. It was with considerable secrecy that the negotiations with Accrington were conducted, the committee of the club being under agreement not to divulge the matter until he gave his consent. Rushby was born in 1881 and should therefore have many years' cricket ahead of him.[20]

It was reported on the same page that weaker clubs in the Lancashire League were agitating for the abolition of professionalism, ten out of the fourteen having failed to make a profit. Clearly Accrington was not one of them. In December, the Surrey Committee made an attempt to woo Rushby back and approached Accrington asking the club to release him from his contract. They were having none of it.[21]

Meanwhile, back at The Oval:

> Although they fell from third place to fifth, Surrey were the only county which beat the Australians and in that fact they can find consolation for many disappointments the greatest of which was the severance of JN Crawford's connection with the team.[22]

It is all too easy to see controversies in the administration and playing of the game as a clash between the amateur ethic and the professional one, as a straight conflict of class divisions. That is only partially true and over-simplistic. Just as in apartheid South Africa, where there were divisions within as well as between the black and white races, so in the Victorian era and its Edwardian twilight before everything was to come unstuck in 1914, there were divisions within the over-schematic upper and lower classes. Lord Alverstone's educational background was Charterhouse and Oxford, Leveson Gower's Winchester and Oxford,

Findlay's Eton and Oxford. Crawford's was Repton and thence straight into a continuation of first-class cricket.

As an amateur, Crawford was accorded more respect than he would have been as a professional; the club's shabby treatment of George Lohmann and Tom Richardson over the previous two decades comparing with the gentlemanly exchanges with Walter Read. Nonetheless, as a player he was expected to toe the line and kowtow to those who saw themselves as his superiors, but as cricketers, were unfit to lace his boots. That he failed to do so perhaps placed a question mark over the emperor's clothes, but their perceived existence was to remain unchallenged.

Earlier, in 1896, the Committee had demonstrated their ability to favour a professional over an amateur (albeit a Surrey professional and Middlesex amateur) when they had declined to play their transpontine rivals if their team included Sir Timothy O'Brien, who had used bad language to one of the Surrey professionals during a match at The Oval. Middlesex had meekly concurred.[23]

As witnessed by his books and correspondence with the other three, Repton had certainly provided Crawford with the ability to write stylish, grammatically correct English, but the pecking order of schools and universities in those days – and indeed for some considerable time afterwards – was determined not by academic achievement, but by social cachet. Whatever the academic standards of the institutions mentioned, it is unarguable that in the public schools hierarchy, Charterhouse, Eton and Winchester ranked above Repton, and the University of Oxford above no university at all. Against the gold-plated establishment represented by his three antagonists, he had no chance. As a son of the cloth, public schoolboy and amateur cricketer, he would be seen by some, including his fellow players, as part of the establishment, but there are gradations within the establishment that go deeper than the lists in *Debrett's* or *Whitaker's Almanack*. The other three involved in the schism were Premier League, Crawford was perhaps Championship or below. As a cricketer, however, he had infinitely more to offer his county, country and the game at large than the other three put together. In conflicts between players and the establishment, it was far from unique. It was the politics of envy; a golden opportunity for authority to triumph over competence – an opportunity taken with no thought for the long-term consequences.

The report to the Surrey Annual General Meeting of 1910 steered away from controversy:

> Mr HDG Leveson Gower captained the side with much tact and skill, besides making several useful scores. Your Committee have the great pleasure to announce that he has consented to continue the Captaincy for the coming season.
>
> Marshal shewed great improvement and your Committee have every hope that he will prove a great cricketer.
>
> Mr JN Crawford did excellent work.

It was also announced in the Annual Report that Morice Bird had been appointed vice-captain, *de jure* recognition of what had been Crawford's *de facto* position. At the same meeting, there was one last, desperate throw of the dice by Parson Crawford in a motion to rescind the Committee's resolution: 'That the Committee of the Surrey County Cricket Club be asked to rescind the Resolution passed with regard to Mr JN Crawford.' He had stood for the Committee but not been elected, an indication perhaps that while the membership might have had some sympathy with Jack, it did not extend to his father, who not untypical of a Victoria *pater familias* dominated the family but was seen as an interfering busybody who went too far in pleading their cause and fighting their battles for them.

On the grounds that Parson Crawford's motion was critical of the Committee, the President ruled it out of order. Lord Alverstone was Lord Chief Justice of England, so his ruling was accepted both by the proposer of the motion and the Annual General Meeting. The rules of the club, while having plenty to say about the membership, are silent on the respective powers of the Committee and the AGM. The layman's general understanding, however, would be that the Committee is elected by the AGM to act on its behalf and if the membership does not like what it is doing, then it can replace the Committee and express disapproval of its actions. Apart from totalitarian regimes (and it is arguable that the Surrey Committee was veering in that direction), votes of no confidence are seen as being permissible in democratic and pseudo-democratic organisations from the House of Commons, through Yorkshire County Cricket Club to the parish council.

However, though the motion was disallowed, debate was permitted and seems to have been conducted in a respectful and dignified manner by both the President and the Rev John Crawford.

> Following the re-election of officers, Lord Alverstone referred to the resolution of which the Rev JC Crawford had given notice ... He pointed out no resolution of this kind could be moved, chiefly for the reason that it amounted to a vote of want of confidence in the Committee, and was not in order: The general meeting had no power to deal with resolutions of the Committee. Lord Alverstone added that the Committee had determined that the matter could be discussed if the meeting wished.
>
> The Rev JC Crawford said that he found himself in an awkward predicament. When he sent in his resolution he did not intend to raise any question on the merits or demerits of his son's action: few people understood the case, and if they began to discuss it they might go on forever. But for several reasons he wished to ask the Committee publicly to rescind their resolution. In the first place it was not a nice thing to have on the minutes of a great club against a young player, and in the next it would be a recognition of the work of a cricketer whose heart and soul were absolutely in the welfare of the side – whether he were playing for his county or for England in South Africa or Australia. Furthermore, it would be a graceful compliment to himself, who had been a member of the club for twenty-seven years, during twelve of which, with the exception of one season, one of his sons had represented the county.
>
> Lord Alverstone, after thanking the Rev JC Crawford for the very restrained way in which he had made his proposals, said that no one would be more pleased to move the rescission of the resolution than every member of the Committee, if Mr JN Crawford would only come forward, as a gentleman and a sportsman, and apologise for what had occurred; but so far no word of an apology had been received. The Committee had sent messages of goodwill to Mr JN Crawford before he left England and since he had settled

in Australia, and he himself was still in correspondence with him and on friendly terms. The matter was then dropped.[24]

So the Committee, under some pressure from the captain and President, had won a contest on what was never going to be a level playing field. As committees often do, they had taken a decision as a group that some of them at least might not have taken as individuals.

Their decision was the subject of much criticism both at the time and in later years. Neville Cardus wrote that Crawford's break with Surrey was a sad deprivation of fame and pleasure to himself and a grievous loss to English cricket. 'It is as certain as anything in a man's life can be confidently postulated,' wrote Cardus, 'that had he continued to play in English cricket in the rising years to his prime, he would have taken his place among the select company of England's captains.'[25] Elsewhere, Cardus writes that 'with Crawford, the style was the man himself – and the handsome boy who never grew old'.

An article by Robert Trumble, while paying appropriate recognition to his on-field performances, asks whether Crawford's attitude that apologies were due to him, rather than from him, could possibly have helped defuse the dispute. Under a sub-heading 'A Difficult Man', Trumble argues that Crawford found it impossible to put himself in the shoes of another, and had he done so, he would have appreciated Leveson Gower's position. He could not possibly expect to take on the captain, the President and the Committee and win. He is right, of course, but Jack doubtless took the view that he had to have a go.

When Geoffrey Boycott was dismissed by Yorkshire in 1983, the members were able to have the decision reversed and the committee resigned *en bloc*. Those days, however, were more than a couple of generations ahead. Long after the turbulent events of 1909, the age of deference consigned to history, Benny Green took an alternative view in more trenchant terms.

> Exactly what Alverstone, Leveson-Gower and company thought they had achieved by their maladroitness we cannot know. Possibly they assumed that after an appropriately chastening spell in the wilderness, their young heir-

> apparent to the captaincy of the side would duly apologise and return to the fold. Or perhaps the club was content to forgo the services of one of the world's most prodigious all-rounders for the sake of its own authority. Either way the Surrey committee must be held accountable for a degree of idiocy rarely met with even in the realms of cricket administration.[26]

What Crawford's personal emotions were we shall never know. It was not an age where people, men especially, were encouraged to wear their hearts on their sleeves and 'let it all hang out'. The requirement was rather for the stiff upper lip and, especially for the public school educated, an emphasis on being 'manly' and not having emotions – still less, showing them.

Like some hero of Greek tragedy, Crawford's hubris had been his downfall. He had taken on the gods… and lost.

FAMOUS SURREY CRICKETER LEAVING FOR AUSTRALIA.

Mr. J. N. Crawford, the famous Surrey cricketer, left London for Australia yesterday. He is going to take up a scholastic appointment at Adelaide. The picture, taken at St. Pancras, shows Mr. J. N. Crawford at the carriage window. With him are his brothers, Mr. R. T. Crawford and Mr. V. F. S. Crawford (in overcoat).—(*Daily Mirror* photograph.)

courtesy of Mirrorpix

Jack leaves for Australia with only his family to bid him farewell.

9

Return to KangarooLand

South Australia 1909/10

Crawford's new life took him to the other side of the world. It wasn't Botany Bay and it wasn't 'farewell to old England for ever', but it was Adelaide, a new life and the last he would see of his native land for almost a decade. There would inevitably be regrets at leaving friends and family, but he took with him at least one happy memory.

> The happiest memory I shall take with me,' said JN Crawford before leaving for Australia, will be the memory of the first Surrey and Australians match at the Oval this year, when I captained the Surrey team, and we beat the visitors by five runs.[1]

Jack boarded the St Pancras-Tilbury boat train on the morning of 28 October. It was quite a contrast to the scenes of two years previous when he had made the same journey with the MCC touring team. This time there was no tumultuous farewell, no kissing of anyone else's sisters, just a quiet family send off. Surrey representation was conspicuous by its absence, but a few journalists and photographers captured the moment. Under the heading 'England's Latest Loss' the *Hereford Times* reported:

England has lost, probably for several years, one of her foremost amateur cricketers in the person of John Neville Crawford, the Surrey all-round player, who has left for Adelaide, there to take up a scholastic appointment. Although he will not be twenty-three until December 1st, Mr Crawford, who was educated at Repton, has played for six seasons in the Surrey eleven, for which he first did duty against Kent in the Canterbury week of 1904. He has played for the Gentlemen both at Lord's and the Oval, and has represented England in Test fixtures in MCC teams, in Australia and South Africa as well as in this country, though he has never done duty for the Mother Country against the former on home soil. There is no necessity to make more than bare reference to the regrettable dispute with the Surrey County authorities which originated with the return Australian match in mid-July, and resulted a few weeks later in a complete breach. Without a doubt the loss of his services has been and will be severely felt by Surrey, whilst, in spite of the fact that there had been rumours a couple of years ago that he might accept a colonial appointment, there can be little doubt that his acceptance of the offer has been influenced by recent events.

Crawford elected to travel by the earlier boat special which left St Pancras just after half-past nine a.m. Whether the early hour and dirty morning were responsible or not cannot be said but at any rate it was a disappointment not to find any of his fellow cricketers present except those of his own family. The Rev JC Crawford and Mrs Crawford were there to travel to Tilbury to bid farewell to their boy, also his brothers VFS and RT, the latter of whom is making his mark on the concert stage, and his numerous sisters, including Mrs Elliott. A group of journalists were welcome additions to the little party at the Midland terminus, and the 'snapshotters' were busy, the flashlights drawing together quite a little crowd. JN appeared in the best of health and spirits, and expressed thanks to those who wished him Bon voyage. One naturally felt disinclined to discuss with him the events of last season though the 'Parson' had a very few emphatic remarks to make on the subject. JN seemed very pleased at the receipt of a letter from Tom Hayward wishing him hearty good luck and Mr FL Fane, the ex-captain of Essex, who was one of his colleagues in a South Africa in 1905-6, likewise in Australia two years later, also wrote expressing good wishes.

Crawford hopes to be able to play some first-class cricket in South Australia and it may be that he will be found playing for that state against the English XI in the Colonies in the season of 1910-11.[2]

Under the heading 'A Cold Send-Off', *Sporting Life* expressed similar sentiments.

> JN Crawford whose name has become a household word wherever cricket is played and understood left London en route for Australia by the 9.33 boat train from St Pancras yesterday morning to take up a mastership at St Peter's College, Adelaide. His departure means that English cricket has lost a great player – a player who should in the natural course of things have proved one of England's most valuable assets in Test matches in the years to come.
>
> The departure to a foreign land, his severance from all the grounds upon which he has played the game so well, of a player who has represented not only his country in England, in South Africa and in Australia, can only be regarded as an event of importance to English cricket, and so it was surprising, to put the case mildly, that there was not a big gathering of his contemporary players to bid JN Crawford 'bon voyage' at St Pancras yesterday. The press were present in force, so were the photographers of a number of journals, but apart from a few personal friends, his relatives alone were present to see him upon his new start in life, his father the Reverend JC Crawford, his mother, his brothers VFS and RT, and his sisters all accompanied the voyager as far as Tilbury.
>
> JN Crawford and his friends and relations arrived early at St Pancras station and the ex-Surrey cricketer, looking splendidly fit, appeared in the best of spirits. He communicated to a representative of the *Sporting Life* that he had no idea of going to Australia until last Saturday when a cablegram arrived offering him a post at St Peter's College and it was not until Monday last that he decided to leave this country. St Peter's College, Mr Crawford explained to our representative, is a large school having fourteen or fifteen masters and some 600 pupils. He himself is to fulfil a position as ordinary master but will no doubt have to keep an eye on the sport of the school. Pressed to express an opinion upon his unfortunate rupture with the Surrey club, Mr Crawford declined to say more than that he considered himself unjustly treated. Before he left St Pancras Mr Crawford was several times photographed – with his brothers, with his sisters and with the rest of the family, and as he waved *au revoir* to London from the window of a first class carriage, it was impossible not to regret that the keen, lithe figure that had hit so hard and bowled so cunningly was lost to English cricket.[3]

During a stopover in Fremantle, Crawford was sought out by the press and in a frank interview, after observing the proprieties and saying how much he was looking forward to playing in the country, commented on individual players and the high and improving standards of cricket in both Australia and South Africa.

> JN CRAWFORD AT FREMANTLE. Among the passengers in transit by the RMS *Otway*, which called at Fremantle yesterday, is Mr JN Crawford who is en route to Adelaide, where he has accepted an appointment on the staff of St Peter's College. During a short interview Crawford informed a *West Australian* reporter that he was looking forward to his stay in Australia. 'From what little I have seen of the people here,' he remarked, 'their generous hospitality and genial warmheartedness make my approaching stay in Adelaide all the more pleasurable in anticipation, quite irrespective of the attraction which Australians have for me in connection with their cricketing ability. Look at the last Australian Eleven – splendid lot of even, plucky players, who won the rubber through sheer merit. They were not brilliant, taking them all round, but, of course, Bardsley and Ransford stood out as the "lions" of the tour. Of the two, I think, Ransford is the more brilliant cricketer, although both are superb fieldsmen. That's where the Australians shone at home: they completely outclassed the English players in the field. Yes, those two left-handers meant a great deal to your side, and they are a perfect nuisance to bowlers and fieldsmen alike, in fact all left-handers are. I sometimes think they ought not to be allowed to play. Then Noble's captaincy was perfect; he is the best leader in the world. Just does the right thing at the right moment, and while he has certainly had luck with him at times, especially in the matter of the toss, yet he worked with perfect judgement all the time.'
>
> Asked as to the prospects of an Australian combination against South Africa in the triangular tests, Crawford was sceptical. 'There is no mistake about it,' he said, 'but Australia will have her work cut out to beat the South Africans. They are not only good cricketers but they are of the type which is very hard to beat. They are not as good as Australians in the field, but their bowling is superior. They are mostly of the "googly" type but each has some distinctive characteristic which makes them the harder to play. The matches

should certainly be interesting ones, and Australians will have to put their best combinations out.'

Crawford hopes to play for South Australia against New South Wales about Christmas time.[4]

Crawford was spot on about his debut. He was met in Adelaide by representatives of East Torrens (the club for whom he would be playing), St Peter's College and the South Australian Cricket Association. He was told that South Australia had beaten Victoria in the first Sheffield Shield match of the season, and he was wanted to play in the South Australia side against New South Wales starting on 18 December.[5]

A new life beckoned. There was an element of mutual admiration between Crawford and Australia. He had obviously enjoyed his previous tour there two years earlier and the Australians clearly had a huge respect for Crawford's cricket. Coupled with £50 towards his passage as an incentive to arrive in time for the second Sheffield match, the offer of a post of resident master at St Peter's College at an annual salary of £160 per annum was snapped up.

As long as the resolution of the Surrey committee remained in force, Jack was not going to play regular first-class cricket. To play for another county would require a two-year residential qualification. The period of residence required before being eligible to play for an Australian state was three months, and was usually disregarded anyway. It was also an opportunity to escape the stifling constraints of English society where Crawford slotted into neither the upper class nor the working class, but was sandwiched uncomfortably in between.

Discussions had taken place the preceding English summer, principally with Victor Trumper, who had approached Clem Hill, the South Australian captain. South Australia were the weakest of the three states competing for the Sheffield Shield, having won it only once, in the second year of the competition 1893/94, while New South Wales and Victoria had, apart from that single instance, carved up titles between them.

The influence of Trumper in facilitating the arrangements was recognised in the press.

> Although it has not been officially stated (says the *Australian Observer*) that it was Victor Trumper who suggested to members of the South Australia Cricket Association that they would probably get JN Crawford to come to the state if a suitable position could be found for him, it is significant that the New South Wales player had something to do with it, so it was only after Trumper passed through Adelaide on his way home that negotiations were opened up, and Crawford was offered, and accepted, a position as a resident master at St Peter's College.[6]

Within a week of his arrival in Adelaide, Crawford was playing grade cricket and shortly afterwards, having taken a little time to adjust to the different pace of the pitches after two years away, was very soon producing the goods for South Australia.

> Crawford arrived at Adelaide on December 6th and five days later took six wickets for 39 runs for East Torrens against Adelaide. Since then he has shown such excellent all-round form in the matches with New South Wales and Victoria that the winning of the Sheffield Shield by South Australia must be attributable to no small extent to his skill. With Clem Hill still able to make runs as prolifically as ever, and many of the younger brigade developing into players of the very front rank, South Australia possesses today perhaps the strongest team it has ever had ... The advent of Crawford strengthened the side enormously.[7]

The question arose, however, as to whether he should have played at all. If a joint resolution of the State Associations had been adhered to, he would not have been able to do so until the following season, but common sense kicked in and rules were sidestepped in the interests of a higher standard of competition.

> 'Laws,' someone once said, 'were made to be broken.' Especially would such seem to be the case concerning the appearance in Sheffield Shield matches of players not qualified to do so. In the annual report of the New South Wales Cricket Association for 1893-4 it was stated:
>
> 'The Associations of Victoria, New South Wales and Queensland have adopted a resolution to the effect that no player shall be eligible for selec-

> tion in inter-colonial matches unless he has been a bona-fide resident of the colony for three months immediately preceding the match to be played.'
>
> The rule, however, has frequently been violated, and the latest instance – that of JN Crawford, who played for his state eleven days after his arrival at Adelaide – will probably result in the qualification being discussed again at an early date.[8]

It was not an oversight. The legality of Crawford's playing without fulfilling the required residential qualification had already been identified before his selection and although the New South Wales Association initially advocated adherence to the letter of the law, Victoria, maybe because of the tradition of opposing anything New South Wales supported, was happy to be more flexible. In the end pragmatism prevailed.

> Though JN Crawford will have been at Adelaide only two weeks, South Australia expects to play him against New South Wales next month at Adelaide. As a matter of grace the Englishman's playing in this match may be permissible, but it will, one believes, be generally acknowledged that if the residential qualification be strained in this case, as it has been in others where South Australia and Queensland are concerned, it would be better to delete the few months residential clause from the records. One does not expect New South Wales to decline to agree to JN Crawford playing; but without references to the personal aspect, it should be decided (says an Australian writer) that, unless there is a birth qualification, the residential clause should be rigidly applied.[9]

Just before the match, the New South Wales Association had cleared the way with a statement: 'The Cricket Association has informed the South Australian Association that, while it is satisfied that JN Crawford is ineligible to play for the State, in view of Victoria's decision, it waives the objection.' The legalities neatly side-stepped, Crawford made his Sheffield Shield debut against New South Wales on 18 December: 'Crawford, who evidently found the wicket too fast, made only 14 ... Crawford bowled splendidly and deserved his success.'[10] Clem Hill's 205 was the major component of a South Australian total of 397 and Crawford's six for 59 in the second innings saw his new team to victory by an innings and four runs.

The *Brisbane Courier*, quoting a piece in the *Adelaide Register*, gave a taste of what the Australian public would have missed had he not been allowed to play.

> A MAN AND A CRICKETER. To watch JN Crawford bowling at the conclusion of the match against New South Wales last Tuesday was to see a magnificent example of tireless energy and resource. No man could look on and fail to be impressed by the personality of the latest addition to the ranks of South Australian cricket – a state that has given the world one of its finest exponents of the game. So far as Crawford is concerned, it was not actually a new experience to Adelaide cricket however because when he was here with the MCC English team in 1907 he excited the admiration of everybody by the determination with which he bowled on the hot day when Clem Hill and Hartigan made their famous stand. On that occasion some of his comrades became tired beyond the limit of endurance, but when the ball was thrown to the young man, who was then but twenty years of age, a few minutes before stumps were drawn, he handled it with the same vim as when he was put on hours earlier. It was the same thing on Tuesday. New South Wales required 68 runs to avert an innings defeat, and six wickets were left to do it in. The pitch was perfect, the batsmen were good, and Crawford was brilliant. So were the other bowlers, but JN, hat off, shirt sleeves rolled up, and with determination allied to a great heart made the public look to him to perform the feat. He performed it. Steadily, surely, the runs crept up to the total of 213 required by New South Wales. The 200 drew into sight when four men still remained to be dismissed. The 180 appeared, then 185. Two runs later two wickets fell. Whitty got both of them. Ten more runs came before the ninth man departed (Crawford's wicket) and 200 arrived without disaster. It went forward still further, and a boundary hit assisted to bring the dangerous total of 200 up. Then the end came. Crawford concluded a brilliant performance by clean bowling the last man, and the ex-Surrey player pulled down his shirt sleeves, gathered up his hat and walked off the field. For an hour and a half he had bowled at the batsmen in the true sense of the term. His every action denoted personality: he was an inspiration to the team. Nothing was too hard work for him and he was just as keen and tireless at the end as when he started.

> This man is going to have a splendid influence on South Australian cricket and the traits of his character indicate that not alone as a cricketer will he shine.[11]

Against Victoria at Melbourne, in the match starting on New Year's Day 1910 he demonstrated the folly – unthinkable now – of batting without gloves as well as showing some form with the bat.

> The game started with an accident, Sewart (who batted without a glove) being hit on the hand by a ball from Crawford and compelled to retire ... Crawford, fourth out (at 296) made 75 out of 208 in three hours and a quarter and hit seven fours; he adopted quieter methods than is customary for him as C Hill was scoring so rapidly. No other member of the side reached 20.[12]

Crawford's performances, along with those of Clem Hill, were instrumental in South Australia's capturing the Sheffield Shield for the first time in more than a quarter of a century, the match with New South Wales in Sydney being decisive.

> Much interest centred on this match, as a victory would enable South Australia to regain the Sheffield Shield for the first time since 1893-4 ... Crawford was bowling admirably and was chiefly the cause of the low scoring. Gradually Crawford tired and the runs came more readily. The Surrey man, however, it was who was responsible for the break-up of the partnership [between Kelleway and Minnett], which had realised exactly 100 for the ninth wicket in sixty-three minutes ... Hill and Crawford, who, batting freely on a wicket eased by light rain, put on 100 for the third wicket in seventy minutes ... Crawford ... played a faultless game. It was a capital win for the visitors considering how unrepresentative a side they had.[13]

Jack even had the satisfaction of scoring the winning boundary.

The Sheffield Shield safely in the Adelaide Oval trophy cabinet, Crawford then ended a highly satisfactory season by helping East Torrens to the South Australian Premiership. It is one of the strengths of Australian cricket compared with its English counterpart that there is the possibility of a seamless transition from grade to state to international cricket in a way that rarely happens with the club and county system in England. The wheels are oiled by the presence of first-class cricketers in the grade sides. It was absolutely to be expected then that when not required by the state side and when his duties at St Peter's permitted, he should turn out for one of the grade teams. Even before his arrival, it had been arranged that he should play with East Torrens who had taken the Premiership the season before and would do so again in his first season with them.[14]

> Half a dozen Saturdays ago or perhaps a little longer than that, interest in this year's cricket premiership lost its keenness on account of the overlordship of the strong East Torrens eleven ... At all times East Torrens looked good enough to represent South Australia by themselves. With the exception of three drawn games they won every match and if the scores were not phenomenal they at least carried a good deal of weight behind them. Crawford did not twinkle with the bat but stood almost alone with the ball. East Torrens certainly earned their premiership with one of the best club teams that the state has seen for a long while.[15]

Jack's batting performances had been very modest – 96 runs in seven innings – but his bowling – 23 wickets at 11.63 – made a significant contribution to the Premiership winning side. Later, when in a coaching position with SACA, having moved to Glenelg, he turned out for that club, one of the weaker sides in the competition at the time. He impressed for both teams, first with his bowling then with his batting, keeping East Torrens at the top and moving Glenelg up the table.

Any contact with friends and family during the Australian winter would have elicited the information that Surrey were struggling on the bowling front without him.

> Smith, of Surrey, had a most successful time last week ... In the absence of JN Crawford and Rushby a great deal will depend on him .... It is probable, however, that the need of another bowler of the first rank will be felt before the season is very far advanced, especially if the weather improves and cricketers experience a succession of hard, true wickets, for EC Kirk will appear very seldom if at all and Hitch, although possessing plenty of pace, is not a

> bowler who inspires one with a great deal of confidence. Lees, most willing of workers, is, fortunately, still available.[16]

> Smith was not altogether fortunate in the support he received, the loss of Rushby and JN Crawford being sadly felt. Rushby, by the way, having had enough of Lancashire League cricket, will be back in the Surrey eleven next summer.[17]

Surrey had released Marshal, paying his passage back to Australia and voting him a pay-off of £50 (though they later got away with £30) provided he was out of the way in a couple of weeks, by 1 July, but not before playing in a club match for AH Marriot's XI against Ashford where he had the impressive figures of 16-3-28-10 in a total of 81 all out.[18]

On the family front, Reggie, playing very little first-class cricket these days, had a successful season with Wanderers, 852 runs at 31.55 and 127 wickets at 10.69.[19] 'Pa' Crawford, aged sixty-one, had headed the Cane Hill batting averages and Frank had left Leicestershire and was going off to something completely different: tea-planting in Ceylon.[20] He left in December.

During the southern hemisphere close season, however, press notices announced that:

> It is understood that JN Crawford, the ex-Surrey cricketer, has forwarded an apology as the 'result of correspondence with Lord Alverstone' to the committee of the Surrey Club for his refusal to play against the Australians during the last tour.[21]

The timing suggests that the apology may have been catalysed by family pressure following the previous month's Annual General Meeting of the Surrey Club, but it gave Crawford another option should the South Australia adventure go stale in the future and also opened the way for possible participation in the England-Australia-South Africa Triangular Tournament in England originally envisaged for 1909, but subsequently postponed to 1912.

The media were a few weeks ahead of the committee. Letters had to travel by sea at the time and took longer to be delivered than those sent by email today, but it was not until several weeks later that the matter was put before the committee. They were non-committal. The President was asked to send a reply and the matter was postponed.[22]

As well as his cricket coaching skills, Jack's singing talents were also in demand at St Peter's and he seems to have fitted in well with the social life of the school. At the Old Blues dinner in July, 'An orchestral programme was given under the direction of Mr C Cawthorne. Messrs JN Crawford and C Degenhardt and Master R Saunders sang.'[23]

The 1911 Australia cricket team – some thought Crawford should be among them. In the centre of the back and middle rows are Crawford's South Australia teammates, Algy Gehrs and Clem Hill.

10

SEASONS IN THE SUN

SOUTH AUSTRALIA 1910-13

The following season South Australia came close to winning the Shield again, but a defeat by New South Wales was decisive. They were tied on points, but 'on the strength of averages for and against them, New South Wales were declared holders of the Sheffield Shield'.[1] Jack was able to play in only two matches plus two against the South African tourists. He contributed to a win against Victoria at Adelaide, taking advantage of a rain-affected pitch after the first day had been washed out.

> Victoria made a shocking start against Crawford and Whitty, losing Warne without a run scored, Ransford at 4, Smith and Kortlang at 6, McAllister at 13, Delves at 21 and Kenny at 27 ... At that point Victoria were 7 for 27. They recovered, but insufficiently to prevent South Australia winning by six wickets ... Their subsequent cricket was marked by a faultless innings of 79 not out on the part of Crawford, who adapted his play admirably to the state of the wicket ... Ransford ... was then bowled off his shoulder by a fast ball from Crawford.[2]

An innings defeat in the return match in Melbourne did not help in the quest to retain the Shield: 'Of the others only Crawford who made 69 out of 114 in two hours and hit a six and eight fours did much.'[3]

Two matches for South Australia against the touring South Africans were both lost, though Jack turned in reasonable performances in both. In the first, 'Crawford played a fine and plucky game ... At times the fielding was poor, but not so far as Crawford was concerned.'[4] In the second, with 57 and 40, he was top scorer in each innings.

There was a possibility of Crawford being selected for the Australian national side in the Tests against South Africa. Qualifications for international cricket were more flexible and there were the precedents of John Ferris and Billies Midwinter and Murdoch having represented both Australia and England and Indian-born Ranjitsinhji having played for England, albeit not without some opposition. Had the Board of Control wished to play Crawford in the Australian Test team, they could probably have done so, though in some quarters such a selection might have been seen as cynically exploiting the absence of tighter regulations. In the event, however, 'The Australian Board of Control of Cricket has decided not to play JN Crawford against the South African Eleven on the ground that he has already played for England.'[5]

In the four first-class matches in which he did play, Crawford averaged just under 30 with the ball, just over 60 with the bat including a half century in each match, without concerning himself too much whether he used one of his own bats or someone else's.

> A good workman requires the best material. Therefore champion batsmen are particular nowadays about their bats. On Friday JN Crawford in cracking a ball to square leg broke his bat. He held out a signal for another. With the utmost sangfroid however, he did not wait for it, but calmly borrowed Clem Hill's and found plenty of good wood in it, for he immediately banged a ball for four. A moment later after three more bats were taken out to him, and after carefully trying their 'spring' he chose one of them, but he did not make again a sweeter stroke than the one from the piece of willow which was supposed to have been specially rounded for a left hand batsman.[6]

He continued to excel in grade cricket and unlike the previous season, this time made an impression with the bat, registering his first century in any kind of cricket since that on the same ground on the 1907/08 MCC tour.

> On the Adelaide Oval where East Torrens lost only seven wickets against Adelaide, JN Crawford was responsible for 182 of the score of 309. Crawford is now completing his second season with the East Torrens club, but up till Saturday he had not made a three figure score in district cricket or in interstate matches for South Australia. His effort on Saturday was praiseworthy, and the spectators were delighted as he brightened up the afternoon. Twenty five fours, two sixes and a five were included in his score.[7]

East Torrens again won the A-Grade competition and St Peter's College, in part no doubt as a result of their new resident master's coaching, were triumphant in the B-Grade. Unlike the previous season when his batting had failed to impress, this time he was pre-eminent with both bat and ball: 'JN Crawford headed the batting list with the fine average of 66.68 and in bowling he was top with 28 wickets for an average of 11.39.'[8]

AG Moyes, a pupil at St Peter's at the time of Crawford's tenure, recalled:

> I saw Crawford first at Adelaide, when he hit 114 against South Australia. Later, after a disagreement with the Surrey Club, he came back to St Peter's College, Adelaide, as a master, greatly to the delight of those of us who were in the eleven. He tried to teach us to bowl as he did. Elated in mind, but in agony physically, we stood while he twisted our fingers round the ball in the manner he himself adopted. Then we would hide for a time until our fingers regained their normal feel and begun to function again.[9]

At the end of his second season with South Australia, tiring of schoolmastering, he terminated his appointment at St Peter's College. Rumours were rife in the media that he was to give up cricket and take up farming.

> Mr JN Crawford who has been in South Australia for the past eighteen months has resigned his position as a master at St Peter's College. The res-

ignation will take effect from the end of term on May 6. Mr Crawford who has been a prominent cricketer both for East Torrens Electorate Club and for the State is undecided as to his future movements, but on Friday he said 'I am thinking seriously of going on the land and it is my present intention to remain in South Australia.' Should he carry out his present ideas it is not likely that he will be able to keep up practice in cricket, and the state will lose the services of a first-class player.[10]

In the event it didn't happen. SACA stepped in and he was appointed Oval Clerk at a salary of £200 per annum with duties beyond clerking and extending to coaching and scouting.[11]

There is conflicting evidence on the impression he made at the college. Some have said that his approach was lethargic and indolent and there was relief when he decided to call it a day after little over a year in the job, but evidence from the college magazine is quite the reverse. His appointment was welcomed and his early departure regretted, reported as being 'much to the sorrow of the school in general. He was very popular and the cricketers especially will feel his loss.'[12] The Headmaster regretted his leaving. There may be an element of 'he would say that, wouldn't he?' but nevertheless, even after his resignation, Jack continued to participate fully in the life of the college and its Old Boys.

The headmaster of St Peter's College (Rev H Gardlestone) at the annual meeting of the St Peter's Collegians Association on Wednesday evening expressed his regret at the pending resignation from the College teaching staff of Mr JN Crawford.

After the meeting, 'A smoke social followed and a capital musical programme was carried out by Messrs JN Crawford, K Jones and H Heinemann and a quartet party.'[13]

Outside the college too, his musical talents were in demand:

The members of the Lyric Club were provided with a splendid programme by Miss Vera Jure on Wednesday evening, and exhibited their appreciation. Miss Jure contributed a violin solo and a piano solo. The other items included: Songs 'The Windmill' by JN Crawford.[14]

Meanwhile, earlier in the winter, almost a year after he had submitted his apology to Surrey, he was informed that the resolution that he would not be invited to play for Surrey again had been rescinded.

> On Monday Mr Crawford received a letter from the Secretary of the Club stating that at a meeting held on March 10 the resolution of 1909 was rescinded on a motion of the President, Lord Alverstone.[15]

The committee had taken their time. Jack's main antagonist, HDG Leveson Gower, who had now relinquished the captaincy and been replaced by Morice Bird, was presented with a silver cigar box 'in recognition of his valuable services as Captain of the County Eleven'.

1911/12 was a season which heralded an MCC tour and five-match Ashes series under the captaincies of Clem Hill and JWHT Douglas. Crawford had had a foot in both camps and was perhaps in a better position than most to analyse the strengths and weaknesses of both sides.

> It is nearly two years since JN Crawford, who was a regular player for Surrey, came to South Australia. For some time he was on the staff of St Peter's College, but he severed his connection with that school a few months ago and has now received an appointment on the clerical staff of the South Australian Cricket Association. It is his intention to remain in Adelaide and he will again play in inter-state matches.
>
> 'From my knowledge of the players while I was in England, and from what I have seen in the press since my coming to Australia, I should say that they will give Australia all they want,' said the ex-Surrey man when interviewed by a representative of *The Advertiser* on Tuesday in regard to the English team. 'Much will depend on the success or otherwise of Hordern, the New South Wales googlie bowler. Without wishing in any way to disparage the efforts of the other Australian bowlers I am strongly of the opinion that if Hordern does not "come off" England's chances are very considerable.'
>
> What about the batting strength?
>
> 'I think they will take a lot of digging out. They are a very solid batting side but the team possesses none of the brilliance of men like Trumper. Woolley, Foster and Hobbs may be expected to be the fastest scorers on

the side, and men like Vine, Douglas and Kinneir will take no end of getting out. Smith, second wicketkeeper, is a likely man to knock up 60 or 70 quickly at any time. Warner should make a capable captain and may be expected to contribute a lot of runs, that is if he does not get tangled up with Hordern's "googlies". Then there is a run-getter in Gunn, who was not with us in AO Jones' team in 1907-8.'

And the bowling?

'Well, they ought to have a fast bowler – that is a really good fast man. Such a player is necessary in Australia, if anywhere. The position is that there are few such cricketers in England, and when Brearley refused – the cable messages stated that he had declined the invitation – the selectors might have done better if they had asked Hitch, who is also a wonderful field, to come out. The absence of a fast bowler is sure to be a weakness. Barnes is one of the finest right arm bowlers. He did magnificently when out here with Jones' team. Foster is a fine left arm trundler and this pair will bear the brunt of the attack. Douglas might prove more useful out here, as he is a right-hand fast medium, and his deliveries come very fast off the pitch. Then there is Iremonger to be reckoned with, provided he can get his swerve on the ball. I am of opinion that bowling generally has deteriorated during the past ten years, up to the discovery of the googlie. There are now no fast bowlers, such as Richardson, Jones or Spofforth used to be, and Cotter is not as fast as he was. The Australian bowlers seem to have an advantage over English bowlers out here, and I believe it is owing to the clear atmosphere and the perfect wickets. In England bowlers show as much form as Australian bowlers on their own wickets. With the atmosphere so clear and the wickets so true in Australia it is necessary for a bowler to deceive the batsman in the delivery and flight of the ball, and to become proficient in that takes several years. In this particular the English bowler is placed at a disadvantage on coming to Australia.'

'Strudwick is a fine man with the gloves. I have played with him in the Surrey eleven. He is the nippiest wicketkeeper I have ever seen. He is smaller if anything than Carter but the batsman dares not give him any chances, either of stumping or catching, if he wishes to continue his innings.'[16]

After losing the first Test, England came back to win the next four and avenge their defeats in the previous two Anglo-Australian series. On the domestic front with South Australia, despite Crawford's century and seven wickets in the match, Victoria successfully chased down a target of over 300 in the fourth innings to win the opening match of the season. It was the first time South Australia had played in front of the now iconic new scoreboard at the Cathedral End. It is still there, still functioning and has recorded many centuries in international and state cricket. Jack Crawford's in November 1911 was the first; his innings recalled that for MCC four years earlier.

> Crawford's batting dwarfed everything else in the second innings of the home side. During the two hours forty minutes he was in he made 126 out of 190, hit a six and eighteen fours and combined sound defence with hard hitting.[17]

According to *Wisden*, 'Scoring 35 and 126, and taking seven wickets, JN Crawford was unlucky to be on the losing side.'[18] There was some personal consolation, however.

> One of the trophies which have been liberally subscribed for to mark the acquisition of the magnificent new scoring board for the Adelaide Oval was won on Monday by JN Crawford who notched a century against the Victorians. One trophy was to go to the first South Australian who scored 100 runs and the other to the first one to capture five wickets in a first class match. Crawford thoroughly earned one of the mementos by his brilliant innings against the Victorians. It is all in the game that the couple of chances he gave comparatively early in his innings were not accepted. His was a fine effort when other men were falling comparatively easy victims to the visiting bowlers. Crawford's defence throughout was sound, and he made many good hits in front of the wicket, one of which, off Armstrong, sailed away for six.[19]
>
> CRAWFORD'S SUCCESS SUITABLY RECOGNISED BY SACA MEMBERS
> A pleasant function eventuated at the office of the South Australian Cricket Association yesterday afternoon, when members of that body assembled for the purpose of presenting Mr JN Crawford with a token in recognition of his score of 126 made on November 5 for South Australia against Victoria on the Adelaide Oval.

> Sir Edwin Smith, President of the South Australian Cricket Association, who occupied the chair, said that it was his pleasing duty to join with other members of the Association in conferring an honour on Mr JN Crawford. The members were so pleased with the new scoring board that they decided to present the first scorer of a century or over in an inter-state or international match with a mark of appreciation, and to follow a similar course in the case of the first bowler taking five wickets in one innings. The movement had been inaugurated by three members – Messrs Fraser, McEwan and AE Evans – and the amount of subscription had been limited to 2/6. In round numbers about £14 or £15 had been collected and half of this had been devoted to purchasing a memento for Mr JN Crawford, who was without doubt one of the best all-round cricketers in Australia. He hoped Mr Crawford would long remain with them and had great pleasure in handing over the articles to him.
>
> Mr Crawford, who appeared to be far from comfortable, said that he had felt great difficulty in expressing his thanks to the donors, but he was very pleased to be the fortunate winner of the trophy. He thanked the donors for their generosity. He came out to South Australia as a stranger and had been treated most generously and his greatest joy was that he would be able to do good work for South Australia. A man could not always do well; he might make a duck, fail to get wickets or drop a catch, but he had not to mind that as it was all in the game.
>
> The trophy took the form of a travelling bag, fountain pen, signet ring and umbrella. The travelling bag bore the following inscription 'Presented to JN Crawford by members of the South Australian Cricket Association to commemorate his score of 126 for South Australia v Victoria on November 6, 1911, this being the first century recorded on the new scoring board at the Adelaide Oval.'[20]

What was not appreciated at the time was that, as well as being the first person to have a century recorded against his name on the new scoreboard was that shortly after the turn of the year, he would have six for 141 against New South Wales and be similarly rewarded for being the first bowler to have five wickets recorded against his name on the same scoreboard.[21]

Later in the month he was to renew acquaintance with some of his former colleagues when South Australia entertained the touring MCC.

They were too strong for the state side, however, overwhelming them by an innings and 194 runs, Crawford being one of the few members of his team to emerge with any distinction: 'Except for the batting in the second innings of Crawford and Mayne, the home side's run-getting calls for few remarks.'[22]

Hobbs has pleasant memories, both of Adelaide and of the hospitality received from his former colleague and others, though, writing more than a quarter of a century after the pivotal events of 1909, carefully avoids any mention of the reasons why Crawford might be living in Australia at the time.

> What a treat to see oranges growing in the sunshine and to picture the fogs and chilly air of London, which just then was getting ready for the Fifth of November's guys and squibs. Our reception was delightfully cordial from JN Crawford, Clem Hill and other friends. JN Crawford was living out there at the time.[23]

Visiting MCC captain Pelham Warner had been impressed by the practice facilities at St Peter's College which the tourists used when those at the Adelaide Oval were unavailable because of the South Australia-Victoria match: 'If there are better wickets in this world than at St Peter's College, I have not seen them.'[24]

The next month, Crawford was selected for an Australian XI to play against MCC in Brisbane and against a strong attack, recorded his second century of the summer before being caught behind by his former teammate Herbert Strudwick from the bowling of Sydney Barnes, who was later to account for thirty-four wickets in the Test matches: 'Two thousand spectators witnessed the continuation of the match between the MCC team and an Australian Eleven. Crawford batted brilliantly for 109 minutes.'[25] At a rate of around a run per minute, he made 110.

For South Australia it was a poor season. Unlike the previous two years, they were never in contention for the Shield and after their initial defeats by Victoria and the MCC tourists, they went on to lose to Victoria again, this time by an innings and 135 runs, then twice to New South Wales, by 361 runs in Sydney and eight wickets in Adelaide. For

Crawford too, it was one of his least distinguished seasons. He had just one five-for – his six for 141, which took fifty-two overs – and apart from his century against Victoria and century and half-century against MCC, he passed 15 only once in seven innings.

When all that was over, however, he recovered some form with East Torrens and registered centuries in consecutive matches. Against Glenelg, 'JN Crawford played a fine innings for 157 which included five sixes and eighteen fours.'[26] Against North Adelaide:

> It had been expected that the match between East Torrens and North Adelaide on the Adelaide Oval would be productive of tall scoring. The easterners are in excellent form this season and so far have carried everything before them. Particularly good scores have been made by them in the majority of the matches, and in the two games previous to that started last Saturday their figures were 480 and 5 for 332. East Torrens won the toss from Norths on Saturday, and, occupying the crease throughout the afternoon, knocked up 391 for the loss of four wickets. The first two men were out for 98 but the partnership between LW Chamberlain and JN Crawford produced 193 runs. Crawford who made 157 in his previous game was particularly aggressive and he posted 109 runs in ninety-two minutes. He played freely all round the wicket, and his hits included two sixes and eleven fours. A couple of difficult chances were given and the catch which terminated his innings was brought about in brilliant style by Finch at cover-point.[27]

Trevor Mead, East Torrens scorer, has kindly summarised Crawford's statistics for the club for the three seasons he was there. They are nothing if not impressive.

BOWLING

	1909/10	1910/11	1911/12	**Total**
Runs	268	319	334	**921**
Wickets	23	28	23	**74**
Average	11.65	11.39	14.52	**12.45**
Best	6-39	6-20	4-25	**6-20**
Five-fors	3	1	0	**4**

BATTING

	1909/10	1910/11	1911/12	**Total**
Matches	6	7	8	**21**
Innings	7	7	8	**22**
Not Outs	0	1	0	**1**
Highest score	25	182	157	**182**
Runs	92	400	655	**1147**
Average	13.14	66.66	81.88	**54.62**
100	0	1	4	**5**
50	0	2	1	**3**
Catches	2	4	7	**13**

Once again, Jack continued his singing during the winter, visiting Taxunda with a concert party, being met at the station by the Taxunda Brass Band and entertaining at a banquet and social at Wallace's Hotel.[28] Then he returned to the College to sing again at the Collegians Annual dinner, as well as leading the school song which was 'heartily entered into'.[29]

After a disappointing season in 1911/12, South Australia bounced back to reclaim the Sheffield Shield. It was not unconnected with the fact that Crawford himself had a much better season, his Shield batting and bowling averages being 48.28 and 27.28 respectively. More than that, however, he was promoted from his clerical position to become chief coach.

> JN Crawford, the well-known English cricketer, has been appointed chief coach at the Adelaide Oval, with JC Reedman as assistant. The English chap is trying quite a lot of little jobs since arriving in wool land. The assistant is, of course, the old South Australian representative player of a few years ago.[30]

'Quite a lot of little jobs' is a bit of an exaggeration. The first move from St Peter's to SACA had perhaps been a sideways one that enabled him to concentrate more on state cricket and to abandon school cricket. The move from clerk with its ancillary duties of scouting and coaching to chief coach was, however, an upward move, though coupled with the rumours of wishing to go 'on the land', it was a reflection of a restlessness which can characterise twenty-somethings as they try to find a suitable career ladder and step on to it. In Crawford's case, the job was to provide him with the experience which two years later would send him across the Tasman to yet another country.

The season began with a win in a non-Shield match against Western Australia in Adelaide.

> The home side led by 201 runs on the first innings, Crawford taking seven for 31, including a hat-trick, as Western Australia collapsed to 69 all out in seventy-five minutes and ninteen overs.
>
> The sensational bowling of JN Crawford was responsible. He and L Howard, both fast upon an excellent wicket, proved too much for the visitors: seven wickets were down for 16. Crawford at one time had six wickets for 9 runs, including the hat-trick. The Westerners seemed unable to play the bowling at all and sent the ball into the air on all sides.[31]

Clem Hill chose to bat again – according to the press, to get a good gate on the following day – extending the lead to 611. Jack's contribution was negligible in the second innings, but he did win an interesting side bet with Algy (DRA) Gehrs on which of them would hit the most sixes.[32] Gehrs had 119 with twenty-one fours, but no sixes. Crawford had 7 runs which included one six! He then took four for 40 in the second innings as South Australia won the match by 365 runs.

It was a portent of things to come. In the pre-Christmas fixture at Adelaide, New South Wales were despatched by an innings and 53 runs and, although the return match in Sydney was lost, South Australia beat Victoria twice to win the Sheffield Shield for the third time in all and the second in four seasons. The second win was in every way Crawford's match. While it is not quite true to say that he won the match single-handedly, Victoria were never likely to recover from his first innings 163, followed by bowling figures of 22.5-7-66-8.

His ability is remembered in the following way by AG Moyes:

> In those days the wicket at Adelaide, and on other Australian grounds, shone like a dress shirt. Nowadays both are out of fashion. But Crawford could

> spin the ball at fast-medium pace, and when the ball left his hand there was a crack as of a stick breaking, and the ball would spin on the shiny surface ... This man was a grand cricketer. In the days when there were giants in the game he was one of the men who mattered. His vitality was amazing, his energy beyond measure. He put everything he had into the game; in the hot Adelaide sun it came out again in perspiration. At each interval Crawford hung his saturated flannels on the fence behind the dressing-room: he was always 'wet with honest sweat' when he left the field.
>
> As a bowler he was tireless, and he never became ordinary. Just as you imagined the time had arrived for him to rest he would come along with something fresh. In all he did there was fire and hostility. Now and again he would release from his fingertips the one we called 'man-killer'. This flew high and fast, with such a force that a speed bowler need not have been ashamed of it; those of us who fielded in the slips were forced to beg him to signal it. When he gave the signal, as he walked back with that springy, athletic stride, we crept back a few paces and hoped for the best.
>
> As a batsman he was entirely a forward player, getting his power from a last-minute stiffening of the wrists. His bats were usually hollowed in the middle from consistent pounding, for he hit very hard, and was never afraid to lift the ball over mid-off with a stroke that is now out of fashion. His style in his forward play was perfection, and he could carry the longest boundary. I saw him one day at Sydney reach forward to Macartney; the ball carried on to the green hill near the sight-board and never rose above ten feet all the way.
>
> One day at Adelaide we were watching a batsman wend his way sorrowfully to the dressing room. Clem Hill stood there with us. Suddenly he turned and said, 'There are grand cricketers in this game; and then there is Jack Crawford.' How true it was! He was a man who could have been one of the greatest cricketers ever to play; might have gone down in history as one of the champions of all time. Today there is no one in the game with the all-round skill that he possessed.[33]

Although the Board of Control had decided not to play him in Test matches, he was clearly a presence on the national scene and invited to play for the Rest of Australia against New South Wales in Victor Trumper's testimonial match. The beneficiary had 126 not out and 61, but Crawford made little impact in a match originally scheduled for four days, but extended to five because of time lost to weather on days two and four.

Just before the beginning of the season Crawford had moved to the seaside suburb of Glenelg, about nine kilometres from central Adelaide. The press speculated that the move might mean the end of his time with East Torrens and so it turned out, as he now threw in his lot with the local club which was later to be a launching pad for the careers of Ian and Greg Chappell, but at the time Crawford arrived was at a low ebb in its fortunes.[34] He played as often as his state commitments allowed and his presence made a difference.

The scorecards suggest that in mid-summer Adelaide heat, he often bowled through the innings, taking seven for 95 against West Torrens in a total of 194 and eight for 111 in Adelaide's 259.[35]

In the return match against West Torrens, in which Crawford did not play:

> It would not be fair to describe the Glenelg combination as a one man team but it is rather a curious circumstance that during the present season their success or failure seems to coincide with the presence or absence of their crack bowler JN Crawford. Saturday's play was no exception to the rule as the seasiders were treated to an afternoon's 'leather hunting' by their doughty opponents and only succeeded in disposing of six of them at a cost of 305 runs.[36]

When he did play it was quite different, although despite his six for 84 and seven for 33 against Adelaide University on a rain-affected pitch, Glenelg still managed to lose by 69 runs.[37]

He then finished the season with a flourish.

> JN Crawford (Glenelg) dominated the game in which his team played Port Adelaide at Alberton. He secured eight wickets for 66 (a repetition of his previous week's fine performance). The local men were dismissed for 128. Crawford clean bowled five men, caught and bowled one had two others caught and helped Hack to get a wicket.[38]

> The ex-Surreyite, JN Crawford put up another fine performance in Adelaide cricket on Saturday. Playing for Glenelg he smacked up 72 out of a total of 132, only one other batsman getting double figures. Crawford is connected with the South Australia Cricketing Association in an official capacity and is handed over to the weakest team. Glenelg would have been utterly annihilated this season had it not been for the great all-rounder who, by the way, wears spectacles when batting.[39]

The *Register* summed up Glenelg's and Crawford's season as follows:

> Glenelg have advanced from eighth to fifth position through the efforts, almost entirely of one man, JN Crawford. Without him they lost heart and were generally easily beaten. Although the team rarely made extra big scores, and were slow in making runs at any time, the fire and sling of Crawford's bowling generally had the result of dismissing the opposing team fairly easily. 'JN' was considered not to have done much in the way of batting but he had almost the best average among the seasiders. His bowling was phenomenal and he now holds the record for having secured most wickets during a season.[40]

There was, however, a downside – one which has echoed through club and school cricket wherever performances have been dominated by a professional among amateurs or a superstar among ordinary mortals. The rank and file were not getting much of a game. Glenelg's official history comments:

> It could be said that Crawford's genius inhibited the rest of the team, particularly the bowlers, who were not getting enough time at the crease. His colossal efforts had only lifted Glenelg to fifth position. Of course, his absences were caused by appearances for the state team.[41]

The record was 66 wickets at 10.18, a considerable achievement in a competition that had been running almost forty years, especially when he was not available to play for his club every weekend, missing three matches out of twelve. Not until the 1926/27 season was the record broken, by leg break and googly bowler Norman Williams.[42] For good measure, Jack also topped the batting averages with 381 runs at 34.6.

His combined figures for East Torrens and Glenelg over the five seasons he played in Adelaide District cricket were 1659 runs at 48.79 and 155 wickets at 11.77. Twice he topped the district batting averages.

Towards the end of the season there was some debate in both hemispheres on possible change to the LBW law, some expressing the view that if the ball were hitting the wicket, the batsman should be given out, wherever it pitched. As always, Crawford was ready to give a firm, well argued opinion.

> An animated controversy is taking place in the London newspapers on the oft-debated question of the desirability of altering the 'leg-before-wicket' rule of cricket. The law as it stands reads: 'The striker is out if with any part of his person he stops the ball, which in the opinion of the umpire at the bowler's wicket shall have been pitched in a straight line from it to the striker's wicket and would have hit it.'
>
> The well-known old cricketers, Mr AG Steel and Mr Robert H Lyttelton, are at the head of the agitation for an alteration so that the batsman would be out if his legs prevented the ball from hitting the wicket, no matter where it pitched; and on the other side are Mr PF Warner and other well-known players.
>
> 'Absurd,' was JN Crawford's opinion of the proposal. 'They tried it in England six or seven years ago, but they soon dropped it as being unsatisfactory. Only about two matches were played under that arrangement and each side in a contest between the MCC and Leicestershire – I believe it was – made only 70 or 80 runs and a large proportion of the batsmen were out lbw.'[43]

The proposed new law never was introduced, though there was a change from the 1937 season when, provided the batsman were hit in line, he could be given out to a ball pitching outside the off stump, giving rise for a brief period to a new scorebook entry 'LBW(N)'.

The New World of Cricket: Edgar Mayne, PS Arnott
and Jack Crawford in front of Ottawa Cricket Pavilion.

11

PLAY BALL

NORTH AMERICA 1913

After the Triangular Tournament in England in 1912, the Australian team made its way home via the United States and Canada, playing in Philadelphia, New York, Bermuda, Winnipeg and Victoria. While they were there, a few of them took it upon themselves to begin negotiations for an Australian tour of North America the following year. In the days before air travel became the norm it was a massive undertaking, covering the major provinces of Canada and much of the eastern United States. Only five of the matches would be first-class, the remainder at a lower level (a few, much lower) in places that were not dedicated to cricket. The total fixture list was fifty-five matches (increased to fifty-seven by two 'fill-up' matches), spread over five months and many thousands of miles. It was a privately arranged tour, no sanction being given by the Board of Control, but that was of little concern to the Americans, who welcomed the visitors with typical transatlantic hospitality and enthusiasm, although there was a little resentment in some of the more 'official' circles.

> Twelve Australian cricketers for America are booked to leave Sydney on May 5 by the *Niagara*. Among the names mentioned as those of the party are ER

> Mayne (who has done the organising at this end), GC Campbell, JN Crawford, WJ Whitty, HL Collins, PS Arnott, W Bardsley, CG Macartney and A Mailey. Some of these are uncertain. The guarantee for a number of games is said to be satisfactory, but in light of the experiences of the Australian baseball team in America, players who go may undertake a risk. It will not be an official Australian team, but in a country like America, where the distinction will not be generally understood or appreciated, it may not mean much, the comment in a Philadelphia newspaper notwithstanding.
>
> An attack on the Australian team which visited America appears in the *Philadelphia American* of Mar 1, 1913. Among other things is the statement, 'The American cricketer thinks that a general opinion prevailed to the effect that our foreign opponents last summer composed an official Australian side. It would seem that no very resolute effort was made to dispel this erroneous impression.' It would be as well for the Philadelphians to remember for future reference that an official side from Australia could visit them only through arrangements made with the official body in Australia.[1]

The mood seems to have been entirely harmonious with no hint of the misbehaviour which characterised the Australian tour of England the previous summer.[2] The venture was described as 'not for money-making, but for pleasure', though Crawford estimated each player would make about £200.[3]

In the nineteenth century, as the quintessentially English game of cricket had been spread with missionary zeal through the British Empire and her colonies and former colonies, cricket may well have become one of America's major sports. The world's first international cricket match was not, as commonly supposed, between Australia and England in 1877, but between the United States and Canada in 1844. In 1859, George Parr had led the first English tour to those two countries. Around the time of the Civil War cricket rivalled baseball in popularity, but after that became a distant second.

The USA would not have been strong enough to provide serious competition in the triangular tournament of 1912. Anyway, Abe Bailey, who spearheaded and financed the South African involvement, saw it as an event designed to cement and strengthen imperial bonds. Nevertheless, despite the eventual dominance of baseball, deep pockets remained.

The game of cricket was particularly strong in Philadelphia, and there was enough of it elsewhere to justify a tour of the continent long enough to occupy most of the northern hemisphere summer and some way into the fall – fifty-three matches were planned.

The party had a brief stop-over in Auckland en route:

> A team of Australian cricketers will pass through Auckland by the *Niagara* next month en route to Vancouver. Twelve berths have been booked. When seen in Adelaide on Thursday Mr Mayne, who has charge of the arrangements, confirmed the news that the trip had been definitely arranged. 'We should have a great time,' he remarked. 'In fact it should be the tour of our lives.'
>
> 'It is not like an English trip,' he stated. 'Everything cannot be decided in a day or two, and it would place a man in an uncomfortable position if I said he was going and then the whole affair fell through. Victor Trumper has given me to understand that he will go and the Americans expect him, and would be keenly disappointed if he did not turn up. I suppose he is known better than any other Australian over there and the Americans are simply mad to see him.'[4]

Unfortunately Trumper was unable to fulfil his undertaking due to financial exigencies and the Americans were to be 'keenly disappointed'.

The journey across the Pacific was broken by a stop in Fiji where the tourists began their impressive tour record with a comfortable 138 run win against Suva. A further stop in Hawaii saw them take the opportunity of swimming and surfing and, along with the townsfolk, seeing an Olympic Champion in action.

> CRICKETERS ARRIVE. With the Moana pier and beach thronged with interested townsfolk and tourists, including the members of the crack Australian cricket team, who were through passengers on the new RMS *Niagara* en route to Canada and the United States for a series of matches, Duke Kahanamoku, champion short distance swimmer of the world, yesterday afternoon, gave his first public swimming exhibition since his return to Honolulu from Stockholm and the Olympic Games. It was at the request of the Australian cricket team that Duke gave the exhibition yesterday, the mem-

bers sending a wireless message to WT Rawlins, setting forth their desire to see the champion in action.

Most of the players took the opportunity of getting a swim at Waikiki yesterday afternoon and several of them sampled the delights of surfing.[5]

Duke Kahanamoku had won gold and silver medals at the Stockholm Olympics and was to win two golds at Antwerp in 1920 and a silver in Paris in 1924. He was an early beach volleyball player, helped to popularise the sport of surfing and went on to a career in politics and acting. The cricketers seem to have had an enthusiastic welcome, their athletic appearance attracting admiring comments.

The Australian cricketers are a husky aggregation of athletes, and if looks go for anything they should put up a strong argument against the best that Canada and America can produce. The men are the crack players of Australasia, but they have done considerable playing as a team and are not merely a collection of individual stars. The Australians made a smart appearance, and wore straw hats with the distinguishing mark of a green and gold band with crossed cricket bats.[6]

Their arrival in mainland America was even more enthusiastic, a half-holiday being declared for their match against Vancouver.

In America, from our special correspondent with the team.

Victoria. We arrived safely this morning and the reception we got will never be forgotten by any of us. Thousands of people came on the wharf to see the *Niagara* come in: and the first thing we saw was a big green and gold banner with the words 'Welcome to the Australian cricketers'. Mr RB Benjamin, who will manage the team, was there to meet us, and I think, all the cricketers in the place must have turned out. We said 'good bye' to all the passengers and they wished us all good luck and I can assure you we made many friends on board. Messrs Chapman and Alexander the well-known evangelists travelled with us from Auckland, and Mr Chapman told me he had never met a finer lot of young fellows and he took a photo of the team. Dr Roland Pope, who has travelled with several Australian Elevens said that he had never known a team to leave such a good impression behind at the end of a voyage as this one. He will travel with us and we are very pleased to have him.

As soon as we got on shore we were taken for a motor drive round town, and in the afternoon had some practice, which we all enjoyed. In the evening we were the guests of the Victoria Club at the theatre, and saw the famous actress Miss Maud Adams, playing Peter Pan.

All sorts of entertainments await us, and this looks like being the trip of a lifetime. My one regret is that we haven't got the champion of champions with us and we are all sorry that Victor Trumper could not get away, as I am sure he would have enjoyed the trip.

We played our first match today against Victoria and had an easy victory. The game started at 10.45 in glorious weather. Quite a good crowd turned up, and they saw some brilliant cricket. It was a matting wicket on grass and was certainly a sporting one. The outfield was rather rough but our fellows fielded like champions and Austin Diamond made two wonderful catches.

Mailey, Emery, Macartney and Crawford bowled well, and turned the ball a lot. Although they didn't get many runs a couple of the local batsmen shaped very well. Ackroyd looked like a good batsman and H Orr has played a lot of cricket in England (Bedfordshire). On going in to bat our fellows played very well considering it was the first match after three weeks on the boat. Victoria could only get 76 in their second innings and the bowling was altogether too good for them.

Tomorrow we are to play Vancouver and we shall meet a much better side. A public half holiday has been declared for the match. On Saturday we play British Columbia and then go on to Edmonton.[7]

Most matches were reported in the Australian and New Zealand press by the 'special correspondent', anonymous at the time, but easily identifiable in later years as a number of the reports are repeated verbatim in Charlie Macartney's 1930 book *My Cricketing Days*.

In the United States, too, the visit was also eagerly anticipated, Crawford being singled out for special comment.

The invasion of this formidable team of cricketers will furnish the admirers of the game in this country a regular treat, as the team comprises some of the greatest players the world has produced.

Jack Crawford is one of the greatest all round players in the world, at times making some remarkable scores, and a bowler of the first grade besides being a beautiful and sound judge of the game.[8]

New York newspapers also reported on the first match against the United States and Canada in Philadelphia.

The Australian cricketers led the United States and Canada eleven by 159 runs when play ended for the day on the first day in the test match between the two teams at the Germantown Cricket Club. Neither team scored heavily although the wicket appeared fast and in excellent condition.

The Australians went to bat first and scored 233 runs in spite of the fast fielding of their opponents. The entire side of the United States and Canada was retired in their first innings for only 90 runs while the Australians scored 7 runs without the loss of a wicket in the last five minutes of play.

The visiting players on the United States-Canadian side were unable to do anything with the bowling of the Australians. FC Goodman, the Montreal star, was bowled by Mailey before he had secured a run, while HS Reid and PE Henderson, the Toronto players, were only able to score 2 each. AA Hoskins, the New York representative played very cautiously and was not out for a total of 8 runs.[9]

It was scarcely a Test match and the cricket vocabulary is a little different, but the flavour of the first day's play is captured before the Australians went on to dominate the second innings too, to win by 409 runs, Bardsley making 142 not out and Crawford, adding to his first innings five for 38 with three for 42, including the wicket of the adhesive Hoskins, promoted to open the innings. 'Our Special Correspondent' gives the Australian perspective:

The first match ever played between Australia and a combined team from the United States and Canada was commenced at the Germantown ground on July 4 – the great day of the year in America. We won the toss and went in on a good wicket.

HS Reid and PE Henderson came from Toronto, FC Goodman from Montreal and AA Hoskins from New York. The remainder of the Eleven was made up of Philadelphia players. It was a fair side and, if their batting had been on a par with their bowling, it might have been a more interesting match. As it was, after dismissing us cheaply enough for 233, their batting broke down badly and the whole side was out for 90. Their batsmen do not wait to get a sight of the ball. This is accounted for by their club matches only lasting one Saturday afternoon and unless each batsman gets runs quickly and then out, half the side would not get a hit, and the games would not be finished. They also bowl ten balls to the over in these club games so as to save time by not having to change over so often. This comes a bit hard on a fast bowler.

Our start in the match was anything but a good one, as Cody was out at 15 and Macartney, after being missed at 5, was caught for 10. When Bardsley had made 10 he was bowled off his pads. Crawford played fine cricket and looked set for a good score when Clark bowled him with a good one which came back from the off. Mayne made top score with 85. Arnott, Diamond, Campbell, Emery and Mailey all reached double figures, but the score was rather disappointing on a good wicket. Pearce, Goodman, Clark and Hoskins bowled well and the fielding was excellent.

None of their batsmen troubled us much and only three of them succeeded in reaching double figures. Newhall and Anderson shaped the best, but the majority of them were in too much of a hurry to get runs and got themselves out. Crawford and Mailey bowled splendidly.

In our second innings we declared with nine wickets down for 416. Some fine batting was seen, and Bardsley reached the century after being missed in the slips at 40. Cody, for the third time in Philadelphia, just missed the century.

The bowling of the combined team was not as good as in the first innings, and their fieldsmen dropped one or two catches. On going in a second time they did a little better than in the first innings but never looked like getting a big score. Our fellows fielded brilliantly in both innings. Everybody tells us that the cricket played by this team was the best ever seen in Philadelphia.

The attendance was rather disappointing and it seems that the public will not patronise cricket in Philadelphia now as they did fifteen or twenty years ago. One can see photos hanging on the clubhouse at international matches that took place twenty years ago, where the pavilion and ground are packed with people, but nowadays a few hundred are all that attend a big

> cricket match. All sorts of reasons are given for the lack of public interest in the game. Some say that golf and automobiles have taken the young fellows away from cricket.[10]

The touring party was particularly impressed by the facilities. Charles Macartney later recalled:

> The ground of the Philadelphia Cricket Club was especially well appointed. In addition to the splendid playing areas there were about a score of tennis courts and a 13-hole golf course had its first tee just behind the players' dressing rooms. These dressing rooms not only had their full complement of shower baths, but were connected by a short underground passage with a magnificent swimming pool. During our stay in Philadelphia the weather was extraordinarily hot and humid and consequently this swimming bath was not overlooked by the Australian team. Every evening of our stay there was marked by a gathering of some description, dinners taking pride of place.[11]

After the reasonably serious cricket of the 'Test match', that on the diversion to Bermuda was rather more light-hearted.

> The week spent at Bermuda, in the Atlantic, (two days sail from New York) was most enjoyable and little incidents during the cricket matches there were very amusing.
>
> During the progress of one match when JN Crawford was batting, he hit a ball over the fence into the trees which knocked one of the dusky spectators off a branch. Although he fell to the ground he was uninjured and showed his splendid teeth in smiles at the guffaws of his brethren … One of the matches at Bermuda was played against a native eleven, who had great hopes of defeating us. To make the match last the required time we were hard put to it to keep the local side at the wickets, and in our endeavour to do this some most remarkable catches were made. Mailey was fielding in the slips to Crawford's bowling, and Jack was keeping them as wide as the matting would allow but the batsman would persist in chasing them. As expected he eventually touched one and Mailey put his hand out thinking to miss the ball when it stuck fast and the catch brought forth roars of applause. Another great catch was made by one of our men in pure self-defence. It came so hard

> and straight that he had no time to evade the ball and had he not caught it might have received a very nasty injury.[12]

The Australians watched some baseball while in the USA and admired the athleticism of the players, comparing it with what was then, thanks to its English origins, a skilful game, but a more leisurely one with more time for social interaction in the intervals.

> 'I have seen a number of games of baseball since I have been over here,' said one of the Australian players, 'and I am bound to confess that it is a rattling good game. Your fielding is wonderful but I have several times wondered whether your baseball man could catch a hard cricket ball thirty feet from the batter with bare hands.'
>
> 'We don't pretend for a moment that cricket is a hard athletic pursuit. It is simply a healthful outdoor pastime. It is a game of skill and the very pace at which it is played, with its long intervals for luncheon and tea, allows of much social intercourse between the players and the onlookers.'[13]

At Chicago there was the opportunity of interface with some of the White Sox baseball players. Charles Macartney recalled in later years:

> At Chicago we were the guests of Mr Charles Camisky who was the controller of the White Sox baseball team. He not only entertained us, but gave us the use of his baseball park on which to play the match set down for that city. Before the match began we were indulging in the usual knock-up, and some of the baseballers came out to watch. We invited them to have a strike, and they accepted, but we regretted it afterwards. These men had absolutely no idea of hitting a ball that bounced, but anything on the full was treated with scant courtesy. Not appreciating the fact that the blade of the bat was the correct part with which to hit a cricket ball they belted the full-tosses with any part of the bat and as a consequence, had we not stopped them, all our bats would have been devoid of fronts, backs or edges. They were surprised when we explained things and remarked that with a baseball club there was no need to consider edges and suchlike.[14]

Jack Crawford did not need a baseball bat when playing in Exhibition Park in Yorkton, in one of his not infrequent big-hitting moods, to dispatch the ball so far into the open country that a boy was sent after it on a bicycle. Neither boy, nor bicycle, nor ball was ever seen again.

It was at White Sox Park that Jack had his most spectacular performance of the tour – at least in statistical terms. Against Chicago, he had ten for 27 (albeit against a team of sixteen players) in a total of 110, then himself made 111 in the Australians reply of 372, thus giving a whole new dimension to the American idiom 'ballpark figure'.

He did not play a major role in another statistical spectacular, 633 for 8 at Brockton Point in Vancouver, making just 33 in the wake of centuries by Campbell, Macartney and Bardsley. The runs were made at almost eight an over – and conventional six-ball overs this time, rather than the more eccentric ten.

The sole defeat of the tour came against Germantown in early August in a match in which Crawford did not play, but two days later in a minor match against what was termed a West Indian Coloured XI in Brooklyn, Crawford and Macartney totally dominated proceedings. Macartney's match figures were fourteen for 13, while Jack had a more modest return of five for 9.

> A new record in international cricket games in this country was made yesterday at Celtic Park in the match between the Australians and the united West Indian eleven. The home players were all out for thirteen runs and the innings was completed in forty-eight minutes of playing time. The bowling of CG Macartney and JN Crawford was a revelation. Macartney sent down thirty-six balls and captured seven wickets for as many runs. Crawford secured three wickets in one over, although he delivered as many balls as his partner. But five runs were scored against him and he had the players in difficulties throughout.[15]

Even that bizarre innings was eclipsed a few weeks later when, in the first of three matches against the Winnipeg Cricket Association, the locals were dismissed in their second innings for just 6, four of which were byes. Crawford had four wickets without conceding a run while Macartney who had eight for 12 in the first innings, was more expensive with six for 2. Crawford's sister Audrey had married in Winnipeg earlier in the year and it is entirely possible that he took advantage of the coincidence to pay her a visit.

A quarter of a century later, Herbie Collins was to recall:

> I can speak with a first-hand knowledge of Crawford's ability. People who have seen both men consider him a better all-rounder than Hammond.
>
> When playing against Winnipeg, Ontario, we decided to let Winnipeg make a few runs in the first innings. When we went in they had a bowler who skittled a few of our batsmen with remarkable shoots or grubbers. Crawford and Macartney were our opening bowlers. They were told not to mess about as the position was serious. Crawford's first ball went to the boundary for four byes. The Winnipeg side were all out for six runs. Macartney took six for none and Crawford four for two.[16]

Such was the scale of victory that a temporary stand collapsed, as though in sympathy with the disappointing performances of the home side.

Although not of the margin as the crushing victory at Winnipeg, most of the fixtures were complete mismatches. The Australians were only defeated once and of the remaining matches, disregarding the fill-ups, three were drawn, the remainder won, most very easily. Crawford finished the tour with 213 wickets at 5.85.

Five of the matches were first-class, three against the Gentlemen of Philadelphia and two against the United States and Canada. Four were won by huge margins, one rain-affected with the tourists in a strong position. Crawford's batting performances were modest, an average of 24.5 with a top score of 58, his bowling rather better, two five-fors and a six-for, 33 wickets at 10.87.

Towards the end of the tour, there were reports that the team was stranded and financially destitute.

> The New York correspondent of the *Daily Citizen* says that Mayne's Australian cricket team is stranded owing to poor gates received last month. They have a perpetual struggle to pay their railway fares and hotel-keepers are tired of waiting for some good gates. The members are moodily wondering

> whether they will have to walk across the continent and work their passage from San Francisco or Vancouver.[17]

The claim was strongly denied, with supporting evidence.

> Mr SJ Down, father of Mr GS Down who is treasurer of the team, when seen tonight said he believed that the rumour was unfounded. In all the letters that he had received from his son the only reference to money matters was in a letter written on June 18, in which he said the financial part looked good. A month later his son sent £20 as a present to his sisters, so that did not look as if they were stranded. His last letter was received a fortnight ago and gave no hint of financial difficulties. He could not believe that the story was true for his son would have sent him a cable message at once and he would have had any money he wanted by return.[18]

The father of Arnott, a member of the Australian cricket team in America, cabled to his son, 'Is the team stranded?' and received the following reply: 'No; publicly deny. Tour a great success.'[19]

In an end of tour interview, Edgar Mayne reacted strongly to the adverse publicity and also summed up other aspects of what seems to have been a highly satisfactory and enjoyable tour.

> Unexpected arrivals by the *Marama* from Vancouver yesterday were Messrs E Mayne, W Bardsley, SH Emery, A Mailey, HL Collins, L Cody, JN Crawford, A Diamond and GI Down, members of the Australian cricket team which recently toured the United States and Canada. Two other members of the team – Arnott and Campbell – are at present in England, while Macartney is returning by the next steamer.
>
> In the course of an interview with Mr Edgar Mayne, Captain of the team, a *Herald* representative gleaned some interesting information about the tour. Before touching on the tour, however, Mr Mayne expressed surprise at the nature of the messages published recently about the players. He could not understand why messages had been sent from America stating that the team was stranded, as the success of the tour was assured from the outset. Never at any time were the players in financial difficulties and the statement that the hotel proprietors in America were tired of waiting for their money from the team was given a straight-out denial. 'We are disgusted with reports

published in Australia,' said Mr Mayne, 'and we cannot understand why steps were not taken to verify them.'

Mr Mayne preferred not to say anything as to the amount each man would net, but he was emphatic about the financial success of the tour. From a playing point of view, too, the tour was a great success, as only one game was lost out of about fifty-five played.

Certainly the opposition was not very strong, but taking everything into consideration the record is one to be proud of. A team from the Philadelphia Club, consisting of twelve players had the honour of lowering the visitors' colours, but had the Australians not taken a risk in leaving JN Crawford out of the team, it is probable that they would have gone through without defeat. At Philadelphia the Australians played on a fast turf wicket and as most of the games previously had been played on slow matting pitches, the visitors were unable to time the ball, chance after chance was given in the slips, and it is of interest to mention that one of the slip men took no less than nine catches. He also accepted another chance at cover-point, making his record for the match ten catches. The Philadelphians were certainly the best players encountered by the tour, but the team was by no means as strong as when JB King, considered by many to be the finest bowler in the world, was a member. There are, however, some promising colts in the city, and as the two grounds are among the finest in the world the game may yet make considerable headway.

The best teams met with in Canada were at Toronto and Winnipeg, but wickets in the Dominion were as a rule very bad. Little trouble was taken in preparing the grounds and it was quite impossible to play decent cricket on matting laid on the rough ground. In Canada quite a number of ex-county men from England were met, but owing to the high price of land good grounds were almost out of the question. A good deal of interest was taken in the team in Canada and at a public reception the Premier (the Rt Hon Mr Bordon) stated that if he could find time he would like to bring a Canadian team to Australia.

As the team was not after records no averages were kept during the tour. The order of batting as a rule was decided by ballot and the instructions to the batsmen in most cases were 'Go in and have a hit'. Still there were plenty of centuries and many fine bowling figures were obtained. Everywhere the team was treated royally and practically all the interesting portions of the

> states were visited. Several days were spent in the Rocky Mountains and a visit was also paid to Niagara Falls.
>
> The Australians, who are all in excellent health, will continue their journey to Sydney by the *Marama* today.[20]

It was time for Crawford to return to cricket in surroundings more used to it – the Adelaide Oval.

Arthur Sims and Victor Trumper in front of a scoreboard showing their mammoth eighth-wicket partnership in New Zealand. It was Crawford's first match of the tour.

12

Second Schism

South Australia 1913/14

1913/14 was a modest season for South Australia, but with an all-round ratio pushing two (39 with the bat and 20 with the ball) and five five-wicket hauls in four Shield matches, it was a more successful one for Crawford than some might have anticipated, given the arduous and exhausting North American tour which had occupied most of the time between last season and this.

He played only two matches for Glenelg, but took fourteen wickets in them. His on-field performances, however, continued to impress, not least that at Sydney in the pre-Christmas match with New South Wales where South Australia won a tight encounter by 19 runs.

> According to a Sydney writer, the Sheffield Shield match between South Australia and New South Wales provided some very good and interesting cricket. Despite the absence of Clem Hill, DRA Gehrs and WJ Whitty, the southerners made an excellent fight, and thoroughly deserved their success. JN Crawford was the star performer for the visitors right throughout the match. In each innings he batted splendidly and with commendable restraint. He seemed a certainty for the century in the first innings and in point of fact the quality of his play thoroughly deserved the three-figure distinction. His off-driving was very powerful and beautifully timed, and

he showed admirable judgement and control in lifting the ball into the unguarded parts of the field. To fine leg he made many neat and effective strokes, and he was ultimately out to Mishima trying to force an over-tossed ball high into the outfield on the on-side. His double, 91 and 40, were the results of really high class play and these scores taken in conjunction with his effective bowling show him to be still one of the leaders in the first-class arena.

In the first innings he sent down thirty-six overs for 89 runs and five wickets – a very fine piece of bowling, and he was equally successful in the second. At all times a most pertinacious and untiring bowler, on this occasion Crawford appeared to have regained some of the 'snap' which characterised his deliveries when Australian cricket first made his acquaintance. His fast ball on Saturday was very much in evidence, his variations of pace were cleverly disguised, and all the time his bowling showed its natural tendency to hurry off the pitch in a way that we have not seen in Crawford's bowling for some time. In this form there are many successes and many years of them for the ex-Surrey amateur.[1]

He followed up with seven for 78 in the return against New South Wales and had match figures of eleven for 145 in the match against Victoria. With two defeats in four Shield matches, however, the trophy was once again fought out between New South Wales and Victoria.

However, Crawford's full attention was not on the cricket field – or at least, the Adelaide Oval. Rather, he was looking further afield and wondering where his cricket would be played the following season. Jack was getting itchy feet.

Crawford was among an Australian party embarking on an end-of-season tour across the Tasman Sea to New Zealand. It was due to a lucrative offer received on the trip that his relationship with the South Australians began to fracture.

Thanks to the enthusiasm and enterprise of Mr Arthur Sims, the Canterbury and New Zealand player, a wonderfully strong side came across the Tasman. There were five famous Australian players, VT Trumper, MA Noble, WW Armstrong, V Ransford and F Laver, together with JN Crawford, the famous

> ex-Surrey and South Australian player, to excite universal interest. The others were: HL Collins and AA himself.
>
> The team veritably smashed its way through the Dominion. Fifteen matches were played, and only in a few games was there the slightest sign of competition. Some huge scores were made: against Auckland 658 (including three separate centuries), against Poverty Bay 461, against Canterbury 653 (two centuries), against Manawatu 510, against Southland 709 (three centuries).[2]

The tour was an unofficial one, expenses met by Sims and profits shared between the players; attractive for them, but less appealing to the Board of Control who declined to sanction the initiative.

Crawford had not travelled with the main party, his departure from Adelaide being delayed by his final Sheffield Shield appearance. His arrival was eagerly anticipated by the New Zealand media.

> The Australian team arrived in Auckland this morning. Crawford, however, will not arrive until next week.[3]

> Arrangements are complete for the match Australia v Auckland which will be commenced on Eden Park (Kingsland) at noon tomorrow and to be continued on Saturday and Monday. It is not considered likely that JN Crawford will reach here in time to be included in this match.[4]

> JN Crawford, who is to join the Australians in New Zealand, is a passenger by the *Willochra* for New Zealand.[5]

> Mr JN Crawford, the well known English and South Australian cricketer, arrived from Sydney today by the *Willochra*.[6]

It was rumoured that he was not in the best of health and that his medical advisor had recommended a rest from the game.[7] That is not unlikely and is scarcely surprising. He had, after all, had two full seasons in the Sheffield Shield, interspersed with club cricket and separated by a massive, exhausting tour of North America. It was, nevertheless, hoped 'that New Zealanders will see something of this brilliant player in action'.

Medical advice was defied and New Zealanders did see a brilliant player in action, both on the tour and in subsequent seasons.

The tour was already half over by the time Crawford arrived. Within a couple of days, however, he was playing in the Australian side against Canterbury at Lancaster Park. He was eased in gradually, bowling only half a dozen overs in the first innings – to an eccentric field – and batted at number eleven, scoring 2. It made little difference to a massive total. The tourists had lost six wickets for 118 and were not far ahead of Canterbury's 92 all out. Arthur Sims and Warwick Armstrong engineered something of a recovery before Victor Trumper, contributing 293 of an eighth wicket partnership of 433 with Arthur Sims, propelled the score to 653 and the lead to 561. Crawford, now presumably recovered from his journey, dismissed five of the top seven batsmen, finishing with figures of 23-6-60-5 in a victory by an innings and 364 runs.

> Crawford came on and Woods late cut his last ball for four, well placed. Crawford was mixing in a few long hops. The field on the off was curiously placed for him, five men standing in a direct line parallel with the wicket, Trumper at mid-off, then Collins forward cover, Mailey at point, Sims ten yards from him and Cody third man.[8]

The next match was absolute mayhem. It was a non-first-class two-day fixture against Fifteen of South Canterbury at the Temuka Oval, but despite its minor status it was deemed worthy of a mention in Crawford's *Wisden* obituary fifty years later.[9] Never was the discrepancy between the hosts and the tourists better illustrated. Technically the match was drawn, as the Australians were more interested in piling up a huge score than in winning it. In a total of 922 for 9 in 113.3 overs, Crawford had 354, including fourteen sixes and forty-five fours and contributions to partnerships of 298 in sixty-nine minutes for the eighth wicket with Victor Trumper and 213 for the ninth with Monty Noble.[10]

> McGregor and Cody took the score to 180. Crawford was the next man, then Ransford and Trumper. They piled the runs on rapidly, breaking records. Crawford hit fourteen balls out of the ground and made 50 in thirteen

> minutes and 50 in ten. Trumper pleased the onlookers immensely by crisp, safe batting. Over 200 runs were scored in the last hour. The bowlers were frequently changed and all the eleven men were tried.
>
> JN Crawford, a lithe, wiry player, always on the move, was keenly watched. The South Australian champion takes a long run to the wickets, bowls wide close to the return crease, and gets them down fast, and, to the general astonishment, was able to make the ball swerve from a foot to eighteen inches.[11]

> Crawford gave several chances, almost all of which would have been accepted by a first-class field. He opened his shoulders to everything, and, barring the chances he gave, could be likened to Jessop. He hit fourteen sixes and forty-five fours.
>
> The bowling was good until at the finish when fatigue broke it down and the batsmen did what they liked.[12]

Another newspaper reported that on two occasions during the innings, fifty runs were scored in five minutes.[13]

While in Canterbury, Jack took the opportunity to visit an old family acquaintance and be reminded of his father's sporting prowess.

> An interesting incident of the visit of the Australian cricket team to Christchurch last week was the discovery that Mr JN Crawford's father, the Rev JC Crawford, was a member of the West of England football team at the time it was captained by Mr F Wilding KC of this city. The Rev JC Crawford was a great football player and had the reputation of being the finest place-kick in England. Mr Crawford, when in Christchurch, took the opportunity to call on Mr Wilding.[14]

Of the eight first-class matches on the tour, six, including the so-called 'Test' matches (New Zealand was not granted Test status until 1930), were won comfortably. Two were drawn. It was a complete mismatch.

> No great amount of comment is necessary about the second test match between the New Zealand and the Australian visitors which was concluded at Eden Park on Monday. The visitors' display was practically a repetition of

their performance against Auckland. Again Waddy, Dolling and Armstrong scored centuries by bright and irreproachable batting, while JN Crawford ran up 134 in very quick time. Crawford does not take long to start, and once he gets going the bowling suffers very severely.[15]

Apart from that century in a total of over 600 in the last of the matches against New Zealand in Auckland, Crawford did little to distinguish himself beyond a half-century in Dunedin, a five-for and two four-fors. He was, however, in serious negotiations about the next stage of his career.

Dunedin, capital of the province of Otago, had been a major business centre in the nineteenth century, but by this time was beginning to feel the effects of the 'drift north'. It was anxious to retain a prominent position in commercial and sporting circles, so there was money around to make Crawford an offer he would find difficult to refuse to play for the provincial team and coach its Colts. The figure they offered – £350 per annum – compared favourably with the £300 he was making in Adelaide.

From March onwards, New Zealand newspapers were becoming increasingly animated about the possibility of Otago recruiting Crawford as their coach and the improvement in standards likely to result.

A little bird whispers (says the *Christchurch Sun*) that JN Crawford of the Australian team is being persuaded by leading cricket enthusiasts in Dunedin to take up his residence there, and act as coach to the Otago Association. New Zealand cricket will score if the brilliant Surrey and South Australian remains in the Dominion.[16]

Crawford is the prominent member of the Australian team mentioned by me last week as likely to settle in Dunedin as coach. It is understood that he had been approached with a lucrative offer for a lengthened engagement.[17]

REPORT OF THE EXECUTIVE OF THE OTAGO CRICKET ASSOCIATION. The Chairman (T T Ritchie) mentioned that negotiations had been proceeding with Mr JN Crawford with a view to securing his services as coach, but that nothing definite could be arranged pending his return to Adelaide.[18]

Says a Southern paper: 'Otago are on the look-out for a good cricket coach, and are prepared to spend from £300 to £400 a year if they can get the right man. I have heard it rumoured that they have their eye on JN Crawford, a member of the Australian team now touring New Zealand.' ... Later news says 'he has been approached with a good offer for a long engagement'.[19]

JN Crawford, the international cricketer, has advised the Otago Cricket Association of his preparedness to accept an offer of a three-year engagement.[20]

CRICKET COACH FOR DUNEDIN. Cable message was received on Saturday morning by Mr TT Ritchie, who has been conducting the negotiations on behalf of the Otago Cricket Association, notifying the acceptance by JN Crawford of an appointment for three years as coach in Dunedin.[21]

Arrangements in connection with bringing to Dunedin of JN Crawford were advanced another stage at last night's meeting of the Otago Cricket Association. Many supporters of the game have promised substantial sums towards securing the services of Crawford, who is to be engaged for three years at a salary of £350 yearly. He will undertake to coach the young players and assist Otago representative cricket.[22]

MR CRAWFORD'S ENGAGEMENT. The arrangements in connection with bringing to Dunedin Mr JN Crawford, the well-known international cricketer, with a view to stimulating the game in this province, were advanced another stage at a meeting of the Otago Cricket Association on Monday evening when Messrs JJ Clark, TT Ritchie and A Martin were appointed a sub-committee to confer with a similar number of gentlemen representing those supporters of cricket outside the association who have been interesting themselves in the movement. It is understood that a position will be found for him, but that he will undertake to coach our young players and assist Otago in her representative matches. The sub-committee was empowered to make all necessary arrangements with regard to this coaching, and a scheme is projected that will ensure our young and promising players being thoroughly taught. It was decided to make arrangements whereby Mr Crawford will be able to take up residence in Dunedin in June, so that he may qualify to take part in the representative matches.[23]

Definite arrangements have been made with Mr JN Crawford who has played such a prominent part in Test cricket in the old world, and in interstate and other first-class cricket in Australia, to act as coach for the Otago district teams. Since word was received on Saturday that Mr Crawford was willingly favourable to consider the question of taking up his residence in Dunedin as coach, several cablegrams have passed between the Cricket Association and Mr Crawford. Yesterday the president of the association finally completed the agreement with the new coach. Mr Crawford will leave Adelaide at once, and may be expected to arrive in Dunedin next month. In order that he may be qualified to represent the Otago district, it is necessary that a player should reside in the province for at least six months before his first match, and, so as to avoid delay in Mr Crawford's case, several gentlemen have guaranteed the money promised him, as they are confident that cricketers and the public will come to the assistance of the association in its effort to advance district cricket. If the matter had not been promptly settled there was a strong probability of Mr Crawford being lost to Otago, as the South Australians were naturally reluctant to lose his services, and strong efforts have been made to keep him in Adelaide.[24]

A private cable advises that JN Crawford has signed an agreement at Adelaide to sign as cricket coach in Dunedin for the term of three years, and that he will leave Sydney for here on Saturday, 6th June.[25]

Once the move was decided, Jack was keen to get to work improving the standard of New Zealand cricket.

In conversation with a *Post* reporter, Mr Crawford said he was strongly of opinion, from what he had seen during his previous visit here, that cricket was on the up-grade in this Dominion, and there was no reason why it should not become as popular as football. New Zealand, especially Christchurch, was fortunate in having many fine cricket grounds although they might not be so fast as the Australian pitches. Mr Crawford strongly advocated the sending of a New Zealand team to tour the Old Country. Although visits to Australia were a great help, a tour of England would be

> even more beneficial, as the players would meet many more players. 'I am certain,' Mr Crawford added, 'that the last visit of the Australians did much to improve cricket here. The cricket at home, however, is of an even higher standard than the Australian game, and I think that in three years' time New Zealand should be able to produce a team worthy of being sent to England. I certainly intend to do all I can to help the game while I am here, and will keep my eye on the promising players.'[26]

The enthusiasm spilled over into other sports. One newspaper was quick to point to the new coach's hockey talents and the Otago Rugby Union, approached by the Otago Cricket Association with a request, agreed to donate the gate money from one of the end of season matches towards the funding of the appointment.[27]

However, in signing a contract with Otago, Crawford was reneging on an agreement with his current employer. Before the departure for New Zealand, Crawford had sent the South Australian Cricket Association what it described as an 'arrogant letter' requesting leave of absence from his employment to join the party due to embark on an unofficial tour to New Zealand and seeking assurances about the renewal of his contract. Both requests were granted and he crossed the Tasman with his future in Australia secured. However, Crawford used that agreement as a negotiating ploy with the Otago Association, who offered him a salary of £350 per annum and negotiated with the SACA to secure his release.

The chain of events leading to Crawford's severance from South Australia is detailed by Chris Harte.

> Jack Crawford wrote to the Association in early December 1913 and in an arrogant letter said that he required two months leave of absence from the end of January, and also wanted to know if his agreement with SACA (which still had six months to run) was going to be renewed as otherwise he would have to look elsewhere for another position. G&F (Ground & Finance) considered this note two weeks later, expressing surprise at the tone of the content before instructing Riley (Secretary) to tell his junior clerk that as he was also the Association's coach there was no way he could just go off in the middle of the season. Added to this, the renewal of his contract would be considered in a couple of months.

A month later, on 16 January 1914, Riley called a special G&F meeting to consider further correspondence from Crawford. After a lengthy discussion they agreed to the request for six weeks leave, and also offered a new three year contract. Two weeks into his leave, Crawford returned to Adelaide and met with Riley. He wanted his salary doubled if he was going to sign a new contract, and furthermore he was going to New Zealand in a week's time for discussions with various cricket associations.

Mostyn Evans (treasurer) and Harry Blinman (from G&F committee) saw Crawford the next day and offered him £160 as an annual salary plus he could keep all coaching fees: This would total around £300 per annum. Crawford agreed and signed a new contract on 18 February before going to New Zealand.

Then, on 11 March, Mostyn Evans received a cable from the Otago Cricket Association, Dunedin which read: 'Will your Association agree to release Crawford from his engagement if we can offer him a substantial inducement to remain here? We ask for your hearty co-operation to assist us further the game in New Zealand.'

Another special G&F meeting was called for the following day during which feelings ran high. Eventually it was agreed to reply to Otago: 'If Crawford personally makes an application to cancel his agreement this Association will be prepared to release him.'

Crawford also received a cable: 'SACA is very surprised, after the way you have been treated, to receive a communication, sent at your request, from the Otago Cricket Association asking us to release you from your agreement. A reply has been sent to them. Wire us immediately if you wish to be released from your agreement.'

Crawford replied acknowledging receipt, returned to Adelaide a month later and informed G&F that he had been offered £350 a year plus a half share in a sports store if he moved to Dunedin. The committee immediately washed their hands of him and started to hunt around for a new coach.

Jack Crawford had treated the Association very badly particularly when it is realised the amount of money that was spent on him. Crawford's resignation was formalised on 5 May 1914.[28]

So much for what went on behind the scenes. The Committee, however much they might have felt exploited and let down, were sufficiently dignified and respectful of tradition to organise a farewell luncheon where the tributes exceeded the usual courtesies.

> During his sojourn in Adelaide for the past four years Mr Crawford has done more for the cricket of the state than any other man, and this fact was appreciated by those who met at the South Australian Hotel on Wednesday to bid him bon voyage. Mr Mostyn Evans presided and at the conclusion of an excellent repast referred in fitting terms to Mr Crawford's connection with cricket in Australia. He had been only a few years in South Australia but he had made many friends. Those who were present regarded him with more than kindly feelings and they would follow his career with interest. It was unfortunate that the South Australia Cricket Association do not realise what it was losing. Crawford had done much for the cricket of the state and no obstruction should have been thrown in the way of retaining his services. (Hear, hear). Mr Clem Hill was entrusted with the duty of presenting Mr Crawford with a set of gold sleeve links and an umbrella, and he paid a nice tribute to the abilities of the departing cricketer. He said that if he were asked to go round the world to find a man to substitute for Jack Crawford he would reply that there was not a cricketer in the world who could take his place. He admired the pluck and enterprise of New Zealand in securing Mr Crawford's services and he was convinced that the class of cricket in the Dominion would be improved 100 per cent under his tuition within a comparatively short space of time. He too regretted that the South Australia Cricket Association did not realise what it was losing. Personally he regarded Crawford as the best all-round cricketer in Australia. (Applause)
>
> Mr Darling said it was not the first occasion on which he had met Mr Crawford as he was caught at point off his bowling at Hastings in their first encounter. He had not had opportunities to meet him since but had watched his career and he regretted that the necessity had arisen to sever his connection with South Australia. He wished Crawford luck in his new sphere of life and if cricket did not improve in New Zealand it would not be the fault of the man.
>
> Mr Crawford in reply said he regretted his departure from South Australia where he had made so many good friends, but it was a case of doing the best he could for himself. He did not want to go away as his feelings were wrapped up in South Australia but other matters had to be considered.[29]

Chairman Edwin Smith made a measured and dignified statement for public consumption, supported by his Committee:

> Sir Edwin Smith who presided at the annual meeting of the South Australian Cricket Association on Wednesday evening referred briefly to the departure from South Australia for New Zealand of JN Crawford. He said the committee had granted the terms asked by Crawford for a continuance of his services, and he would not say whether the player should have remained here or not. What he would say was that the committee had behaved nobly towards Crawford and showed no desire to stand in his way. He was glad to know the committee were making an effort to secure another man from one of the other states.[30]
>
> Mr BV Scrymgour said at the time of Crawford's departure the action of the committee was viewed by some in a wrong light. Crawford received an invitation to join the Australian team for New Zealand, and asked for, and was granted, leave of absence. As his term with the Association would expire in two or three months from the time, Crawford was asked if he would renew his contract. He demurred, and before he left for New Zealand the committee met him by agreeing to give him £5 a week, instead of £4, for an extension of his contract for another three years. Then Crawford was asked, 'Suppose you get a better offer in New Zealand, what will you do?' Crawford replied, 'I should turn it down.' However, after he got to New Zealand the Otago Association cabled, 'Will you release Crawford from his engagement.' The committee were surprised at the request and wired to Crawford acquainting him with the request, and asking him if he desired to be released. Crawford's reply was, 'Don't want release; have refused offer of £350 per annum.' Crawford returned to Adelaide and soon afterwards sent a letter to the Association stating that as he had received an offer of £350 a year with the prospects of an interest in a sports depot, he thought it would be a splendid opportunity and would be glad if the Association would release him from his engagement. The committee realised that Crawford was one of the best all-round cricketers in the world, but there was a limit to which they could go in keeping him in the state, and that £250 was as much as they were prepared to give. Crawford did not give the committee the option of offering £350 a year nor did the committee approach him on the question. They had acted as true sportsmen and in granting him a release, he did not

> think that anything the committee did was unfair to Crawford, the public or the Association. They were sorry Crawford had gone, and they wished him good luck.'[31]

In any dispute very rarely does the whole fault lie on one side. In the split with Surrey, while there was an element of insubordination about Crawford's stance, it was the Committee's self-interested and myopic attitude that led to the loss of a talented all-rounder. Now, however, the actions of the SACA's committee and officials were impeccable, dignified and beyond reproach. Clearly they were anxious to retain his services because of his contributions on the field, but not to an extent where they were prepared to tolerate his attitude, deviousness and playing off one offer against another. Eventually, irrespective of his value as a player they were doubtless relieved to have him out of their hair. Yes, he had helped them to two Sheffield Shields, and precipitated a success for the state unprecedented in pre-Bradman days, but the time had come when the asking price had just become too high.

Crawford left Australia for New Zealand in May. However, what he left behind has dogged his reputation for years – a suggestion that Jack lived a debauched lifestyle in South Australia, culminating in the abandonment of his wife. Rumour has spoiled Crawford's reputation, much of it unfairly.

There have been further suggestions, based on hearsay and anecdotal evidence a couple of generations later, that at a reception at Government House in January 1914, before the match with the touring New Zealanders, Crawford invited two ladies from Adelaide's 'upper class' to a threesome (maybe his personal interpretation of the song 'Three for Jack' which he had sung at the concert in far-away Coulsdon). They readily concurred and were found in bed together at the hotel, after which he was invited to leave. The SACA were aware of events.

The stories come from interviews by Chris Harte when he was in Australia a quarter of a century ago, though because of the distance of time, none involved people with actual experience of events at the time. The key interviewee was CLB Starr, who had played for South Australia, but was a small child at the time Crawford was living in Adelaide. It is easy to see how such rumours develop: dressing room gossip can become exaggerated and distorted, isolated incidents can be taken out of context, painting a quite unjustified Jack-the-Lad image.

Contemporary evidence from local newspapers is that there was no reception at Government House. Social events are reported in great detail including the main guests and descriptions of their clothes and jewellery. While it is not possible to be absolutely categorical and in logic a negative cannot be proven, it is highly unlikely that a function at that level would be overlooked. There was a lunch given by the SACA on the day of the New Zealanders' arrival, but that seems to have been a 'stag' occasion. The function was held at the South Australia Hotel, where he had earlier lived for some time. He no longer had rooms there as he was now living in Glenelg but he doubtless had the contacts and the opportunity for a bit of extra-curricular activity in the afternoon and evening. Whether he availed himself of it is not demonstrable, though some might see a clue in his bowling figures next day of 22-3-80-0.

In correspondence, Chris Harte has also suggested that Crawford made no attempt to ingratiate himself with those from St Peter's or SACA and that he really did not understand South Australian society. That seems unlikely. SACA reflected the upper echelons of Adelaide society, included those involved with state government among its officials with membership fees and admission prices to the Adelaide Oval pitched at a level which excluded the less well off. The class distinctions were not as sharp as those he had left behind in England, but they were there and Crawford seemed to fit easily into respectable society.[32] He remained popular and in touch with the College.

In addition, there is circumstantial evidence to the contrary. The official St Peter's records are utterly complimentary and, according to the college magazine, they were sad to see him leave. After he had left, he was invited back to sing in school concerts and to lead the singing of the school song. If he were *persona non grata* with the college it seems scarcely likely that such an invitation would have been issued. Then, if the SACA were really all that keen to be rid of him because of his alleged misdemeanours, it seems unlikely that a contract of a further three years would have been in their minds in 1913. It is all very speculative and likely to remain so.

Another rumour suggests that Crawford lived a dissolute life in Adelaide and fathered an illegitimate child. His post at St Peter's was residential, so on leaving there in 1910, he was obliged to find somewhere to live. The former South Australian Hotel on North Terrace suited him nicely. He had excellent rooms there which he used for private entertainment, including a number of women, some during the day while their husbands worked in the neighbourhood.

The pregnancy seems to relate to the daughter of a St Peter's housemaster, Ainslie Caterer, who had been on the General and Finance Committee of SACA since 1904 and was one of those who had earlier met Jack on his arrival in Adelaide.[33] Caterer had two daughters of nubile age, so it was clearly biologically possible. It is said that the girl gave birth at a country home in the north of the state.

Genealogical research in Australia has also unearthed no documentary evidence of an illegitimate birth. Like other jurisdictions, the civil registration procedures in South Australia provided that where the mother was unmarried, the father's name was not recorded, unless he agreed that it should be disclosed. There is no record of any Caterer births during Crawford's time in Adelaide and in the local press, where the activities of the social upper crust are recorded in some detail, no mention of any extended absence of the Caterer girls from the state capital. It remains possible that the birth went unrecorded (though that would be illegal) or there was an immediate adoption, so while on the evidence available there can be no certainty, the balance of probabilities is against Crawford becoming a reluctant father.

It has also been suggested that Crawford left behind a young wife.[34] Simply not true. Crawford was engaged but unmarried at the time he left Australia. In November 1912, an engagement was announced between Miss Anita Schmidt, younger daughter of Major DH Schmidt, Beulah Drive, Norwood and Mr John Neville Crawford of Adelaide.[35]

Crawford's fiancée was of German immigrant stock, daughter of Diedrich Heinrich Schmidt and Diosma Augusta Bartels. Diosma's father and Anita's grandfather Adolf Heinrich Friedrich Bartels was born in Hanover in 1819 and, in 1855, married Anna Augusta Weidenbach in Adelaide. Anita herself was the second daughter of four, her sisters Johanna and Maria both dying in infancy. A brother, Paul Berkels Schmidt was born in 1901.

German migration to Australia had begun in 1838 with the arrival of Prussian immigrants in Adelaide and played a large part in settling South Australia and Queensland. After British and Irish, German settlers and their descendants were, until the First World War the largest immigrant group. In South Australia they were and remain prominent in the wine growing regions of the Barossa Valley.

Anita was eighteen at the time she became engaged; young, talented and, as is evident from later portraits, attractive. The pair must have had some feeling for each other during an engagement of two and a half years, for large parts of which Jack was away.

The pair moved in the upper echelons of South Australian society and there are reports of their presence as an item, as later parlance would have it, at a number of social functions, including the wedding of Miss Erica Weidenbach, Anita's cousin, to Gerald O' Dea, the opening of the Tivoli Gardens and Crawford's farewell dinner at the South Australian hotel.[36] It was quite the opposite to the dissolute lifestyle that Jack is supposed to have had.

Lastly, rumours also suggest that Crawford was trying to flee 'a mountain of debt'.[37] It is possible that he left debts, but if so, none of such magnitude for a case to be brought against him in the Petty Debts Court whose cases were recorded regularly in the local media.

To conclude, Crawford's South Australian alleged misdemeanours fall under four headings. Namely, that he left behind a lot of ill feeling, a mountain of debt, an illegitimate child and an abandoned wife. On the evidence available, the first is almost certainly true – he had effectively reneged on a not ungenerous contract. However, the second is possible but unproven, the third is possible but unlikely, and the fourth is definitely untrue... at least, at this point in his life.

Carisbrook, pictured in 1910. It was quite a step down
from Jack's previous home grounds, The Oval and Adelaide Oval.

13

Frustration

New Zealand 1914-1916

In June 1914, Franz Ferdinand was gunned down in Sarajevo. Before Europe sank into crisis, however, New Zealanders were awaiting their new cricket star: 'Mr JN Crawford, the well-known cricketer, is a passenger for Dunedin by the *Maunganui*, which left Sydney on Saturday.'[1]

Crawford had to serve a residential qualification before he could play for Otago but began his coaching duties in August. The venue for coaching was a concrete pitch in a warehouse and by the end of the year he was coaching four times a week at the provincial headquarters of Carisbrook and twice a week at Otago Boys' High School.

The July Crisis quickly escalated and the First World War broke out in the autumn. Even on the other side of the world the financial consequences were widespread and would intensify. Crawford offered to forgo part of his pay.

> A sporting offer has been made by JN Crawford, the coach to the Otago Cricket Association. In view of the financial tightness due to the war, Crawford offered to forgo one half of his honorarium for the benefit of the Association in order that the game of cricket might not suffer through lack of funds to carry it on. The chairman assured him that if it were not absolutely necessary the offer would not be taken advantage of.[2]

Later, in his first public appearance on a cricket field since the Australian tour, he participated in a fund-raising venture for Dunedin orphans affected by the war effort.

> PATRIOTIC DEMONSTRATION FOR PATRIOTIC RELIEF FUND. One of the features will no doubt be the costume cricket match between the University students and the Dunedin Orphans club. This is bound to provide plenty of amusement, and some very clever acts are being worked up by these teams. The orphans' team will be led by Mr JN Crawford in his first appearance as a resident of Dunedin.[3]

The rules of the senior club competition were changed to allow the Colts (and the University of Otago) to enter a team in the first grade, an amendment which caused some disgruntlement among other clubs who were losing their best young players to 'Crawford's Colts', but arguments in favour of keeping the youngsters together as a single entity prevailed.

> JN Crawford, the brilliant Surrey batsman and international cricketer, who has been engaged by the Otago Cricket Association as coach, has not been idle since his arrival in Dunedin. He has selected a number of the most promising colts, and two or three times each week is engaged in coaching them on a concrete wicket. It is proposed to form a team of colts to be called 'Crawford's Eleven' and to play it in the senior competition. Of course this means that the best of the young cricketers will be drawn out of other teams, but clubs must show some sacrifice for the good of the game at large. It is anticipated that the benefits that will be derived by playing Crawford's Eleven in the Senior Competition will be greater than by any other means. Keener interest will also be aroused in the senior matches.[4]

The first outdoor practices were held at the end of October.

> JN Crawford is looking forward to getting his colts out for practice on the turf. So far he has had to do his coaching at night under cover. There will be keen competition for places in Crawford's Eleven for the First Grade competition and interest in the team will be enhanced by the presence of JN Crawford himself. It may be expected that a judicious selection of the

young players will be made so that clubs from which they are drawn will be weakened as little as possible.[5]

The form generally was that of the first of the season but one did notice that the display of the colts who have been coached by JN Crawford was marked by a confidence and freedom of style that told of practice and foretold of dashing cricket in the future. JN Crawford, an electric batsman himself, who believes that the bat is made to hit the ball, and to hit it hard and often, is instilling these methods into his pupils with excellent results.

The Colts' team had its first practice on the turf at Carisbrook on Tuesday evening under Mr JN Crawford, who put the members through a thorough course of instruction. The improvement in several of the colts is most marked and all have profited greatly by the coaching.[6]

The intensity of Crawford's pre-season was vindicated in the opening match of the season.

Splendid weather prevailed for the opening of the cricket matches yesterday. JN Crawford's Colts beat Carisbrook A by 189 to 106. For the former Chadwick made 64, and for the latter Hay compiled 50. Crawford took six wickets for 31 runs.[7]

After that opening, success followed success.

It came perhaps as a surprise that JN Crawford in winning the toss put his side in first on a wicket that could not be accounted to their liking. Probably the coach was of the opinion that a try-out in the circumstances would do no harm, or he may have anticipated a quickly drying wicket and worse conditions for Albion. Whatever his reasons, they were justified by results; but it may have come off either way.

The Colts made a disastrous start, losing four wickets for 12, including Shepherd and Chadwick who each got good figures the previous weekend against Carisbrook A, and JN Crawford. The fall of the ex-English and Australian international was the keenest disappointment of all. Many had no doubt gone to the North Ground to see him going after his failure the previous Saturday. After his captain had gone AW Alloo went out, probably with the idea of steadying things; but he appeared very uncertain and scratched a good deal to the bowling. Later he opened out and hit a six, a four and a three off one over; but his innings generally was not a good one, though the runs were useful. The beginning of all things, as Kipling would say, and the end, was Crawford's bowling. On a wicket that took a lot of the sting out of his pace and caused the ball at times to rise up and look straight in the eyes of the batsman, he came out with the remarkable figures of seven for 11. Out of eighteen overs he bowled no fewer than eleven maidens and the most that was scored off an over was four – two singles and a two. His length was not good and he was frequently short but the batsmen could do nothing with him and five of his wickets were clean bowled.[8]

Crawford's Colts continue their glorious march to victory, and there appears to be no stay to their triumphs. Their latest was a win over Opoho at the Caledonian Ground – a somewhat easy victory if the truth is told.

Crawford, practically recovered from his knee trouble, bowled in his own particular form and mowed his victims down like a machine gun. His methods by this time should be understood, but in case anyone is ignorant of the procedure it is here described: Crawford takes a run of about fifteen to twenty yards, his bowling hand working all the time he is making his dash to the crease; the ball flies from his hand as if driven by a cannon shot but there is no explosion, and before you realise what has struck you are walking back to the pavilion. The coach captured seven of the enemy for 21 runs and, as if this was not enough, rubbed it in by hitting up in inimitable style 40 of the best with the bat.

Next to Crawford, the best innings on the Colts' side was that of Bell, whose batting was marked by freedom of movement and crispness of execution. He is essentially a batsman of promise. AW Alloo played steadily for 23. A nervous starter, this batsman is worth watching when he gets going; but he has to get over the beginning. For the rest, the Colts batted confidently and were not afraid to go for the bowling.[9]

The Colts secured another good win on Saturday, beating St Kilda by 147 runs. The Colts batted first, and to such purpose that with 239 runs on for six wickets the innings was declared closed. Alloo played a splendid innings for 74 and Galland also batted well for 59 not out. St Kilda made a poor start against the bowling of Crawford and Alloo, the side being dismissed for 92.[10]

Crawford had five for 36 in that victory, and more were to follow.

> The Colts secured their eighth consecutive win this season and their second over Carisbrook A. There appears to be no stay to Crawford's team and the side looks like going through without a defeat.
>
> As in the majority of the other engagements, it was the coach himself who was largely responsible for the victory. His not out innings of 135 – his first century by the way on a local ground – was a sound effort, and chanceless withal. He started quietly, getting the measure of the attack as he went along, and hitting an occasional four as the right ball came along. Gradually Crawford opened out with lusty strokes on both sides of the wicket and finished up with a perfect burst of pyrotechnics, hitting twenty-six off the last over: 4, 6, 6, 4, 4, 2. It was such an exhibition of vigorous batting as is rarely seen, and brought the spectators to the edge of their seats in pleasurable excitement. Between the fireworks the wicket was impeccable, the shots being executed with masterly skill and execution, while the strokes throughout were marked by perfect timing and delightful power.
>
> As in the first meeting of the teams at the beginning of the season, Crawford proved the A's undoing and with almost as startling results. In the first match Crawford secured six Carisbrook A wickets for 31 runs. On Saturday the coach was satisfied with eight for 50![11]

The Colts went on to win the competition, Crawford having led from the front. Whether such success would have been more permanent cannot be known. The pre-season practices had coincided with the outbreak of the First World War. The popular belief that it would be all over by Christmas was exploded and the end of the season had coincided with the beginnings of the Gallipoli campaign.

Since its inception in 1906/07, the Plunket Shield, the inter-provincial competition decided on a challenge-match system, had passed to and fro between Auckland and Canterbury. Otago was anxious to break that duopoly and Crawford's influence as player and coach was part of the plan. His experience was such that he was immediately installed on the selection committee and appointed captain of the side. He was also appointed Assistant Secretary of the Association. More than at Surrey or South Australia, he was now a big fish in a smaller, less talented pond;

but in total contrast to his treatment five years earlier, his ability and experience were recognised with commensurate responsibilities.

> The Shield has never been held by Otago and if ever they had bright prospects of winning it, it is on this occasion, for they will have the assistance of JN Crawford, admittedly one of the best all-round cricketers in the world.[12]

> The Otago Association have reverted to the selection committee of three for representative matches, the chosen ones being Messrs A Martin, F Williams and JN Crawford. Mr Martin was given thoroughly to understand at the last meeting of the Otago Cricket Association that the change was in no way a reflection on his work last year, but rather that the circumstance of having Mr Crawford here made it desirable to make use of the ex-South Australian's knowledge and experience in the picking out of the very best eleven to do battle for the Dark Blue this season.[13]

His personal performances were impressive, those of the team less so. His brief career with Otago began on Christmas Day 1914 (about the time the war was supposed to be over) and in the four first-class matches played by the province, he averaged 67.4 with the bat, a highest of 178 not out in the New Year fixture with Wellington, and 12.93 with the ball, taking thirty wickets in seven innings. Team performances, however, were more modest. They lost the Christmas fixture to Canterbury, drew with Wellington and had a win and a draw against Southland.

> As in the match against Canterbury so in the match against Wellington it was the Otago coach who stood out head and shoulders above the other members of the team for sterling work with bat and ball. JN Crawford was regarded as the white hope of the team and well has he fulfilled the duties that were expected of him. To the coach practically all the honours are due for saving the credit of Otago, though this fact is not consoling when estimating the present standard of Otago cricket. In half a season Crawford has done much to improve the play of a number of the colts; but the real influence of his work will not be felt until he has completed his course of three years and brought the colts right through the various stages until they become not a unit of Otago cricket but the whole of it.[14]

It was never to happen. This was the last full season before Otago and all the provinces were to become severely depleted by their involvement with events on the other side of the globe.

Before that, however, Crawford continued to give his all for both club and province. He was prepared to play against medical advice and as well as his playing and coaching did some umpiring

> JN Crawford developed a 'knee' during the week and was advised not to risk complications by playing on Saturday; but he did play and though more or less handicapped he was still a factor to be reckoned with, and contributed materially to the Colts' success. Much of the sting and pace was taken out of Crawford's bowling: but in the brief time he was at the crease he gave a dashing exhibition of batting, scoring 25 in about three overs. Some men can make 100 with less fascination. By the way, Crawford anticipates no serious trouble from his knee. Beyond a little stiffness, it was nearly all right on Tuesday when he was umpiring in the Otago University-Canterbury College match at Carisbrook.[15]

As in Adelaide, he made no attempt to cocoon himself from the local community, turning out for the Gymnastic hockey team and, referred to as a first-class golf player, coaching that sport at Queenstown and the Lakes.[16]

He made his singing talents available, singing 'The Drum Major' for the Mosgiel Patriotic Fund at 'a large patriotic meeting … held in the Coronation Hall … under the auspices of the Otago Patriotic and General Welfare Association'.[17] Then, for the Belgian Relief Fund:

> Last Sunday evening a sacred service of song was given in the Warrington Presbyterian Church. The service was got up by Mesdames Wilson and Begg, the Misses Grant and V Campbell, and Messrs A Martin and JN Crawford, all of whom had come out to Warrington for the weekend. The residents who were present got a great treat and the Belgian Relief Fund benefitted to the extent of £4.2.6d.[18]

Along with some masters he played for the High School XI against an Old Boys team, also for the Belgian Relief Fund.[19] Later in the war, as the significance of cricket diminished, he became more involved in fundraising efforts for the Orphans' Club and the Returned Soldiers Conference.[20]

On 15 April 1915, in St Paul's Cathedral, Melbourne, Jack Crawford, cricket coach, married Anita Schmidt ('rank or profession: home duties').

Crawford's Colts duly acknowledged the forthcoming event with an early wedding present.

> During the interval between the innings in the match Otago v Colts at Carisbrook on Saturday the members of the latter team presented Mr JN Crawford with a handsome oak tray, as a token of esteem and in celebration of the approaching marriage of their coach and captain.[21]

Despite the grandeur of a cathedral wedding it was a quiet celebration, partially if not entirely accounted for by the fact that five days later, Anita's elder sister, Diosma, would be marrying in Adelaide. Anita, being under age, had her father's permission to marry, but the family clearly considered it impractical to split themselves between the two ceremonies. No guests are mentioned in the newspaper report, though there is a fairly detailed description of the bride's apparel, which clearly doubled as both a wedding and going away outfit, though the 'going away' and honeymoon comprised pragmatically the return journey to Dunedin.

> At St Paul's Cathedral, Melbourne, on April 15 the marriage was very quietly celebrated of Mr John Crawford of New Zealand, formerly of Adelaide, and Anita, daughter of Mr DH Schmidt, Kenilworth, Norwood. The bride wore a smart navy blue coat and skirt with cream lace underblouse and a becoming black panne velvet hat with a floral wreath. The Rev Kelly conducted the service.[22]

There is no mention of the groom's outfit. By the time of the marriage Crawford was settled (insofar as he ever settled anywhere) in New

Zealand. Anita was from Adelaide, which Crawford had left in August 1914, so the assumption has to be that Melbourne was a convenient meeting point for the marriage. Bernard Whimpress has expressed the view that Melbourne was a peculiar choice and suggests an elopement. It would have added a colourful romantic streak to the Crawford story and been consistent with some of the rumours about his earlier behaviour in South Australia, but the truth is more mundane. The certificate of marriage clearly states that the union was with the written consent of her father.

There were suggestions that the couple might spend a week or two in Australia before returning to Dunedin, but within eight days of the wedding, they were in New Zealand.[23]

> Arrivals on the *Wimmera* on 23rd April include JN Crawford and Mrs Crawford.[24]

New Zealand probably offered an escape for Anita. Until 1914 there was a healthy symbiosis between those of British and those of German descent, but the First World War soured relations and, in New South Wales, 7,000 'enemy aliens' were interned. Numbers were lower in South Australia, but up to 400 of German or Austro-Hungarian background, some of whom had become naturalised British citizens and some of whom were taken from ships in Australian ports, were interned at the Torrens Island Internment Camp.

Anita was doubtless relieved to be away from all that, but the patriotic fervour which permeated the Empire embraced anti-German sentiment. It cannot have been an easy start to married life for the young couple. Very soon events proved too much.

There was no first-class cricket in 1915/16 and the club competition was seriously curtailed. The first grade was reduced to six clubs, the Colts being among the casualties. Jack was farmed out on a match by match basis to some of the remaining clubs, playing for Albion, St Kilda and Dunedin. His form continued to be devastating and, as he had done so often in the past at first-class level, but more often in club encounters in five countries, he destroyed the equilibrium of what might otherwise have been a well-balanced and closely fought encounter.

> Although cricket in Dunedin as elsewhere this season has fallen away owing to the war, there is never a Saturday passes but something happens to revive the interest, says an Otago writer. The latest was a 200 not out by Jack Crawford, the international, for St Kilda against Harry Siedeberg and Co (Carisbrook). The fine weather and the good pitch suited the ex-Surrey all-rounder and he bagged them wholesale with both bat and ball. Crawford was in daring mood and he banged the bowling to all points of the compass, knocking fours and sixes like shelling peas. It was a thrilling and sensational innings and at any other time would have attracted marked attention. With the ball Crawford bagged six for 30, five of them clean skittled.[25]

> JN Crawford did some hurricane scoring the other day. Batting against time, for the Albion team in Dunedin, he made 96 runs in half an hour.[26]

With war crippling the New Zealand domestic season, the Otago Association found itself committed to paying a star player and coach with little for him to actually do. In legal terms, it was a classic case of frustration of contract. There were insufficient funds to pay him and a severe shortage of people to coach, almost all having been caught up in the patriotic fervour and answered the call of the Empire. The negotiations were prolonged and embellished by complaints about the lateness of Crawford's report on the one side counteracted by complaints from him that players were missing practice.

He agreed to forgo part of his salary on condition that he might be allowed to offer his coaching services to clubs as a free agent. Agreement could not be reached on the amount to be forgone. The Association suggested a reduction to £200; Crawford had earlier suggested £245, but now increased that to £300, a figure around three times as high as the total amount in the coach's fund. The Association countered with £150 and agreement to terminate the contract. Crawford reverted to his original figure of £245 and eventually a compromise figure of £200 was agreed – which was where negotiations began, except that it had now become a severance payment rather than a salary reduction. The Annual Report glossed over the acrimony:

> Owing to the war it was impossible to obtain funds to pay Mr Crawford and it was also difficult to get colts to coach, and the contract was terminated with deep regret on June 1, 1916. Had times been normal we are sure that Mr Crawford would have made Otago the foremost province in the Dominion.[27]

There was over a year still to run on the three-year contract, but it was all academic. Two months later, the Military Service Act was on the statute books to mop up those eligible from the minority who had not already volunteered for war service and cricket was pushed further into the background.

The *Auckland Star* summed up the sorry state of Otago cricket.

> The engagement of JN Crawford as coach to the Otago Cricket Association has been terminated by mutual consent and by the payment of a lump sum in lieu of his engagement which had another season to run. The history of Otago cricket so far as the engagement of coaches is concerned, has been a chapter of misfortune not due to any fault of the coaches, but to a series of circumstances which militate against the utmost benefit being derived. Upwards of £2000 have been spent during the past ten years by the association in its efforts to improve cricket here. Hundreds went at various seasons in pursuit of the Plunket Shield through special trips being taken to Auckland which held the coveted bauble for several years. Several hundreds were expended on coaches, before the engagement of JN Crawford with comparatively poor results but with the engagement of the English coach it was thought that the troubles were over. Crawford was engaged during the visit of Arthur Sims' famous team to Dunedin, for three years, at a salary of £350 per annum. Guarantors were forthcoming for the amount and it was anticipated that with the assistance of cricketers and an occasional appeal to the public for funds the coach's salary would be made up. Before Crawford had got started on his first season's work the war broke out. That was the beginning and end of the trouble, though bad weather and other circumstances also militated against the success of the scheme. Despite the effects of the war Crawford did good work amongst the young cricketers, and those colts in

> the first grade during his first season, but last season the influence of the war on the game was most marked; interest dwindled and very little coaching was done. In the circumstances and, in view of the fact that cricketers would, on account of enlistments, be fewer than ever during the coming season, the association decided to offer Crawford a lump sum to terminate the agreement (which has another season to run) and an arrangement to this end has cleared its liability, but it has been at the expense of a formidable overdraft, and in its extremity it has decided to make a fresh appeal to the public and supporters of the game.[28]

Jack was now jobless and, for a while, ill.[29] What made the future even more uncertain was that, after little more than a year and a half of marriage, Crawford abandoned his wife.

> On or about the 28th day of November 1916 the said John Neville Crawford separated himself from your said Petitioner and has never co-habited with her and he has deserted your Petitioner without lawful cause for a period of over two years and upwards.[30]

Crawford's life was as unsettled as it ever had been. There were rumours that he would return to England either immediately or for the first cricket season after the war; that he had already left New Zealand; or would remain there, in Dunedin or Christchurch or Wellington.[31] He was still in Dunedin in late November and still in demand for his cricket, though there were rumours that he was about to join up.

> The statement by a Wellington writer recently that JN Crawford is going into camp with the next draft of reinforcements is indeed news to Jack Crawford, who is still in Dunedin. By the way, Crawford was out at Carisbrook on Saturday when Grange was playing Carisbrook. Grange had only nine men, but a very strong nine, and they wanted to bat Crawford, but the Carisbrook captain declined to allow the northerners to play the international, giving rise to an incident not exactly in keeping with the best traditions of cricket.[32]

For a while he had a job as a Clerk with the Dunedin City Corporation, but only until his enrolment in the New Zealand Expeditionary Force.[33]

Form of attestation of voluntary recruits and of men called up for service under the Military Service Act, 1916, who are willing to be attested in this manner.

Volunteer

[H.F. Form No. 2]

ORIGINAL

NEW ZEALAND EXPEDITIONARY FORCE

ATTESTATION FOR GENERAL SERVICE. *13919.*

QUESTIONS TO BE PUT TO THE RECRUIT.

1. What is your name? ... 1. *John Neville Crawford*
2. Where were you born? ... 2. *Coulsdon Surrey England*
3. Are you a British subject? ... 3. *Yes*
4. What is the date of your birth? ... 4. *1-12-1886*
5. What are the names of your parents? ... 5. Father: *John Neville Crawford* Mother: *Alice Crawford*
6. Where were your parents born? ... 6. Father: *Kent England* Mother: *Kent England*
7. If they are of alien origin, when and where were they naturalized? 7. Father: Mother:
8. How long have you been resident in New Zealand? ... 8. *1 years*
9. How long have your parents been resident in New Zealand? ... 9. Father: *Still at Home* Mother: *Still at Home*
10. What is your trade or calling? ... 10. *Clerk*
11. Are you an indentured apprentice? If so, where, and to whom? 11. *No*
12. What was the address at which you last resided? ... 12. *4 Clark St City Dunedin*
13. Have you passed the Fourth Educational Standard or its equivalent? 13. *Yes*
14. What is the name and address of your present or last employer? 14. *City Corporation Dunedin*
15. Are you single, married, widower, divorced, or legally separated from your wife? 15. *Married*
16. If married, a widower, divorced, or legally separated from your wife, how many children under sixteen years of age have you? 16. *None*
17. If single, how many persons are absolutely dependent on you? 17.
18. Have you ever been sentenced to imprisonment by the Civil power? If so, when and where? 18. *No*
19. Do you now belong to any Military or Naval Force? If so, to what corps? 19. *No*
20. Have you ever served in any Military or Naval Force? If so, state which and cause of discharge. 20.
21. Have you truly stated the whole (if any) of your previous service? 21. *Yes*
22. Have you ever been medically examined for service with the New Zealand Expeditionary Force? If so, when and where? 22. *[illegible] 19-12-16*
23. Have you ever been registered for compulsory military training under the Defence Act, 1909? If so, where? 23. *No*
24. Have you ever been rejected as unfit for the Military or Naval Forces of the Crown? If so, on what grounds? 24. *Yes for eyesight*
25. Are you willing to serve in the New Zealand Expeditionary Force in or beyond the Dominion of New Zealand for the duration of the present war with Germany and six months thereafter, if your service is so long required? 25.
26. For which Reinforcement draft do you volunteer? ... 26.

NOTE.—Your discharge will not be granted before you return to New Zealand unless permission for discharge elsewhere be obtained from the G.O.C. New Zealand Expeditionary Force.

I, *John Neville Crawford*, do solemnly declare that the above answers made by me to the above questions are true, and that I am willing to fulfil the engagement made.

Signature of Recruit: *J. N. Crawford*

Signature of Witness: *[illegible] Donaldson [illegible]*

Oath to be taken by Recruit on attestation.

I, *John Neville Crawford*, do sincerely promise and swear that I will be faithful and bear true allegiance to our Sovereign Lord the King, and that I will faithfully serve in the New Zealand Expeditionary Forces against his Majesty's enemies, and that I will loyally observe and obey all orders of the Generals and Officers set over me, until I shall be lawfully discharged. So help me, God.

Certificate of Attesting Officer.

The above questions were read to the above-named recruit in my presence. I have taken care that he understands these questions, and that his answer to each question has been duly entered. The said recruit has made and signed the declaration and taken the oath of allegiance before me, at *Dunedin*, N.Z., on this *5.11.17* day of *July* 1917.

Signature of Attesting Officer: *[illegible] Moffat [illegible]*

NOTE 1.—If any alteration is required in the attestation, the Attesting Officer should be requested to [illegible]

NOTE 2.—The recruit expresses a preference to enlist for *Infantry* (Branch of service)

Attestation showing that Crawford joined the New Zealand Expeditionary Force as a volunteer, not a conscript, having previously tried unsucessfully to enlist.

14

In the Army

1917-19

Compared with many of his contemporaries, Crawford had an easy war. He joined up late, spent most of his time at camp, where he managed to play some cricket, and arrived in England when it was almost all over. By contrast, Jack's elder brother Frank, coming to the conflict from Ceylon where he had been involved in tea planting, experienced Gallipoli and the Somme, never fully recovered and, weakened by dysentery and shell shock, was to die of pneumonia at the young age of forty-three. Many did not make it as far as that.

In fairness, Jack did make an attempt to enlist – several times according to the *Daily Mirror*, but as that newspaper places him in Australia at the time, its report might not be entirely accurate.[1] Unsurprisingly, having worn glasses from childhood, Crawford was rejected on the grounds of his eyesight.

Until 1916, recruitment was on a voluntary basis and at first there was no shortage of volunteers. However, the escalation of the war and the large number of casualties meant that more recruits were required. The Military Service Act came into force in August, introducing conscription. Those eligible for service who had not already enlisted had their names entered on reserve rolls and were balloted on a monthly basis. Jack's name is not to be found there – he was not considered eligible – but, in July 1917, Crawford joined the New Zealand Rifle Brigade at Trentham Camp, near Wellington. His form of attestation confirms that he did so as a volunteer and that he had been earlier rejected on 19 December 1916 because of his eyesight. The medical requirements had been relaxed, along with the earlier practice of taking single men only, meaning that he was now considered suitable.[2]

Crawford's eyesight was given as 6/24, which meant that he could see at six metres what a person with standard vision could see at twenty-four; equivalent to being able to read as far as the third line on the Snellen chart, the conventional test of visual acuity used by eye-care professionals. Spectacles improved it to 6/12, better, but that was still below average. Photographic evidence shows that he bowled without glasses – presumably reducing his chances of a caught and bowled – but wore them for batting and fielding. He had a different pair for reading and brother Reggie was later to recall how in a club match, Jack was bowled for a duck – his usual batting glasses had been hidden and surreptitiously exchanged for the pair he used for reading.[3]

The newspapers which followed his cricket career with Otago now pursued his continuing career with the armed forces and, although they were mainly concerned with events in Europe, they continued to report in some detail on cricket, including the fortunes of Trentham Camp in the Wellington First Grade competition. Military metaphor has always had a place in sports reporting, but those reading a sentence beginning 'the Trentham soldiers are eager for the fray' might well have thought this reflected an enthusiasm to get to the front. They would have been nonplussed with the conclusion that 'as JN Crawford and HB Lusk, two international players are at present in camp, the soldier team will have a pretty solid foundation on which to start building up the side'.[4]

Well before Jack arrived at the camp, there was press speculation that he was on his way and the camp commandant and adjutant were doubtless pleased to have him, though not necessarily for military reasons.

> It is said that JN Crawford, Otago's coach and English and Australian international player, is coming into camp with the next draft of Reinforcements

> ... The Camp Commandant of Trentham (Lieut-Colonel Potter) and the Camp Adjutant (Captain Bell) encourage the playing of cricket by the soldiers. During last week a cricketer soldier was sent into town to purchase material required and came out with a good supply.[5]

Crawford himself was originally less keen.

> JN Crawford, the international cricketer, says that the report that he is going into camp at Trentham with the next batch of Reinforcements is news to him. He is still in Dunedin and if nothing turns up in New Zealand, it is more than a possibility that he will return to England.[6]

Nothing turned up but he did not return to England, instead joining the army in July 1917. Crawford was mentioned in a strong squad of cricketers (including some with international and first-class experience) lined up to do duty in the Wellington first-grade competition, albeit with the recognition that it was all subject to their not being required for duties at the front.

> The soldiers in Trentham should have a good team in the Wellington first-grade competition this season. JN Crawford and HB Lusk, Frank Shacklock (the old Notts, Derby and Otago player), P Dwyer (East Christchurch, West Christchurch and Victoria University College), D Hamilton (Southland), and E Smyrk (Petone) are also in camp. NC Snedden (Auckland and New Zealand), ER Caygill (Canterbury) and EE Crawshaw (Canterbury) may be off to the front too soon for them to play in the team.[7]

Cricket filled in the time while they were waiting to be called to the theatres of war, though an accident to Crawford's first finger reduced his effectiveness as a bowler.

> NORTH v TRENTHAM AT BASIN RESERVE
> When play was suspended the previous week North had batted for 263 to which the Trentham men had responded with 86 for three wickets.
>
> JN Crawford and JA Bruce, the not out men, resumed batting at 223, the Englishman proceeding slowly, probably as a result of an accident to

> the first finger of his right hand, sustained while following his duties at the camp. It handicapped him considerably while batting but later on in the day the mishap caused him a lot more trouble – his bowling lost all of its sting through the finger which put the swing on the ball being out of action. However this pair of sound batsmen went along quietly until the total reached 126, at which stage Crawford dragged a ball well outside his off-stump into his wickets. Just prior to this mishap, he had made a couple of sweet off-drives, the pace with which one of them swished along the ground being really remarkable. He seemed to be settling down, but the stroke off which he was dismissed proved that he was short of practice.[8]

Jack continued to dominate entire matches, as he had in club and school cricket in earlier years.

> At Petone the Trentham team made merry at the local team's expense, JN Crawford getting the satisfactory total of 138. After he passed his century the Englishman treated the spectators to some spectacular batting, getting 27 runs in one over. The soldiers declared their innings closed at 300 for eight wickets, others to get runs beside Crawford being JA Bruce (80), NC Sneddon (27) and HB Lusk (33). Petone were beaten by an innings, their two strikes producing 109 and 80.[9]

Despite the damaged finger, he had five for 34 in the first innings. Trentham won the competition which, as might be expected, Crawford dominated with batting and bowling averages of just over 55 and 10 respectively. Some thought that he might have been used less to give others a chance and that the batsmen might have been kinder to the bowling of the Returned Soldiers team. The correspondent of *Free Lance* took an alternative view.

> By the way, some people are complaining about the various teams scoring so freely against the returned soldiers, declaring the century-scorers to be anything but sports. I cannot agree with this contention. The main object of the playing of cricket is to score runs, and it is better sport in my opinion to play the game right up to the hilt, rather than that the batsmen should throw their wickets away when they have put a tidy score to their credit.

> Another argument might be made that the Trentham team, being so much stronger than the others, should not use JN Crawford as much as they do at the bowling crease. If it is right that the batsmen should not score runs against the weak bowling of the Returned Soldiers team, it surely is right that the Trentham side should give the batsmen a chance of making a decent tally against them by resting the dashing Englishman oftener than they do, which would be a foolish argument without the shadow of a doubt, but not more foolish than the one I have heard in several places. 'Play the game' is the correct thing every time.[10]

Later in the season, his finger gave him further trouble and affected his bowling.

> TRENTHAM v NORTH. For once in a while JN Crawford was not in form at the bowling crease, failing to muster up his accustomed pace and swing. Early in the season Crawford snipped the top off his index finger in following his soldier duties. On the opening day of the match under review he got a nasty crack on the same finger and it has given him a lot of trouble since, so much so that last Saturday he could not get a fair grip of the ball.[11]

However, he came back with a six-for the following week against the Returned Soldiers and at one stage looked like establishing a new record for the number of wickets in a season in Wellington cricket, beating the previous record of 72.[12] But the record holder, WS Brice of Petone, with whom Crawford was soon afterwards to have a successful but inevitably short-lived bowling partnership for Wellington, came up strongly on the rails to finish the season with 93 wickets; Jack had 89.[13]

There had been no first-class cricket in New Zealand for the previous two summers, but a limited amount was played in 1917/18, Crawford turning out twice for Wellington, both against Auckland, at Eden Park in January and the Basin Reserve in March and April. Wellington won both matches, Jack scoring a century and collecting three five-fors (Brice had two four-fors, a five-for and a seven-for). It was the first first-class cricket he had played in three years and the last for over a year.

Matters more serious than cricket awaited, however. Jack had joined the army as a private. Had it been the British army, his public school background would probably have ensured his entry at officer level. His promotion was, however, rapid. By September, along with eleven of his colleagues, he was upgraded to temporary corporal in the Quartermaster's Department, responsible for supplies, and by the following April to quartermaster-sergeant – also temporary.[14] Because of wartime conditions, promotion was more rapid than it would have been in peacetime, hence the temporary nature of the appointments. Before demobilisation two years later, having failed to qualify for permanent quartermaster-sergeant, he was reduced to the ranks.[15]

The Quartermaster's Department gave priority to married men with children, presumably to reduce the likelihood of their being in the front line of battle. Crawford had no children, but his eyesight meant he was better suited to a clerical support position than one involving contact with the actual fighting. It was a post of no small responsibility, the department being responsible for the control of everything required by the camp and its soldiers from uniforms to scrubbing brushes. The quantities were huge and in pre-computer days a challenge to stock control and record keeping. The experience and responsibilities would, however, stand Jack in good stead in later positions in post-war business life.

> Few business firms in the Dominion conduct their businesses on such gigantic lines as do the CQM stores at Trentham. During the first three months of this year the items issued to soldiers personally – apart from the furnishings of huts – were as follows: 5,557 mess tins and covers, 13,781 jackets, 13,775 trousers, 109 pantaloons, 8,261 putties, 8,702 greatcoats, 8,921 hats and puggarees, 19,190 brass titles, 8,632 palliasses, 8,718 kitbags, 30,798 pairs of blankets, 5,639 pairs of braces, 17,623 boots, 17,498 drawers, 17,500 shirts, 17,501 undershirts, 5,571 shoes, 9,013 denim jackets, 26,238 pairs of socks, 5,535 cholera belts, 5,639 holdalls, 5,594 sea-kits, 8,733 jerseys, 8,088 tooth-brushes, 8,069 housewives, 8,726 knives, forks, and spoons, 8,719 plates and mugs, 17,418 towels, 9,082 waterproof sheets, 9,085 denim trousers, and 8,263 denim shorts. These figures, multiplied by four, give an amazing total of the amount of equipment required in fitting-out the Infantry and Engineers of the New Zealand Army during one year, and of the extent of the organisation required to keep the stocks in such order that there is never a shortage of any particular line.[16]

After a year in training at Trentham it was time to leave for the front and the *Tahiti* sailed from Wellington on 10 July 1918. It was the fortieth group of reinforcements and among the last troop ships to leave New Zealand for Europe. On board was JN Crawford: 'rank QMSergt, regiment number 61208, occupation clerk, next of kin Mrs A Crawford (wife) 4 Clarke St, Dunedin.'[17] There were stops in Australia and South Africa before the *Tahiti* joined a military convoy in Sierra Leone before arrival in Plymouth on 9 September 1918.

The journey was not without its misfortunes. Marcus Hansen of the Specialist Company who travelled on the same troop ship kept a diary which described conditions on board.

> We left the wharf at 1.55 p.m and finally set sail at 5 p.m. Started off in fine weather and all well. There were four companies of infantry, A B C & E and one coy of artillery and our own coy, the 40th Specs on board on this trip and no doubt the total number will be almost 1,200. We are packed in like sardines in the bows of the ship 'tween decks. Our bunks consist of hammocks strung to the ceiling, and we are packed right across the ship longways & sideways & every inch of space is utilised, for underneath are our mess tables which are also our writing tables etc and we have to live down here in rough weather. The food is very good and plenty of it.[18]

Later in the voyage however, after contact with HMS *Mantua* in Sierra Leone, the ship became infected with an influenza pandemic resulting in deaths and a serious weakening in the condition of the survivors.

> The hospital is over full and also a dozen patients on deck ... quite a gloom was cast round the cabin as soon as we were up when three deaths were reported on board. The burials took place at 11 a.m. The Colonel read the service and it was quite a touching scene ... more deaths and burials total now 42. A crying shame but it is only to be expected when human beings are herded together the way they have been on this boat.[19]

There were seventy-seven deaths in all from a total of 1,117 troops and nurses on board, conditions which an enquiry later in the year was advised was not unusual. It had carried more in the past, albeit with no cargo, whereas this time there was a substantial amount of freight on board. The high quality and plentiful food reported by Hansen at the beginning of the voyage was now exhausted and conditions were very different.

> Mrs JR Gibbons, the first witness, said that the transport carried 1,117 men and nurses and was shockingly overcrowded. Hammocks touched everywhere. The ventilation was sufficient for fine weather, but there was none when bad weather came. They had been told that the transport carried 1,288 men on a previous trip but on that occasion she carried no cargo, whereas on this occasion she carried 60,918 cubic feet of cargo and a large quantity of spare stores and Red Cross gifts. The only covered space was reserved for officers and airmen. Soldiers' letters showed that the soldiers starved while the officers were fed like in a first-class hotel. The transport left with insufficient drugs. The medical officers were youthful and inexperienced. One soldier wrote that the men had next to nothing to feed them with while the officers were feeding on poultry and jellies.
>
> Captain Post said the transport was making her tenth trip. She left under better conditions than ever previously and was fitted according to Admiralty instructions. He could not admit overcrowding.[20]

The *Tahiti* docked at Plymouth on 9 September and, despite the condition of the soldiers, they were still expected to parade. A month later, however, they were allowed a week's leave and given a free 'go anywhere' rail pass.

A later publication added the medical detail.

> A serious outbreak was that which occurred on board the troopship *Tahiti* in August 1918. The transport carrying the 40th Reinforcements, including 21 officers, 10 NZANC and 1,080 men called at Sierra Leone towards the end of August where she had rendezvous to form part of a convoy. Contact was made with HMS *Mantua*, a cruiser infected by a serious and fatal form of influenza. Within a few days of the sailing of the convoy influenza broke out on the *Tahiti* and practically the whole ship's complement was affected. A very fatal broncho-pneumonia which complicated the more serious cases,

> caused 68 deaths at sea before landing at Plymouth, and of the surviving sick three died of purulent bronchitis and one sister of cerebro-spinal meningitis. It is hardly possible to realise the difficulties of dealing with such a pandemic on board a crowded transport in a submarine zone, where ventilation was limited by reason of the closing of the portholes at night, and where practically everyone suffered from the disease, including the three medical officers, the nursing sisters and orderlies.[21]

The war was in its final stages when these New Zealand troops arrived in England, the armistice being only a few weeks away. They were posted to Lark Hill for a month, marched up the top of the hill and marched down again, before proceeding to Sling Camp near Bulford on Salisbury Plain. It was a camp which trained reinforcements and casualties who were regaining fitness.

At the end of the war there were 4,600 men at Sling. The discipline was particularly harsh and the men had to wait until there was enough transport to ship them back to New Zealand. Australian troops were in the same position, but there were enough of them and with sufficient skill to participate in first-class cricket in England. The activities of the New Zealanders went in another direction. To occupy them they were given the task of carving the shape of an enormous kiwi in the chalk of Beacon Hill overlooking the camp. It is now known as the Bulford Kiwi, carved in February and March 1919.

New Zealand troops had played a heavy price during the war. Over 16,000 were killed, over 41,000 wounded, a casualty rate of around 58%, one of the highest of any country involved in the war. Those who survived were slowly and gradually shipped back to the other side of the world.

Yet Jack Crawford had no intention of returning with them. Demobilised on 9 April, there was nothing for him in the Southern Hemisphere except a deserted wife and some job-hunting. Circumstances had now returned him to his native land, where a new cricket season was about to begin. After some coaching and classroom teaching at Repton, Crawford resumed first-class cricket with Surrey ten years after it had been so rudely interrupted.[22]

NEW ZEALAND EXPEDITIONARY FORCE. (B.R.—126.

Rank: Q.M.S. Name: CRAWFORD JOHN [illegible] Unit: [illegible] No. [illegible]

Enltd. [illegible] M. or S.: M D. of Birth: 1.12.86 Occupn: Clerk Ht.: 5.11 Wt.: 166 lb.

Hair: D. Brown Eyes: Brown Complexn.: Dark Relgn.: C of E Inocln.: 2

N/K: Mrs Anita Crawford (Wife) 4 [illegible] Street Dunedin N.Z.

Place of Birth: [illegible], Surry, England.

PROMOTIONS, CASUALTIES, MOVEMENTS, Etc.	DATE OF CASUALTY.	AUTHORITY, AND DATE OF SAME.	INITIALS.
~~EMBARKED AT WELLINGTON PER "TAHITI"~~	10-7-18	EMB. ROLL	
COMPLETION DUE N.Z. & COMMENCING FGN. SVCE.	10-7-18	H S	
DISEMBARKED AT ~~PLYMOUTH~~ London	9-9-18	DISEMB. ROLL	
Marched in [illegible]	[illegible]	[illegible]	[illegible]
Paid Res RBB			
Failed to Qualify [illegible]	[illegible]	[illegible]	[illegible]
Marched out to [illegible] (OPL)	8-2-19	[illegible]	
Discharge [illegible] in UK (Demobbed)	9-4-19	[illegible]	[illegible]

Extract from Crawford's Army Record showing he was discharged in England in April 1919.

15

Back to Blighty

Surrey 1919-21

When Jack Crawford embarked for Australia in October 1909, it would never have crossed his mind that one day he might return to England on board an infected troop ship from New Zealand. The one plus point was that he was able to do so free of charge rather than at his own expense, but the circumstances of the journey meant that was scant consolation.

According to the New Zealand press, his family had no idea he was in the country.[1] A month after his arrival, they received the sad news that his cousin, Loris, daughter of Major Frank Fairbairn Crawford, had drowned at the age of thirty. Returning from Ireland, probably after visiting the family of her mother, Frances, she was a passenger on RMS *Leinster* which was torpedoed by a German submarine en route from Kingstown (now Dun Laoghaire) to Holyhead.

The family situation was unrecognisable from the one Crawford had left. His father, aged seventy, had just retired from the chaplaincy at Cane Hill and was now living in Wimbledon. Frank had been planting tea in Ceylon but now returned to England, albeit via Gallipoli and the Somme. All his siblings had married; Edith and Lesley before his departure, Frank in 1917, Reggie in 1912, Audrey in 1913 in Canada, and youngest sister Marjorie in 1916. After a divorce, she was to do so again in 1935. Grandfather Andrew was now well into his nineties, but still had a few years to go.

Crawford also returned to a very different Surrey CCC from the one he had left ten years earlier. The war had taken its toll. The club's war memorial records the names of forty-eight who lost their lives in the war. They include Harry Chinnery, John Raphael and Alan Marshal. Tom Rushby was back, however, and so was Ernie Hayes, with a distinguished war record and MBE.

Jack was not to be demobilised until April 1919, but as early as January he was making overtures about resuming his career with Surrey. Some sources suggest that it was only now that Crawford made his peace with the county, although that had happened several years before by correspondence between London and Adelaide. Crawford asked if Surrey might help find him employment which he needed to enable him to continue as an amateur.

The request was considered first by the Cricket Committee.

> A letter from Mr JN Crawford offering to play for the county in 1919 contingent on some employment being found for him was read. The committee recommend that Mr Crawford be informed that they will be pleased to see him playing for the side, but that they cannot see their way to find him employment.[2]

Lord Alverstone, who might well have been more favourably disposed, had died in 1915. Without him, the main committee had lost none of its recalcitrance of a decade earlier and suggested he might like to consider turning professional.

> The minutes of the Cricket committee meeting, January 6th, as printed and circulated, with the following additions and amendments, were approved:
>
> (a) it was decided to support the recommendation of the Cricket Committee in regard to Mr JN Crawford, but that as an alternative he might be placed on the professional staff subject to his signing the usual agreement.[3]

Even after the devastating effects of the war on the class system, that would have been too much of a change for Jack. The offer was declined and he found himself a job as a master at his old school.[4]

> Reptonians will be glad to hear that Mr JN Crawford has been appointed games master at his old school. It is to be hoped that the ex-Surrey captain will make a re-appearance at The Oval.[5]

Crawford himself was pessimistic about the prospects for post-war cricket. The situation had not improved since he spoke to the New Zealand press two years earlier.

> Mr JN Crawford, the great English All-rounder, who has been located in Dunedin for a few years, paints, according to the New Zealand Press, a rather drab picture of cricket in England after the war, as you perceive on reading the following: 'Remember this: that the playing grounds of the county clubs were brought to perfection only after years of continued, persistent, skilled work, involving in the aggregate an enormous sum of money. At one blow all the work has been undone, for nearly all the county grounds, and many of the club grounds at Home have been taken over by the Government for military training camps. Big draining operations have been undertaken and every inch of ground has suffered the wear and tear of thousands of feet of men training in the one sport that possesses every Briton these days. This is the big financial problem that counties and clubs have to face after the war; and they will, alas, face it with empty purses and few resources....Then of the men, how many will be fit to play the game as we have been used to see it played? When I read amongst the killed and wounded the names of many cricketers with whom I have personal acquaintance, I realise that there are thousands of less-known cricketers who have paid the same price. I am thinking that it will be a very humble start that the game will make; that for a decade there will be but a spark that will require most careful fostering to keep alive. We shall all have to take hold, so that, if not we, at least our children, may see cricket regaining that high position it had won.'[6]

It was a statement made with no recent experience of cricket in England, though doubtless he had kept in touch by correspondence.

In May the Surrey Committee had worked out that, whether or not they were able to find him employment and whether he played as a professional or amateur, Crawford might be free of Repton commitments and able to play for the club by August. The Secretary was instructed to approach him to find out. The reply was positive.[7] It was a move welcomed in the following year's Annual Report: 'The advent of Mr Crawford in August was a source of great strength to the side and his success gave unbounded satisfaction.'

Before that, however, he made an inauspicious return to first-class cricket for the Gentlemen against the Players at The Oval, bowled for two by Cecil Parkin who, unbeknown to either of them at the time, was to become his colleague in league cricket the following season. The Oval faithful, however, still remembered him and showed their appreciation.

> Mr Crawford was given a very generous reception by the spectators who do not easily forget a good man and Mr Crawford was certainly a great cricketer. Whether he is still a great batsman his innings yesterday did not show, for he was bowled by a really good ball from Parkin when he had made only two, but the one or two strokes which he made certainly suggested the master. It is certainly a general wish that he may be seen during the holidays in first-class cricket once again.[8]

The next match, Crawford's first appearance for Surrey for ten years, was against the Australian Imperial Forces, a team of Australian servicemen left over from the war who had not yet been able to return to their homeland. Crawford was back to his belligerent best. In the opposition was 'Nip' Pellew, who had been coached by Crawford at St Peter's College. Crawford's 144 brought back memories of his spectacular innings and included a thoroughly professional last wicket partnership with Tom Rushby. His bowling (one for 85 and two for 84) was less impressive.

> HOW A SURREY IDOL CAME BACK
>
> Hobbs and Knight out for 9! This was the double-barrelled shock for the crowd which at The Oval yesterday had been anticipating some rapid and classic hitting as some recompense for its patience during the uninteresting stages of the long Australian innings.

Crawford was a long time moving, but after he had hit Winning on to the scorebox, he joined Wilkinson in going for the bowling, and the pair put on 143 for the seventh wicket before Wilkinson went for a fine 103.

Crawford then went for his century with his gloves off. He hit six others into the members' stand and it was only a question of how long Rushby, the last man in, could stay. When Rushby was 0 Crawford was 87, when Rushby was 1 Crawford was 120 and while Rushby was finally carrying his score from 1 to 2, Crawford got another 21. So hard and rapidly did Crawford hit that he got his last 100 in an hour and actually scored all but two of the last-wicket partnership of 80 in thirty-five minutes. He hit two sixes, one five and eighteen fours. It was a dramatic reappearance for his old county. The crowd cheered Crawford even more than they cheered him in the old days. The Surrey total was 322. After five for 26, this can be said to be the recovery of the season.[9]

In later years, Herbie Collins was to recall:

It was my great pleasure to be associated with a remarkable Englishman in Jack Crawford. He will be remembered as a player for South Australia for a few years.

After ten years absence from England he was selected in the Surrey team to meet Australia in 1921. On a perfect wicket Hobbs, Knight and Ducat went cheaply. Jack Gregory had three wickets for a few runs when Crawford came in. He handled Gregory as I had never seen the fast bowler handled before. When Crawford finished up with over a century Gregory's bowling figures were four for 109. I had a few overs in that innings, and Crawford hit me clear over the clock. I laughed as Gregory was being pasted, and Gregory's laugh as I was hit over the clock was rude, to say the least of it.[10]

Pellew had 24 and 43 not out in this match and played for South Australia for another ten years. His first-class career included ten Test matches.

Two days later, Jack's friend Digby Jephson paid the following tribute, placing the Crawford brothers' hitting in the context of that of their contemporaries and near-contemporaries.

Well played, old friend! It is fine to see you back in the old side – fine to see you still at the top of your form, and that you are still one of the easiest hitters that the cricket world has ever known. During my long connection with the game, from the time I played with half a bat and a paper ball with GJV Weigall on Broadstairs sands to the days I spent at The Oval and Lord's, I have seen many hitters of many styles of varying degrees of merit.

I have seen Bonnor hit – that splendid specimen of a man, powerful and yet graceful. I have watched the firm-footed Lyons drive George Lohmann six times over the ring at Lord's. I have been playing when CI Thornton lifted Sammy Woods out of Fenners and a hundred times on a hundred grounds have I fielded with and fielded against that wonderful whirler of the bat – Gilbert Jessop. I have studied all these mighty sloggers, and I have studied them closely, and I have never seen anything of the ease or the length of driving of JN Crawford and his elder brother, Frank.

There is no swinging of the bat, like an electric trail; no crouching, no colossal effort; just one stride and a straight bat meeting the ball at the very psychological moment. Away it soars high over the ring, high over the excited spectators, and far over the red-roofed hutch, and, I had almost added, into the next parish. It looks so very simple: it is the maximum of power with the minimum of exertion.

Once at Lord's I saw these brothers Crawford hit against each other. It was at the end of a season, and a mixed side were playing against the Cross Arrows, poor Albert Trott's little flock. JN Crawford made 100 and Frank 75. It mattered not one straw which took the bowling. Ball after ball carried the ropes (the wicket was near the Mound stand) and bounced back off the side of the pavilion, twenty yards or so into the field of play, and we, who were merely spectators of this fifty minutes of wonderful driving, left the ground that night full of delight and great thankfulness that we had turned out and were in at the death of such a stupendous show. Bravo Jack – a great cricketer. And what is better – a real good sort.[11]

The innings set him up for a reprise of some of his innings of a decade earlier. Against Yorkshire:

Mr Crawford came in and some wonderful batting took place. Mr Knight still played stylishly and made runs freely with what seemed to be very little effort, while Mr Crawford drove and pulled with great power … Mr Craw-

> ford and Hitch added 38 in twenty minutes … Then, while hitting out in an attempt to get his hundred before the last wicket fell, Mr Crawford was well caught in the long field when he had scored 92. He had been in only ninety minutes, and did not give any actual chance, although one or two high shots went rather near fieldsmen. He hit with extraordinary strength, and his batting was most attractive to watch.[12]

1919 was the season of the short-lived experiment with two-day county matches. In Jack Hobbs' benefit match against Kent, originally scheduled for four years earlier but postponed because of the suspension of first-class cricket during the war, Surrey were left requiring 95 to win in forty-two minutes. Scoring at eight per over, Hobbs and Crawford reached the target with ten minutes to spare, Kent sportingly remaining on the field despite the pouring rain. It was their only defeat of the season.[13]

For Palgrave (Louis, who wrote *The Story of the Oval* – not Francis, who compiled the *Golden Treasury*, though it would not have been inappropriate as the Golden Age is recalled):

> JN Crawford joined in the fray with a sparkling knock of 92. Here was a display of amateur batsmanship reminiscent of a period twenty-years past, batsmanship that today is chiefly conspicuous, alas, by its absence.[14]

While *Wisden* noted:

> Crawford only played in a few of the county matches, but apart from his share in beating Kent he gave a fine display against Yorkshire. His great triumph was an amazing innings of 144 not out in the second match against the Australians. Not often in modern cricket is a very fast bowler treated the way he treated Gregory.[15]

Business commitments would reduce Crawford's availability for first-class cricket in future years and his last Championship appearance was, appropriately perhaps, against the county which just over a decade earlier had witnessed his highest first-class innings. This time, however, it was at Taunton. Going in with the score at 18 for 4, he contributed 39 of a partnership of 42, took two for 17 and two for 46 and was at the crease in the second innings when Surrey won by six wickets in two days. His bowling was less effective than it had been in pre-war years but, thanks to that innings against the Australian Imperial Forces and a later 92 against Yorkshire, he finished the season with a batting average of 61. Still aged only thirty-two, he had much to offer, but had no opportunity to do so.

The Times summed up Surrey's season and Crawford's contribution to it in the following terms:

> Up to a certain point Surrey did not have a really good side, but when fully represented as they were in some of the later matches, with Mr JN Crawford as well as Mr DJ Knight to support Hobbs, they were stronger in batting than any other county, not excepting Yorkshire. Mr Crawford's real value is not shown by his averages in purely county matches as he made his largest score against the Australians, playing on that occasion an astonishing innings. The miracle of batting by which he and Hobbs beat Kent a fortnight ago, scoring 96 runs in thirty-two minutes was the sensation of the season.[16]

Early in the following year, 1920, Crawford's father intervened, though as Jack was now thirty-three and had over the years demonstrated himself perfectly capable of looking after his own interests, some might say he 'interfered' on his son's behalf.

> The Secretary reported correspondence which had passed with the Rev JC Crawford with reference to his son JN Crawford, pointing out the desirability of finding some appointment for him in order to preserve his connection with the county. The Secretary also reported the correspondence he had had with the President on the subject. The draft letter which the Secretary suggested should be circulated amongst the committee had been approved by the President and it was agreed that the letter be so circulated.[17]

Two months later, however, his father was reporting that Jack had 'accepted a billet in Rochdale'.[18] The billet was with Dunlop Rubber as a Manager in Sudden Mills and Jack was to play for the town's cricket team in the Central Lancashire League. There was to be no county cricket that year, and only two first-class matches, both at The Oval. In the Gentlemen v Players match he made 37 (dismissed again by Cecil Parkin, now his teammate at Rochdale) and 5 and took two for 65 in a match in which he was on the losing side to the tune of an innings and 87 runs. Out of practice and now past his peak, he struggled against the professionals' bowling.

> On his first appearance in first-class cricket (relates *The Field*) JN Crawford received a very hearty welcome from the crowd at the Oval when he went in for the Gentlemen, but finding himself in difficulties from the first he seldom made any of the daring hits for which he is so well known. At the commencement of his innings he had very narrow escapes off Howell, one ball going only a few inches too short to be a catch to Kennedy in the slips, and another dropping to the ground and threatening to go into the wicket; it was not until he had made his third chop at it that the batsman succeeded in warding off the danger. A little later he was missed at the wicket and he would have been in very great danger from a big and high straight drive if Hendren had been able to sight the ball at once. As it was, he at first ran in to meet it, and when he succeeded in getting on the line of the ball it was just too late. After this Crawford made two glorious pulls, and everybody was hoping that some furore would be seen but he was caught in the slips off a bumping ball.[19]

The other match in which he played, Gentlemen of the South v Players of the South, looked to be going the same way but mercifully days two and three were washed out after the Players had reached the other side of 500 on the first.

Not since 1907/08 had Crawford played Test cricket, but in 1921, although clearly some way past his peak and no longer committed to county cricket, there were suggestions that he might do so again. There was, however, an implicit recognition that the observations were based on his form two years earlier. *The Times* correspondent commented:

> I confess that, with a few exceptions, the present-day batsmen do not, when playing bowling of extreme speed, inspire me with much confidence. Some of them seem to have no idea of scoring, except by getting the ball away on the leg side. Very different was the method adopted by Mr JN Crawford in

> his wonderful innings for Surrey against the Australian Imperial Forces team at the Oval in 1919. Seldom or never have I seen a fast bowler – he was just as quick then as he is now – treated as Mr Gregory was that afternoon. Mr Crawford scarcely scored behind the wicket, making nearly all his runs by means of splendid driving. The Selection Committee have many good batsmen to choose from, but there is not one of Mr Crawford's type.[20]

The question was not without interest on the other side of the globe and reaction was mixed. In Adelaide, where he was clearly still remembered and attracting more attention than in the British press, *The Mail* reported the news from London:

> The fact that JN Crawford has been picked in the Surrey team to meet the Australians on Saturday has aroused speculation whether he will be invited to play in the tests.
>
> It is understood he would have been invited earlier but the selectors deem it undesirable to play a man who figured in Australian cricket. Others declare that the objection is groundless, adding that Crawford is likely to deal vigorously with the Australian bowling.[21]

Apart from the Gentlemen v Players match a few days later – his last in first-class cricket – his appearance for Surrey against the Australians was his only one that season. With innings of 1 and 28 and bowling figures of one for 50 and none for 18, he did little to distinguish himself as Surrey failed to repeat the victory of twelve years earlier and lost by 78 runs. As a bowler, Crawford now looked a spent force. The zip of yesteryear had gone.

> Mr Crawford seemed innocuous. The subtle variation of pace was still there and still well concealed, but the ball does not whip off the pitch as it used to. Mr Crawford now bends his left knee at the moment of delivery, and, if memory serves, this trick of style is something new.[22]

Had he played for England he may have made very little difference as Gregory and McDonald ran amok and Warwick Armstrong's team won three and drew two of the five Tests. The golden age was over – for Surrey, for cricket and for Jack Crawford.

The touring West Indians at Elders and Fyffes, 1950.
Crawford is second from the right on the front row.

16

Going Bananas

Club and works cricket 1920-39

His first-class playing career over, Crawford now became a businessman and weekend cricketer. For a short time in 1920 and early 1921, he held a managerial position with Dunlop Rubber in Sudden, Rochdale. The textile mill, which at one time claimed to be the largest in the world with over 3,000 employees, was an offshoot of the Lancashire cotton industry, making cloth for lining Dunlop's bicycle tyres. Like many large organisations at the time, it provided sports and social facilities for its staff, but Jack spent his leisure hours playing for Rochdale as an amateur in the Central Lancashire League.

One of his colleagues there was Cecil Parkin; professional, gritty and northern and, like his club and county, tough, committed and uncompromising. It is a compliment to the strength of the northern leagues at the time that selection committees were prepared to select northern league amateurs and professionals for the prestigious Gentlemen v Players match. In 1919, 1920 and 1921, the selection committee at The Oval, despite their earlier differences, selected Jack Crawford for the Gentlemen. As an amateur, he was perfectly entitled to forgo a Saturday afternoon league fixture to play a first-class one and duly did so.

Such was not the case with his professional colleague, however. Parkin had been invited to play for the Players but Rochdale Cricket Club held the purse strings and he who paid the piper called the tune. He had played in 1919 and 1920, but they declined to release him to play for the 1921 fixture. They graciously conceded, however, that if selected to play in a Test match he would be released. He played in all five Test matches in Australia in the series whitewash of 1920/21 and four of the five in England the following summer when the home side used thirty players.

Crawford would undoubtedly have played more matches for Rochdale had the club itself played more matches, but in 1920 it was suspended from the Central Lancashire League after a dispute involving Parkin. It is a saga the like of which has been played out many times at many levels of many sports and arose from disagreements between players, officials and bureaucracy. On this occasion it began with Parkin walking off the field in a match against Littleborough, having been told by an umpire, for the third consecutive week (he alleged), that LBW appeals could not be given in his favour if he bowled round the wicket. The league demanded an apology, didn't get one, and suspended Parkin.[1] The club played him again against Castleton Moor with their opponents' agreement (the Rochdale pro was box office material) in defiance of the league's decision.[2] Consequently, Rochdale were suspended from the Central Lancashire League and applied to join the Lancashire League.

Meanwhile, Parkin did apologise, although the apology was deemed insufficient. Nevertheless Rochdale were reinstated, but declined to play their next fixture and resigned from the league.[3] The club's stance was endorsed unanimously by its membership at a meeting held in the open air because the club house was not large enough to accommodate all those who wished to attend.[4] Eventually, after the intervention of the Mayor of Rochdale, the status quo was resumed with apologies and handshakes all round. It was a sorry tale of vested interests, wounded dignity, insolence of office and tortuous negotiation.

The following extracts from the local press give a flavour of the controversy:

> Further developments arose last night in connection with the action of CH Parkin, the Lancashire cricketer, in leaving the field in a league match a month ago as a protest against a decision by one of the umpires. A meeting of the Emergency Committee of the Central Lancashire League received a letter from the Rochdale Club stating that Parkin had tendered an apology to that club for his conduct, and asking the League to allow Parkin to play for Rochdale against Oldham today (Saturday) and against Castleton Moor on Tuesday.
>
> The League Committee declined to reverse their previous decision, but agreed to extend the time within which Parkin had been called upon to apologise to them (the League Committee) until 2.30 today and that the Secretary, (Mr R Thompson) should attend the Oldham ground before the match to receive such apology if it was tendered.[5]

> With cricket out of the question owing to rain, all the interest at Watersheddings, Oldham on Saturday were centred on whether Cecil H Parkin, the Rochdale professional, would tender an apology for his recent action to the League through their secretary. Parkin, in an interview, said: 'I shall not apologise. So far as I am concerned the matter is at an end. The whole affair is now in the hands of the Rochdale Cricket Club.'
>
> As Parkin did not apologise by 2.30 he, according to the League resolution, automatically suspends himself from playing again for Rochdale in their Central League matches until such time as he does apologise.
>
> With regards to the resolution passed by the Rochdale Cricket Club on Friday expressing willingness for the facts to be placed before the MCC and to abide by their decision, Mr R Thompson, (the League Secretary), said the MCC had no power in the matter. Rule 6 of the Central Lancashire League states that 'the committee shall have power to adjudicate in all disputed matters in the competition, or in the affairs of the league, and their decision shall be final.'
>
> The Rochdale Club officials have asked that a special meeting of the Central Lancashire League should be summoned for Thursday next to deal with the whole matter.[6]

Nowhere does it seem to have been suggested that the umpires might have been wrong. Parkin himself had powerful arguments to suggest that they were: 'In the Lancashire v Yorkshire match last year I got five Yorkshire wickets that way, including that of George Hirst.'[7]

The following season, however, Rochdale reached the end of their tether with their professional. Despite permission to play in the Gentlemen v Players match being refused, he went off and played anyway. The repercussions brought to an end a rollercoaster three-year relationship in which the club had first supported their professional against the league, then dismissed him. The clear-cut master-servant relationship which in pre-union days characterised the cotton mills of Lancashire spilled over into their recreational pursuits.

> ROCHDALE SUSPEND PARKIN. Parkin is having a varied experience with Rochdale. Last season, when he left the ground as a protest against the decision of an umpire who held that the bowler could not have a batsman given out lbw when the former was bowling round the wicket, Parkin received the keen support of the Rochdale Club. This week he was selected to play for the Players v the Gentlemen but the Rochdale Club decided that he must fulfil the terms of his agreement with that club and be present in the Rochdale ground on Wednesday, Thursday and yesterday. Parkin, however, journeyed to London and appeared in the Players team. On Wednesday night the club's committee met to consider the position. After a long sitting, they issued the following statement to the press: 'The committee have suspended Parkin and have issued instructions for him to appear before them.'[8]

His place in the league match the following Saturday was taken by Wilfred Rhodes – not a bad substitute.[9]

In his autobiography, Parkin makes no mention of either incident and its repercussions, indeed little of Rochdale and none of Crawford, restricting himself to a justification of his actions in the 'misunderstanding' of his apparent criticism of Arthur Gilligan's captaincy in the Edgbaston Test of 1924, a review of his own performances and a potboiler survey of the leading cricketers he has played with and against.

Crawford himself had no part in all this (indeed, he had left Rochdale and the club) but must have seen echoes of his own battles with authority, principally with Surrey, but also, to a lesser extent, South Australia and Otago.

Crawford's reputation was such that with other leading players of the district, including Parkin, Sydney Barnes, RH Spooner and Jack Sharp, He was invited to play in Harry Dean's benefit match at Turf Moor in Burnley.[10]

He is recalled in the club's history, *Parkin to Pepper*:

> One of the most notable amateurs ever to play for the club was JN Crawford, who was in Parkin's side in 1920 and 1921. Although his form was generally disappointing, he revealed in some games glimpses of the stylish batsmanship and clever bowling which gained him a place in the England side which toured Australia in 1907-08 and caused him to have a distinguished career in county cricket with Surrey. Crawford's reason for coming to Rochdale was because he forsook his profession as a schoolmaster to accept an appointment at the DR Mills at Sudden.
>
> At the same period JW Whewell, working on the building of the DR Mills extension, assisted Rochdale and was a wizard of a wicketkeeper.[11]

By his standards, Crawford had a poor season in 1920, scoring 188 runs at an average of 17. He was, nevertheless, the club's leading amateur batsman. There was a possibility that he would play in the Bolton and District League in the 1921 season, but it did not happen.[12] Shortly after the beginning of the season, he was on his way south again.

Crawford took a job with what was then Elders and Fyffes, a banana importing company. His employment there was to occupy the remaining thirty-one years of his working life. Apart from a brief secondment to the Bristol office, he spent the whole of that time in the company's head office in London. His experience as a quartermaster in the New Zealand army equipped him with what we would now term 'transferable skills' and Crawford found a home in the Stores and Export Department. Occasionally, however, he ventured outside the office environment, as in the national dock strike of 1923 and the General Strike of 1926 when, as part of an unskilled and unhardened volunteer workforce, he helped unload boats before the bananas went to waste.

Later, during the Second World War, after the company's headquarters took a direct hit during a German bombing raid and business records were destroyed, he took part in the mammoth task of writing hundreds of letters to secure duplicate copies of correspondence and invoices from customers and suppliers.

Crawford continued to play club cricket, but now halfway into his fourth decade, the emphasis in his game was on batting rather than bowling. He played principally for Merton whose home ground was, and still is, at John Innes Park in Merton. At the time Crawford was there, they ran three teams and were one of several within a few miles of one another, including Wimbledon, Merton Boys Club and Merton and Morden.

Crawford gradually played himself in, scoring 24 and taking three wickets against East Molesey in May, 61 against Epsom and 96 against Mitcham. He become more prolific later in the summer, doubtless enjoying firmer batting surfaces than those experienced both further north and in the spring, hitting form with scores of 106, 60, 91, 90 and 43 in August and September. In addition to those played earlier in the season, opponents were Streatham and Wimbledon.[13] Although there was a bit of league cricket in the area at the time, this was at junior level in the Croydon and District League and the London Wesleyan League. Senior club cricket in the south of England was based on a programme of friendly matches: outside the first-class circuit in which he did not feature after 1921, this was the highest level available.

In later seasons, he also appeared occasionally for other clubs, including Elders and Fyffes. At a time when works, office and factory sides were more prevalent than they have subsequently become, *The Times* reported briefly on club cricket and pointed to a number of distinguished and match-winning performances.

The following season, 1922, he continued to make his mark, mainly with the bat, but supplemented by the occasional bowling performance.

> The most notable performance of the day was that of the Surrey player, JN Crawford, who, playing for Merton against Teddington, made 107 runs and took four wickets for 30.[14]

His century included a six and twenty-one fours. Merton went on to win by 172 runs.[15]

JN Crawford again played well for Merton. He made 40 out of a total of 185 for seven declared.[16]

Wimbledon were beaten easily by Merton. The latter side were assisted by JN Crawford and it was largely due to his innings of 94 that Merton were able to make 241 for the loss of eight wickets.[17]

There are also reports of four for 24 for Elders and Fyffes against the Ellerman Line and later of 52 for Merton against Mitcham.[18] Merton remained his first-call club, but clearly he was still enjoying the game and prepared to turn out for his company team and any others that could make use of his still considerable services. In 1926 he had six for 65 for 'Old Boys' (there is no indication as to whose) against Wimbledon and late in the 1929 season, he had 53 for Mr JA Armstrong's XI against Mr HD Swan's XI at New Malden.[19]

The Cricketer, covering senior club cricket in more detail than it does now, had a number of complimentary reports.

Playing for Elders and Fyffes against Cook and Co., the old Surrey amateur, JN Crawford, did not meet with any bowling success, but he carried his bat for a vigorous 59 not out. A high scoring game was left drawn.[20]

The old Surrey and England player, JN Crawford had a day out for Elders and Fyffes against the Guaranty Trust Co. With the bat he made 46, having previously secured five wickets for 27. It seems a pity that Crawford is not seen in better class cricket, for he undoubtedly retains much of his old skill. Needless to say Elders and Fyffes gained an easy win.[21]

MALDEN WANDERERS CRICKET WEEK. In the Merton game Withy played a beautiful three-figure knock of 122 and the innings was declared closed at 275. Merton responded with 202 for 5, JN Crawford playing a merry little 39, which included one huge hit for six.[22]

> Merton had the assistance of JN Crawford in their match with Wimbledon, and, although he took six wickets for 65, the home side experienced little difficulty in winning by 134 to 65.[23]

By the end of 1926, apart from the occasional match, he played solely for Elders and Fyffes, giving up Merton colours. He does not feature in Merton's batting averages, having not played enough innings to qualify (fewer than five). There is no 'also batted' list and he does not appear in the bowling statistics.

He did, however, turn out for Merton against Mitcham at John Innes Park in a match which attracted a good attendance thanks to his presence in the team and that of William Abel in the opposition. Both were top scorers for their teams, Crawford 52, Abel 59. Merton won a close match, taking wickets with the third and fifth balls of the last over. A collection for the local Nelson Hospital realised £2 10s 9d.[24]

In an end of season charity match for which Jack Hobbs, who was associated with Merton CC, brought a team of celebrity cricketers to Merton to play against Wimbledon and District, Crawford turned out for the latter and was listed on the scorecard as 'Elders and Fyffes'. His father was on the organising committee and was one of the umpires. Afterwards, all the players adjourned to the Palais de Danse.[25]

At the time and for a few decades after the Second World War, works, factory, civil service and office sides were very much part of the club scene and it was an accepted part of the functions of large employers to provide subsidised sports and social facilities for their staff. The Elders and Fyffes ground was in the nearby suburb of New Malden. It is still there, now the sports ground of LSE and used by Fulham Football Club's Academy. The cricket facilities are of sufficient quality for Surrey to use it as a venue for 2nd XI fixtures and a training facility for its own academy. In a way the wheel has come full circle, but there is no indication the ground ever belonged to the banana company.

Part of the ethos of the provision of recreational facilities by large employers was the creation of internal competitions, and one of the last matches in which Crawford played was the final of the Elders and Fyffes'

Challenge Cup held on the company ground at Druid Stoke. It was significant enough to merit a report and scorecard in the sports page of the *Western Daily Press* under the heading 'Banana Men's Big Match'.[26] Amid the tourist and county matches there are details of the match between the Western (Bristol) Branch – where Crawford was transferred in the early part of his career – and the London Branch – where he spent most of his working life. The Western Branch had an easy win by 191 to 82, Crawford, apart from one catch making no contribution. Bowling figures are not given, but if he did bowl he took no wickets. Then, batting at number four, he failed to score, being clean bowled by WF Long who won the match for his team with nine for 32.[27]

The previous year, 1928, he had participated in the first of what was to become a regular end-of-season event on West Indies tours of the British Isles – an invitation XI to play the tourists at the Elders and Fyffes ground in New Malden. West Indies, on their first Test tour, had lost all three of those matches by an innings, but did well enough against the weaker opposition of AH Stockley's XI , losing five wickets in the pursuit of 104.[28] Batting at number ten in a team of thirteen, Crawford was caught and bowled for three.

Jack continued to play both cricket and hockey up to 1939, including some of the country house variety, such as the fixture against Sir Julien Cahn's XI at Stanford Hall, but by the end of the 1930s, into his fifties, Crawford's sporting career was over and he was able to settle down to a life of business and domesticity.[29] On his retirement he was presented with a wrist watch and cigarette lighter and, as well as commenting on his first-class cricket career, the feature in the staff magazine mentions 'the interest and help he gave to the London Sports Club in its early days'.[30]

A wealth of cricket history assembled at Lord's in 1961, the gathering organised by Rothmans. All England players, the 23 veterans played in a total of 449 Test matches between 1899 and 1957. Standing: Laurie Fishlock, Len Hopwood, George Geary, Arthur Wellard, E. W. 'Nobby' Clark, Bill Voce, Jack Durston, Bob Appleyard, George Brown, Peter Smith, E. J. 'Tiger' Smith, George Duckworth, Eric Hollies; seated: Denis Compton, Tom Goddard, Bill Hitch, J. N. Crawford, Frank Woolley, Sir Jack Hobbs, Wilfred Rhodes, S. F. Barnes, John Gunn, H. I. 'Sailor' Young.

courtesy of David Frith

A distinguished gathering of former England cricketers at Lord's in 1961. Crawford is seated, fourth from left.

17

End of the Road

1922-63

Jack had left his wife in New Zealand in 1916, but it was not until April 1923 that Anita filed for divorce. The grounds were adultery coupled with desertion, though as the desertion in itself would have been sufficient cause, no co-respondent is named. Press reports on the case, euphemistically translating adultery as misconduct, mention a West End London hotel. The case was uncontested. The court papers state that Crawford's current address was unknown, but his last known address was Fischer's Hotel, 11 Clifford Street, W1 (no longer in existence and buildings have since been renumbered), the same venue, according to the evidence of a waiter and barmaid that the 'misconduct' occurred.[1] One newspaper report maintains that Anita had to travel to Europe in connection with her work, heard something of him from friends and had him watched.[2]

> In the divorce court on Monday, Mr Justice Harridge granted a decree nisi to Mrs Anita Crawford on the ground of the desertion and misconduct by her husband, John Neville Crawford. Mrs Crawford said that she was married in 1915 at St Paul's, Melbourne and afterwards lived with him at St Clair, Dunedin. There were no children. Without saying anything to her, he left her and did not communicate with her but she afterwards found out that he

> had joined up with the Expeditionary Force and went overseas. He did not contribute to her support, and she had to earn her own living. Up to 1919 she conducted an orchestra in New Zealand.
>
> In December 1922 she obtained an appointment with an Adelaide firm, which necessitated her travelling in Europe. Respondent was at present in England. Evidence was given that respondent had stayed at a West End hotel with a lady who was not the petitioner.[3]

The judge pronounced a decree nisi with costs against the respondent. The abandoned wife did not languish in Dunedin, but returned to Adelaide where she resided for a while with her parents, before travelling to Europe where she developed a new career.[4]

> For some time after her marriage Mrs Crawford lived in New Zealand but soon after the outbreak of the war she went to England. Since that time Mrs Crawford has lived almost entirely in England with the exception of a brief visit to Adelaide in 1922. While in England she became continental buyer to a well-known Adelaide drapery firm.[5]

Anita travelled to London in 1921, returning to Adelaide on SS *Beltana* on 10 November. Describing herself as a 'housewife', she gives her last address in the UK as 'c/o Bank of Adelaide, Leadenhall Street' and the country of her intended future permanent residence as Australia. Towards the end of the following year, she returned to the UK again on board the *Omar*, travelling first class from Adelaide to Southampton and arriving on 8 January 1923.[6]

If the desertion had occurred in November 1916, why wait for more than six years before filing for divorce? The answer is astonishingly simple: until then there had been no need. Now there was.

Anita wished to remarry and within a few months had done so. Her German family had, for very obvious reasons, changed their name from Schmidt to Smith during the war, and her father from Diedrich to David. Anita found another way of changing her surname to the same one. In June 1924, she became Lady Smith, the wife of distinguished aviator and national hero, Sir Keith Macpherson Smith.

The final decree was pronounced on 4 February 1924. Within days the engagement of Anita and Sir Keith was announced.

> The engagement is announced of Sir Keith Smith, aviator, brother of the late Sir Ross Smith, to Mrs Anita Crawford who recently secured a divorce from JN Crawford the international cricketer. Mrs Crawford is a daughter of Mr DH Smith, Secretary of the Naval and Military Club, Adelaide.[7]

Within a few months the couple were engaged, married and had honeymooned in Paris. The press reports were suitably laudatory. Anita was a lady of considerable accomplishment, intellectually and socially accomplished, and of a status that now merited having her portrait painted. If her first husband was a man of some distinction in the sporting arena, her second was one who featured on the world stage. It is possible they met in Adelaide where they both grew up, but given the amount of time both spent in England during and immediately after the war, it is more likely that they met there or at least developed and cemented an acquaintance which had begun earlier on the other side of the world.

> The engagement of Sir Keith Smith to Mrs Anita Crawford is announced, says the *Adelaide Observer*. All the world knows of Sir Keith and his fine courage during the war, and, later, with his brother (the late Sir Ross Smith) he did the famous flight from England to Australia. He is in London at present, associated with the firm of Vickers, Ltd. Mrs Crawford, too, is in London. At least, her headquarters are there, but she aeroplanes to Paris constantly, and from those two world centres buys latest fashions for a well-known Adelaide drapery firm. She is a most charming and brainy woman, capable and extremely versatile, a good business head, yet most artistic, an excellent musician, her favourite instrument the piano, which she plays beautifully. Practical to a degree, she can cook and serve dinner in a manner which would make any chef envious.[8]

> Miss Marian Jones, the Australian artist, whose delicate and sympathetic picture 'Cui Bono?' was so commended last year, is sending in several portraits,

> among them a very attractive one of Mrs Crawford, who is about to marry Sir Keith Smith, the famous aviator.[9]

Despite her new husband's expertise and the assertion that she aeroplanes to Paris constantly, she confesses to a fear of flying and confirms that they travelled there for the honeymoon in a more conventional way.

> Lady Keith Smith, replying to an interviewer who asked whether she flew to Paris, where she and Sir Keith spent their honeymoon, said: 'No aeroplanes for me. I'm frightened of them. We travelled in the good old-fashioned way, like Christians.'[10]

The Smith brothers, Keith and Ross, were of mixed Australian and Scots descent and their education was divided between the two countries. Keith's war record was less distinguished than his brother's as he was rejected for service by the Australian Imperial Forces on medical grounds, but undeterred, he had paid his own passage to England where he undertook ground and training duties. Ross by contrast saw active service in Suez and Turkey and was awarded the Military Cross twice and the Distinguished Flying Cross three times.

After the war, the brothers' chief accomplishment was to fly from England to Australia, more specifically from Hounslow to Darwin, in under thirty days. It was the first time it had been done and earned them a purse of £10,000 from the Australian government and a knighthood each. Sir Ross was tragically killed in April 1922 at Weybridge on a test flight preparatory to an attempt to fly round the world in a Vickers Viking. Sir Keith, however, continued his successful career in aviation working for Vickers and becoming Vice-President of British Commonwealth Pacific Airlines, a director of Qantas and Tasman Airways and in the Second World War vice-chairman of the Royal Australian Air Force Recruiting Drive Committee. He died of cancer in December 1955.[11] Anita survived him by more than thirty years, dying in 1986 and bequeathing her entire estate to the establishment of the Sir Ross and Sir Keith Smith Fund for 'the advancement in the State of South Australia of the science of aeronautics and of education therein'. The brothers have also given their names to an Australian cricket legend who was born in 1919 and christened 'Keith Ross' in their honour: Keith Ross Miller.

The divorce also left Jack free to remarry, which he did in December 1926.[12] His bride was Hilda May Beman, daughter of a Law Clerk. The event seems to mark the beginning of the loosening of hitherto strong family ties and a transition into relative obscurity. Jack and Hilda began married life at 2 Dault Road in Wandsworth.

The Crawford family had already begun to unravel by the time Jack married. In August 1922, Frank, who had never recovered from serving at Gallipoli and the Somme, died of double pneumonia, having for some years suffered from shell shock and dysentery. He was buried with military honours.

> Among the wreaths at the funeral at Merton yesterday of Captain Vivian FS Crawford, the Surrey and Leicester cricketer, was one in the form of a bat in red and white chrysanthemums. This bore the motto, 'Well played. A Great Heart. From his brothers and sisters.'
>
> Eldest of three brothers who gained fame on the cricket field, Mr Vivian Crawford was only forty-three. During the war he served with the East Surrey Regiment and suffered from dysentery and shell shock.
>
> From his residence at Merton, the funeral cortege moved to the church, the coffin being wrapped in a Union Jack and borne on a gun-carriage. The procession was headed by the band of the East Surrey Regiment.
>
> After the coffin had been lowered into the grave, which was lined with leaves, the firing party fired a volley and 'Last Post' was sounded.[13]

The local newspaper looked back on some of Frank's astonishing batting feats as a youngster. With the help of *Wisden's Cricketers' Note Book*, it recalled eight seasons between 1893 and 1900 in each of which he had scored over 1,000 runs, including four over 2,000 and one over 3,000, as proudly pointed out by his father. In only the first of these did he fail to make a century. Five times his highest innings was over 200, including one of 300 and in the first six seasons he took over 100 wickets, including 200 in 1895 and 217 in 1894. It was further pointed out that his initials VFS were interpreted early in his career as 'very fast scorer'.[14]

Nearly four years later, another Crawford died. This time it was Andrew, Jack's grandfather. Having celebrated his one hundredth birthday in 1924, he was finally called home by the grim reaper at the advanced age of 101. In 1926, there were not many more than a hundred centurions in the UK.[15] His last hours were recalled by the local press.

MR A CRAWFORD'S WONDERFUL INNINGS ... FATHER AND GRANDFATHER OF CRICKETERS

Wimbledon's Grand Old Man – Mr Andrew Crawford – died shortly before midday on Monday, at 63, Merton Hall-road, the residence of his son, the Rev John C Crawford MA. The old gentleman, it will be remembered, celebrated his 101st birthday on January 27th last, and to within a day or so of his death retained his faculties to a remarkable degree. On Saturday evening he joined the family in a dinner to celebrate his son's birthday and then seemed quite all right, although, of course, the weakness which had gradually come over him in the last few months was apparent. He retired at about 9.30 and as he dropped off to sleep he remarked in a gentle voice – gentler than usual – that he did not think he would get up on the following morning. On Sunday he seemed uneasy and it was evident that he was sinking. He died quietly at 11.40 the following morning without any pain. Although he had been blind for some time, his hearing and mentality had been wonderfully acute, and on Saturday he actually shaved himself – a personal attention he had always been able to perform. The head of a famous cricketing family he would during every day discuss the progress of matches, and showed his interest in general events by joining in conversation concerning politics. Since his death his family have been almost inundated with messages of sympathy.

Mr Crawford who was born at Bathgate, Linlithgow, was bereaved of his wife in 1878. He never had a serious disease in all his life and, although he was a non-smoker, he enjoyed a glass of wine, and his favourite evening meal was a glass of beer and bread and cheese. His recipe for longevity, as given to a *Boro' News* reporter, was work.

The late Mr Andrew Crawford was for some years second Master of Appleby School, Westmorland, some of his old pupils being the late Sir James Whitehead, Baronet, Dr Percival, late Bishop of Hereford, and many others who also became celebrities. Afterwards, removing to Hastings, he built a school house, but in 1859, he removed to the Maidstone Grammar School and later became a most successful 'coach', only one of his pupils ever failing to pass his examinations. Owing to his defective vision he went to reside with his son in 1891, but did not become totally blind until eight years ago. A man of great learning he felt the hardship of not being able to read everything himself, but took the keenest interest in things in general. For all his wonderful age, to within twelve hours of his death, his mind retained all its vigour, although of late his physical powers were naturally somewhat abated.

In his earlier days, Mr Crawford was a very fine underhand bowler of the old school and in later years had the satisfaction of seeing his two sons – the Rev JC Crawford and the late Major FF Crawford , both playing for Kent. Later still his great delight was to sit in the Oval Pavilion and watch his grandsons, VFS, RT and JN make some of their famous hits.

He was always proud in stating ... that his grandsons never wasted time in picking up invisible stalks and rolling down the turf after each ball.[16]

In 1925, there were worries that an obituary would also be necessary for Jack. He fell seriously ill with appendicitis and at one stage it was feared it may claim his life. He was living at the home of his father, who on his retirement from Cane Hill in 1919 had been obliged to vacate his tied cottage and was now living in Wimbledon. He recovered sufficiently to have an operation in Norwood Cottage Hospital. It was successful. The press took an interest and reported in some detail on his progress.

Mr JN Crawford, the Surrey cricketer, is lying seriously ill at his father's residence. He is suffering from appendicitis and it is feared that poisoning has set in. Yesterday he was reported to be a little better.[17]

So greatly has the condition of JN Crawford, the well-known Surrey cricketer, improved that it will be possible for him to be moved into the Norwood Cottage Hospital next week for an operation.[18]

An operation for appendicitis was performed in Norwood Cottage Hospital yesterday on Mr JN Crawford. The operation was carried out successfully and it was announced later that Mr Crawford was going on satisfactorily.[19]

From his father's house at 63 Merton Hall Road, a three-storey semi-detached opposite the Wimbledon College of Art (now part of the University of the Arts) and a comfortable ten-minute walk from the Merton Parish Church where 'Pa' was curate, Jack moved to 47 Bournemouth Road in Wimbledon, a two-storey semi, the epitome of suburban respectability, before moving again on his marriage.

Jack's family links were now with the relatives of his new wife. His will, dated 1960, makes no mention of the Crawford family. All of his siblings with the exception of Marjorie (and possibly Audrey whose death has not been traced) had predeceased him but, although there were nephews and nieces who might have featured, the bequests are all to Hilda and her family. Hilda's sister, Edith Baker, her husband Alfred and nephew Godfrey received £100, £50 and £800 from a net estate of £4,466.1s.

Perhaps a more telling document, however, is that of the will of Parson Crawford which, written in 1924, nominated eldest daughter Edith as executor and sole beneficiary, subject to putative widow Alice having the right to live in the leasehold property. However, Alice died in 1931 after a marriage of fifty-seven years and a 1934 codicil to her widower's will named Marjorie as reserve beneficiary and executrix, but left a bequest of £50 to Reginald. The Reverend died the following year, so Edith, to whom probate was granted, and Reginald benefited. Frank and Lesley had already died, so that left Audrey – living in Canada, but who travelled back to England in 1933 – and Jack, who does not feature.

Earlier evidence is that Jack was close to his mother. He mentions in *Trip to KangarooLand* that she was not present at Tilbury on his first departure for Australia in 1907 because they had quarrelled the previous day about who loved the other the most.[20] She did, however, travel to Tilbury for the 1909 departure. After her death in 1931 the widening family rift possibly became wider and the closeness which characterised the Crawfords in earlier years was no more, even among the remaining members.

The local press lists the mourners at both Frank's and Andrew's funeral. Jack was among them. There is no record of those who attended Pa's funeral in 1935, just a mention of his playing for Merton at the age of seventy-five, his involvement as a supporter of, and umpire in, the annual charity matches in aid of the two local hospitals, and a comment about Lesley (later Mrs Colley) being the first woman ever to score a century.[21]

The disintegration of earlier strong family ties was perhaps the inevitable consequence of the *pater familias* style of domination by Rev JC Crawford who continued fighting his family's battles, particularly those of Frank and Jack, long after the time when they were perfectly capable of fighting their own. He was obviously and justifiably proud of his family and wished to do his best for them, but there comes a time when they have to fly the nest and do their own thing. For Jack that time came rather late in the day and the severance of family ties, their replacement with ties to Hilda's family and the transition to suburban anonymity and respectability was true to character and marked his final act of rebellion.

The latter part of Crawford's life seems to have been singularly uneventful. In 1934, he and Hilda moved to a new detached house on Conaways Close in the respectable middle-class commuter suburb of Ewell. Nostalgically, he called the house 'Repton', although, apart from his brief coaching spell, his association with that educational establishment had finished some thirty years earlier. Subsequent occupants have retained the name. It is short walk from Ewell East railway station with regular commuter services into London.

Crawford's life was now indistinguishable from that of millions of others who devote their time to work and family; in retirement to gardening, golf or some other hobby. There seems no evidence of any involvement with civic activities, sports or social clubs (apart from the London Sports Club of his employers) or public speaking engagements, although there are reports of his attending a dinner at Lord's in 1953 to celebrate Sir Pelham Warner's eightieth birthday, as well as a Master's Club dinner in 1962, and around the same time receiving a fee of ten guineas for participating in a BBC radio programme to celebrate Sir Jack Hobbs also completing eight decades of life.[22] In 1961 he was present at a gathering of former England players at the Lord's Test match, organised by Rothmans and photographed alongside legends of the game such as Jack Hobbs, Frank Woolley, Sydney Barnes and Wilfred Rhodes.

There is no mention in local newspapers of Jack's death in Epsom and Ewell Cottage Hospital from coronary thrombosis in 1963. There are detailed reports on the FA Amateur Cup Final, and advertisements for the new Hillman Imp and the then popular babydoll pyjamas, but nothing on the passing of one who half a century earlier had been perhaps England's and the world's leading all-rounder. Hilda survived him twenty-eight years, dying in 1991. There is no grave. It was his wish, stated in his will, that his body be cremated.

Crawford's career was a front loaded one, all his major achievements in the first part of his life. Presumably after a first-class cricket career spent in the glare of the public spotlight, having distinguished himself in five countries and been no stranger to controversy off the field, he was quite content to settle down to family and business life and join the anonymous hordes of commuters travelling daily from the suburbs to central London. However, anonymity also had the effect of casting Jack Crawford and his many achievements in the cricket field into relative obscurity. Many have now forgotten the man who was once the greatest schoolboy cricketer and a beacon of hope for Surrey and England cricket.

Kevin Pietersen has been described as a 'high-functioning awkward bugger'.[23] He is not alone in that. Much the same could be said of Geoffrey Boycott, Fred Trueman, Cecil Parkin… and of Jack Crawford. The cases are not identical, but there are parallels. All were self-made cricketers, their success was based on fitness awareness, practice and a commitment to perfecting the skills of the game – in Crawford's case, a Protestant work ethic derived from his clergyman father and close-knit family. Their playing ability was vastly superior to that of most of their contemporaries, infinitely so to that of those who purported to manage them. None could be described as modest; all had an awareness of their own ability and all clashed with authority. All had successful careers in county and international cricket but exercised their right to be different; all missed matches, voluntarily or otherwise, in which they might have played. Given more sympathetic handling, they might have been even more successful. They were mavericks with ego and attitude, rebels in their day and prepared to kick against the pricks. Maybe sport – and society – needs that kind of approach to avoid lapsing into anodyne conformity.

Crawford has been deemed a 'professional amateur', not in the sense that he was a paid amateur like WG Grace or Walter Read, but from his approach to the game – not unlike that of his successors at Surrey, Douglas Jardine and Stuart Surridge. The divide between amateurs and professionals can be considered in a number of ways, the over-simplified being that professionals were paid and amateurs were not (apart from inflated expenses and sinecures such as county secretaryships and assistant secretaryships). Then there was the social distinction, the amateurs being gentlemen and the players hired labourers: no problem for a player from a working-class background who would not dream of becoming a 'gentleman' anyway, nor for those from wealthy aristocratic families who could afford to play for no pay; but a challenge for those like WG Grace, WW Read and JN Crawford from the middle classes. They could not afford to be amateurs in a financial sense but did not wish to be professionals in a social sense. Beyond that, however, there is the question of attitude. Being listed in the amateur or professional column as a result of finance or social status by no means entails remaining in the same column for approach to the game. There have been professionals with an amateur carefree approach like Denis Compton, Keith Miller and Sir Garfield Sobers – not that such a mentality has prevented their being world-class players – and amateurs with a professional approach, keeping fit practising assiduously, thinking about the game and playing hard. In this latter category, Jack Crawford switches from the amateur column to the professional one.

It is incontestable that, in his time, Crawford was outstanding as an all-rounder. It is a matter of surmise, though highly likely, that he was potentially one of the great all-rounders of the twentieth century. Herbie Collins expressed the view that he was better than Hammond. That, of course, is a matter of opinion and may not be shared by all commentators, but it is an indication that he is certainly up there with the best.

There were two huge hiccups in Crawford's career. Firstly, the rupture with Surrey cost him a successful career in England. He could have played for another county – and there cannot be many, if any, who would not have been delighted to have him on their books – but under the rules in force at the time, a two-year residential qualification was required. That would have taken him to 1912 and, although it was not known at the time, within three seasons of the First World War, which cruelly curtailed many a successful cricket career. Indeed, it was that same devastating conflict which pulled the rug from under his feet and caused the second and final hiatus, ending Crawford's promising and successful playing and coaching career in Otago.

Crawford's international career, following his non-selection for the 1909 Ashes series, was left to wither on the vine. He was never again to play for England after that and, despite the possibility of his playing for Australia having been mooted, the Australian Board of Control inevitably took the view that such a selection would have been too controversial.

It has been suggested that Crawford was the least likeable of the characters in my canon of Surrey biography. That may be so, but likeability is a difficult attribute to gauge. It can vary from time to time and much depends on who is making the judgment and when. Certainly Crawford had strong friendships, for instance with Lord Dalmeny and Digby Jephson at Surrey and with Frederick Fane, Ken Hutchings and Richard Young on his MCC tours. Admittedly, they were all from the same background of amateur, public school-style camaraderie, but his relations with his professional colleagues seem to have been cordial and based on mutual respect, if not necessarily likeability. Furthermore, he seems to have mixed well in Adelaide's social circles and retained affable relationships with Clem Hill, Victor Trumper, Herbie Collins and his other Australian colleagues. New Zealand military records have no information on personal popularity and, apart from his club cricket and involvement in sports and social activities at Elders and Fyffes, he seems to have kept himself very much to himself and family in later years. On the other hand, he was probably never on HDG Leveson Gower's

Christmas card list and, although he was doubtless at least likeable to Anita in her teenage years and early twenties, those feelings would have changed later on – if indeed her subsequent career and relationships gave her time to think about it.

Crawford's most unlikeable trait was perhaps his arrogance, however justified it might have been. Nobody likes a smartarse, and at times he was certainly that. Envy is a natural human emotion, so is the wish for popularity and the need to be loved. However, strong managements and strong personalities aim to do the right thing, rather than the popular thing. They do not always coincide. Perhaps it is the ability to transcend those basic instincts and do the right thing, even at the risk of being unpopular, that separates the Jack Crawfords of this world from the rest of the herd.

Likeability is a complex judgment. Perhaps more appropriate to the early twentieth century, where Freudian psychoanalysis was in its infancy and judgments were simpler, would be the question posed by Nigel Hart: hero or villain?

Crawford was both, but primarily a hero. His deeds on the field were unparalleled at the time and many of them still are. His record and reputation vouch for that. It was a brave (though some might say rash) act to challenge the full might of the Surrey Committee. But, life is not lived entirely in a committee room or on a cricket field, however Elysian it may appear to be.

There are two black spots on Crawford's life away from the field. First, the desertion of Anita. There were understandable if not necessarily excusable reasons in the Anglo-German hostilities at the time. The full circumstances are not detailed in the divorce hearing, but whatever other commitments might have been, fifteen months or so does seem a short time to try and get a marriage to work. However, Anita's subsequent life and marriage suggests that she did not come out of it too badly and, as far as can be ascertained, Jack seems subsequently to have settled down to a stable domestic life, albeit one without children. Apart from Edith, he was alone among his siblings in that.

Secondly, on the professional side, the way in which he treated the South Australian Cricket Association was underhand, maybe even despicable. They had smoothed his passage to Australia and treated him very well. The dignity with which they handled his departure contrasted sharply with his double dealing when he played offers from the South Australian and Otago Associations against each other.

His lifestyle in Adelaide may have been a further black mark, but maybe we should leave it to those without sin to cast the first stone. Like Dylan Thomas's characters in Llareggub who lived their lives Under Milk Wood, like most of us, he was not wholly bad or good. Perhaps, like King Lear, he was a man more sinned against than sinning.

Sir Keith and Lady Smith (formerly Anita Crawford, Jack's first wife).

ACKNOWLEDGEMENTS

The resources of the following libraries and archives have been invaluable: British Cartoon Archive in the Templeman Library at the University of Kent, British Library, Flinders University, London Borough of Merton Local Studies Library, London Borough of Sutton Local Studies Library, National Archives, National Library of Australia, Surrey County Cricket Club and Surrey History Centre.

Additional thanks are due to:

Archives New Zealand for permission to reproduce extracts from Crawford's military record.

Alistair Bolingbroke, Secretary, Rochdale Cricket Club, for information on Crawford's time in Rochdale.

Robert Brooke for sharing the results of his research on Frank Foster, whose career ran roughly parallel to Crawford's.

Marion Brown, Document Services Support Assistant, Flinders University Library, for kindly supplying a copy of Susan Millbank's thesis on South Australian cricket.

Andrew Carver, Secretary, East Torrens Cricket Club.

Vicki Clark for reading the manuscript and suggesting that something should be said about Crawford's likeability and more on Rev JC Crawford's domination of the family.

Hubert Doggart, who met Crawford at the Elders and Fyffes match at the end of the 1950 West Indies tour and recalled being told at Winchester by Harry Altham that in his Repton days, Jack was the greatest schoolboy cricketer ever.

Caroline Edney, Secretary, Staines Hockey Club.

Phil Evans of oldukphotos.com for permission to use the photograph of Repton School in 1906.

David Frith for permission to use the photograph of the gathering of former England cricketers at the 1961 Lord's Test from *Pageant of Cricket.*

Bill Gordon, Librarian and Archivist, Surrey County Cricket Club, for his help with locating obscure publications and scanning and improving grainy photographs of more than a hundred years ago.

Richard Gould, Chief Executive, Surrey County Cricket Club, for permission to use the artist's impression of Hobbs and his contemporaries.

Sarah Gould, Heritage Officer, London Borough of Merton.

Gideon Haigh for drawing my attention to press items on Crawford's time in Australia, particular, his popularity with players and officials (and with women), and for putting us in touch with his namesake, Graeme Haigh.

Graeme Haigh, genealogist, for his researches into births and, at the relevant period, the absence of them in the Caterer family.

Chris Harte for sharing information on his conversations about Crawford's time in Adelaide and for permission to use extracts from his *History of the South Australian Cricket Association.*

Tony Kingston for drawing my attention to the hymn tune 'Repton', named after Crawford's old school.

John McKenzie for permission to use Rev JC Crawford's letter of September 1897.

Andrea McKinnon-Matthews, Archivist of St Peter's College, Adelaide, for information on Crawford's time there.

Trevor Mead, East Torrens Cricket Club, for statistics from Crawford's time with the club.

Howard Milton for access to the Cricket Society Library.

Roger Packham for sharing his knowledge of the Crawford family and drawing my attention to a number of articles.

Scott Reeves of Chequered Flag Publishing for rescuing the book after it had been first accepted then declined by the Association of Cricket Statisticians and Historians, and his subsequent professional and sensitive editing.

Melanie Sambells, Communications Executive at Mirrorpix, for permission to use the photograph of the three Crawford brothers on Jack's departure for Australia in 1909 and her attempts to trace the copyright of the RIP drawings.

Alan Scholtz, Honorary Secretary, Glenelg District Cricket Club, for information on Crawford's two seasons there.

Kathleen Shawcross, Archivist, London Borough of Sutton – it was rumoured that Crawford had played for Sutton CC (my own club) in the 1920s, but closer investigation revealed that it was another player entirely, JM Crawford, occasionally misprinted as JN.

Dominic Sibley, for kindly contributing a foreword to the book.

Paul Stevens, Archivist of Repton School, for supplying information from the *Repton Register* and *Repton Cricket 1901-1951*.

Iain Taylor, for pointing us in the direction of several articles on Crawford.

Cliff Thomas, Glenelg District Cricket Club, for sharing information arising from his work on the recently published history of the Club.

Wray Vamplew, Emeritus Professor of Sports History, University of Stirling, for his help with research into Crawford's time in Adelaide.

Bernard Whimpress for first-hand knowledge of Crawford's time in Adelaide and drawing my attention to his article on unanswered questions in *Cricket Lore*.

Peter Wynne-Thomas for kindly providing me with the JN Crawford section of his index to *The Cricketer*.

The Head Groundsman of LSE and the security staff of Fulham Football Club for information on the ground and pavilion formerly used by Elders and Fyffes.

Another six! An illustration from *Trip to KangarooLand*.

STATISTICS

Further details are available in Hart, *Famous Cricketers: JN Crawford* and on Cricket Archive.

TEST CRICKET

BATTING

	05/6 SA	07 SA	07/8 Aus	**Total**
Matches	5	2	5	**12**
Innings	10	3	10	**23**
Not Outs	1	0	1	**2**
Highest score	74	22	62	**74**
Runs	281	26	162	**469**
Average	31.22	8.66	18.00	**22.33**
50	1	0	1	**2**
Catches	6	1	6	**13**

BOWLING

	05/6 SA	07 SA	07/8 Aus	**Total**
Overs	100.3	29	237.4	**367.1**
Maidens	19	6	36	**61**
Runs	322	86	742	**1150**
Wickets	9	0	30	**39**
Average	35.77		24.73	**29.48**
Best	3-69		5-48	**5-48**
Five-fors	0		3	**3**

ALL FIRST-CLASS CRICKET

BATTING

	Matches	Inns	NO	High	Runs	Ave	100/50
1904	9	15	1	54	229	16.35	0/1
1905	13	19	3	142*	543	33.93	2/0
05/6 SA	11	18	1	74	531	31.23	0/3
1906	30	44	5	148	1174	30.10	1/6
1907	28	44	6	103	1158	30.47	1/6
07/8 Aus	16	24	1	114	610	26.52	1/3
1908	29	41	4	232	1371	37.05	3/5
1909	22	37	2	95	794	22.68	0/5
1909/10	3	5	1	73*	178	44.50	0/2
1910/11	4	8	2	79*	368	61.33	0/4
1911/12	6	11	0	126	390	35.45	2/1
1912/13	6	11	0	163	393	35.72	1/1
13 N Am	5	6	0	58	147	24.50	0/1
13/14 Aus	5	9	1	91	313	39.12	0/1
13/14 NZ	5	5	0	134	190	38.00	1/1
1914/15	4	7	2	178*	337	67.40	1/2
1917/18	2	3	1	110	156	78.00	1/0
1919	8	12	4	144*	488	61.00	1/1
1920	2	2	0	37	42	21.00	0/0
1921	2	4	0	42	76	19.00	0/0
Total	**210**	**325**	**34**	**232**	**9488**	**32.60**	**15/43**

ALL FIRST-CLASS CRICKET

BOWLING

	Overs	Maidens	Runs	Wickets	Average	Best	5/10w
1904	262.5	58	745	44	19.93	7-43	3/1
1905	306.5	72	868	47	18.46	8-24	3/1
05/6 SA	250.3	58	627	34	18.44	6-79	2/1
1906	886.3	237	2394	118	20.28	7-85	6/2
1907	827.1	208	2102	124	16.95	7-60	12/2
07/8 Aus	566	115	1663	66	25.19	5-40	4/0
1908	728	147	2106	98	21.48	7-132	3/0
1909	345.2	82	994	36	27.61	6-83	2/0
1909/10	107.1	13	378	20	18.90	7-92	2/0
1910/11	125.5	28	418	14	29.85	5-42	1/0
1911/12	276	63	811	21	38.61	6-141	1/0
1912/13	222.3	32	762	33	23.09	8-66	2/1
13 N Am	116.2	21	359	33	10.87	6-40	3/0
13/14 Aus	265.5	51	697	34	20.50	7-78	5/2
13/14 NZ	135.5	30	388	21	18.47	5-60	1/0
1914/15	134.3	27	388	30	12.93	6-37	4/1
1917/18	87.1	18	242	16	15.12	5-47	3/1
1919	197	32	607	20	30.35	3-62	0/0
1920	37.3	1	156	4	39.00	2-65	0/0
1921	36	1	137	2	68.50	1-50	0/0
Total	**5903.5**	**1294**	**16842**	**815**	**20.66**	**8-24**	**57/12**

Two of Jack's schism correspondents:
Lord Alverstone and HDG Leveson Gower

Schism Correspondence

Surrey County Cricket Club, Kennington Oval
20 May 1908

Dear Crawford,

At the committee meeting today a resolution was passed unanimously and by acclamation congratulating you on your fine captaincy of the XI, and the whole XI, on the result of the match Surrey v Australia, and the fine cricket. With good wishes, I am,

Faithfully yours,
(signed) Alverstone, President, SCCC

Hornton Lodge, Kensington
20 May 1909, 9am

Dear Crawford,

I must send you a line of congratulation on the result of yesterday's match. It confirms the opinion which I have long entertained of your thorough knowledge of the game, and I think your judgment and you putting on Lees for the last wicket was a master stroke. Considering that the luck was rather against us, it was a great win. Rushby hitting the wicket without dislodging the bails was an extraordinary incident. Wishing you good luck all through the season, I am,

Very truly yours,
(signed) Alverstone

Surrey County Cricket Club, Kennington Oval
15 July 1909

Dear Crawford,

The committee have learned with very deep regret of your refusal to captain the Surrey XI today, and the reason you gave for refusing. No one knows better than you the difficulties which beset the captain of a county team and the absolute necessity of maintaining the highest standard of good conduct on the part of the professionals. The reasons which led Leveson Gower to leave out Marshal and Rushby are known to you, and I need not tell you that the Committee not only approve of Leveson Gower's action, but are grateful to him for taking the responsibility. The committee feel that until you send to Leveson Gower an expression of your regret and an apology for your refusal to play today you cannot be invited to play for Surrey. Should you wish to see me I will of course see you at any time, but I trust you will feel that what the committee ask is only that which is due from you as a gentleman and a sportsman.

Faithfully yours,
(signed) Alverstone

Coulsdon
17 July 1909

Dear Lord Alverstone,

I do not understand your letter. I merely declined to accept the responsibility of skippering a team v. the Australians which did not include Rushby, Lees and Davis. I knew of nothing against the three, nor could I learn of what you insinuate. I do not know who was responsible for the second eleven sort of team furbished up for such an important match, but I apologised to the Australians for it, and explained my reasons for standing down. There seems to be some impression amongst a few of the Surrey committee that I am some young professional instead of being a young fellow who has had an experience of cricket that has seldom fallen to the lot of anyone, and my request for an alteration to the team last Thursday should have had some weight, and was but the outcome of a sporting desire to avoid the criticisms which have already appeared on the subject in most of the papers. Believe me, dear Lord Alverstone,

Yours very faithfully,
(signed) John N Crawford

Hornton Lodge, Pitt-Street, Kensington
19 July 1909

Dear Crawford,

I very much regret the terms of your letter of the 17th. The team for Thursday last was chosen by Leveson Gower, the captain of the eleven, as you know perfectly well; it was in no sense a second eleven sort of team as you suggest, but be that as it may your refusal to play unless a particular professional, Rushby was included, when Leveson Gower had good reason not to play him, cannot be justified.

No single member of the committee regards you as a young professional, and you have no right to make such a suggestion. We one and all regard you as a brilliant amateur with great experience, if it were not so we should not have invited you as we have to captain the eleven. If leading amateurs do not show loyalty to their captain, there is an end of true sport in cricket. I sincerely trust that on reflection you will see that in justice to yourself and the club the proper

course open to you is that indicated in my letter of the 15th, and that I may have the pleasure of seeing you playing for Surrey in many great matches.
I am, faithfully yours,
(signed) Alverstone

19 July 1909

Dear Lord Alverstone
On Thursday last, as acting captain of Surrey, I telephoned through to the official captain, who should have been present to welcome the Australians, about the extraordinary composition of the team, and stated that Lees, Rushby, and Davis (all of whom are playing at Lord's today) ought to be in the side. The only answer vouchsafed in explanation with regard to their not playing was that Lees was of no use to the club. Had I been told why Davis and Rushby were in disgrace (which seems now to have been condoned), I should have upheld the official captain in every way. But to give the acting captain a weak bowling team, and say in effect that 'You must skipper this team whether you like it or not, and if you don't skipper it you must apologise to me', placed me in the unpleasant position of having to decline the responsibility of skippering such a side. Had it been an out match I should have had my choice of thirteen players and in common courtesy, the official captain might have asked whether I could manage with the team he had picked.
Believe me, yours very faithfully,
(signed) John N Crawford

Hornton Lodge, Kensington
20 July 1909

Dear Crawford,
I have just received your letter of this date. I must at once correct two important statements therein. First, I understand from both Leveson Gower and Findlay that you knew on Thursday morning the reason why Leveson Gower had decided not to play Rushby against the Australians. His being played at Lord's has nothing to do with the matter. Had Smith been fit Rushby would not have been included. The second which is more important is that you were asked to apologise on Thursday morning. No question of apology was ever suggested at all until it was reported to the committee that you had declined to play unless Rushby was included, thereby actually reversing Leveson Gower's decision and putting him in a most difficult position. The committee unanimously decided that an apology was due from you. You know as well as possible that the whole difficulty has arisen from your declining to play with the team which Leveson Gower had chosen. You say in your previous letter that you apologised to the Australians for the character of the Surrey side. I am wholly unable to understand from what point of view you can justify such action.
I am, faithfully yours,
(signed) Alverstone

23 July 1909

Dear Lord Alverstone,

It is awfully good of you to take so much trouble over this matter as you are doing. I am perfectly astounded to be informed that the official captain and Findlay assert that I knew (or know now) the reason why Davis and Rushby were not to be played. Lees only was mentioned as being 'no good to the club'. But if the official captain chose the team what is the good of the Selection Committee? I withdrew from skippering the side because Davis, Rushby and Lees could not be done without in such an important match as the Australians, which I was anxious to win, and which would have been won if Rushby had been playing in addition to the other two. With regard to your reference to an apology I merely remarked that the team was given to me in a 'stand and deliver style'. 'If you don't skipper this team I have selected you will have to apologise to me for it', and for which you afterwards asked, and which under the circumstances I am not prepared to offer. Rather is one due to me. I again reiterate that as the acting Captain I was entitled to the courtesy of being consulted in the selection for such an important fixture, when any circumstances for or against it could have been discussed. Again thanking you for all the trouble you must have been put to over this matter in your earnest desire to smooth things over, believe me, dear Lord Alverstone,

Yours very faithfully,
(signed) John N Crawford

Eastbourne Cricket and Football (Association) Club, The Saffrons
29 July 1909

Dear Jack,

Just got your wire sent on to me from my office. Considering the line you have thought to adopt towards me with regard to Surrey cricket at which I am not only extremely surprised but also extremely hurt, I must cancel my invitation to you for Scarborough and in this CI Thornton quite agrees. The MCC Committee who are responsible for the England side to South Africa this winter have asked me to let you know that under the circumstances they will not now require your services.

Yours sincerely,
(signed) HDG Leveson Gower

The Sports Club Ltd, St James Square
4 August 1909

Dear Jack,

I had not sufficient time to speak to you today. The matter between yourself and the Surrey cricket committee is now in their hands as outlined to you by Lord Alverstone's letter, and a reply to that letter must be received from you before any further action can be taken.

Yours sincerely,
(signed) HDG Leveson Gower

PS – I shall also have to consider with them the letter I had from your father on the subject.

Hook Wood, Limpsfield, Surrey
5 August 1909

Dear Jack,

When I saw you at The Oval last Tuesday I had not seen all the correspondence that has passed between you and Lord Alverstone. This was laid before the Surrey Committee today, I could not have believed that you could have written such letters and said such things about me. There could, under the circumstances be only one course for me to adopt. Either you or I must give up playing for Surrey. The Committee have decided this question, and if the members and the public want to know the reason they shall have the whole facts from me. I shall let the professionals know. After what I have done for you and have tried to do for you in many ways which you know of, the manner in which you have treated me seems to me to be on your part an act of the deepest ingratitude.

Yours truly,
HDG Leveson Gower

Surrey County Cricket Club, Kennington Oval
6 August 1909

Dear Crawford,

I am directed by my committee to send you a copy of the following resolution which was passed at a committee meeting held yesterday.

'That in view of Mr Crawford's conduct in declining to play for Surrey on the morning of the Australian match after previously communicating to the secretary his intention to play and his subsequent letters to Lord Alverstone the committee resolve that he be not invited again to play for Surrey.'

Yours faithfully,
W Findlay (Secretary)

Hotel St Cloud, Eastbourne
7 August 1909

Dear Findlay,

Kindly convey to the committee my acknowledgement of their resolution which surely might have been accompanied by thanks for past services.

I fail to see why I should practically be branded as a criminal because as acting captain in the second match against the Australians, I declined the responsibility of skippering a team which did not include three essential players in Davis, Lees and Rushby – an independence which I trust will still remain in spite of the awful example made of me to every amateur in the United Kingdom.

Yours faithfully,
(signed) JN Crawford

The above correspondence was sent by Crawford to the *Sporting Times.* Such was the attention that it attracted the following spoof in *Punch*:

An English Cricketer's Love Letters

The following correspondence was thrust in our letterbox last week with the demand that it should be printed in our next issue. We have not the least doubt that it is unauthentic – or premature, at any rate; but at the same time it certainly seems to convey the atmosphere of the authorised letters. It may be, of course, that our contributor has only got hold of the rough drafts.

24 December 1909

My dear Crawford,

A Merry Christmas to you. I hope you are keeping fit for next season; we must try to beat the Australians. Can you possibly drop in for tea tomorrow?

Yours affectionately, Alverstone.

July 1909

My dear Crawford,

We are all horrified at your conduct in refusing at the last moment to play against the Australians, when you had promised Leveson Gower to do so. Unless you can see your way to making a public apology to the Committee, in the presence of Apted and the other groundsmen, it will be our painful duty never to let you have the Saturday half-holiday again.

Yours very truly, Alverstone.

My dear Lord Alverstone,

All I said was that I wouldn't accept the responsibility of captaining a team which consisted entirely of Harrison, Platt and Ducat. No reason was given to me why the others weren't asked, and I think I ought to have at least been consulted, seeing that it was entirely owing to my captaincy that we won the last match. A lot of people look upon me as a sort of professional, instead of being a very young man with an experience and knowledge of the game unrivalled even by WG Grace.

Yours sincerely, John N Crawford.

My dear Profumo – I mean Crawford,[1]

My instructions are to the effect that, anyhow, you are quite old enough to know why all the Surrey professionals except three are in disgrace; if you didn't know, you ought to have guessed. The fact that they are playing today against Middlesex has nothing to do with it. If the wicket had been soft some of them would have been left out. Will you apologise?

Yours faithfully, Alverstone.

My dear Lord Alverstone,

It is awfully nice of you to write me such jolly letters. The official Captain, which I won't sully my pen with his name, only told me that Hobbs wasn't good enough for Surrey, and never said anything about the others. Under the circumstances, I don't see why I should apologise to him or to anybody – except Noble.

Yours sincerely, John N Crawford.

My dear Jack,

Awfully sorry I hadn't time to nod to you when I saw you today, but the Committee have ordered me to cut you. I will write you a nice long letter when I get home.

Yours ever, HDG Leveson Gower.

My dear Jack,

I am amazed, revolted and disgusted at your conduct. To think that you should refer to me in this way in your letters to Lord Alverstone, when you know how good I have always been to you! You bad boy! I shall tell Strudwick how wicked you have been. Under the circumstances I shall have to cancel your season ticket to the White City – and Kiralfy quite agrees with me in this.[2] It is also obviously impossible that we should both go with the MCC Team to South Africa, and so I have asked the South Africans to choose which one of us they would rather played against them in Test Matches. They have unanimously chosen *me*.

Yours ever, HDG Leveson Gower.

Dear Crawford,

At a Meeting of Surrey stockbrokers it was decided that the following resolution be sent to you: 'that in view of young Crawford's refusal to play against the Australians and the bad style and construction of his letters to Lord Alverstone, he be asked never to play cricket again. And "jolly good riddance".'

Yours sincerely, W Findlay.

Dear Findlay,

Why I should be practically branded as a criminal for refusing to take the field eight short when you might at least have thanked me for past services, I'm sure I don't know. Anyhow, I hope that others will do the same.

Yours for the very last time, John N Crawford.

Notes

1 In the Beginning

1. *The Times*, 9 August 1883.
2. Bailey, Thorn & Wynne-Thomas, *Who's Who of Cricketers*, p.243.
3. Packham, *The Crawfords of Cane Hill*, p.14.
4. *Wimbledon Boro' News* 7 March 1935.
5. Census of Population 1861.
6. Census of Population 1871.
7. Censuses of Population 1881 and 1891.
8. Not Glengrove as reported in *Wisden* 1907 and other sources which have repeated the error.
9. Census of Population 1891.
10. Again, not Henley, as similarly reported and replicated elsewhere.
11. Censuses of Population 1891 and 1901.
12. *Cricket*, 28 April 1898.
13. 'Special Article No 4: The Art of Bowling – JN Crawford' in *Star* (Canterbury), 9 October 1908.
14. *Cricket*, 25 October 1900.
15. *Cricket*, 11 July 1901.
16. *Surrey Mirror*, 29 September 1905.
17. *Surrey Mirror*, 12 February 1909.
18. *The Times*, 25 February 1935.
19. *The Times*, 27 March 1902.

2 My Boy Jack

1. *Cricket*, 27 March 1902
2. Monro, *Repton Cricket 1901-1951*, pp.6-7
3. Monro, p.8.
4. *Wisden* 1904, p.cii.

5. *Cricket*, 18 June 1903.
6. *Nottingham Evening Post*, 19 August 1903.
7. *Surrey Mirror*, 11 September 1903.
8. *Wisden* 1905, p.cxxxiv.
9. *Wisden* 1906, p.cxviii.
10. *Wisden* 1906, p.cxxii.
11. *Wisden* 1907, p.cxiii.
12. *Cricketer*, 30 July 1921
13. It was in fact nine.
14. Actually 63 wickets.
15. *Cricketer*, 24 May 1963.
16. Robertson-Glasgow, *More Cricket Prints*, p.46.

3 Confidence and Ability

1. Lord Alverstone's report to Surrey AGM, *Cricket*, 14 May 1903.
2. Meredith, *The Demon and the Lobster*, p.113.
3. Hobbs, *My Cricket Memories*, p.16.
4. *Wisden* 1905, pp.174 & 175.
5. *Cricket*, 11 August 1904.
6. *Surrey Mirror*, 12 August 1904.
7. *Cricket* 11 August 1904
8. *Cricket*, 18 August 1904.
9. *Evening Post* (Angus), 19 August 1904.
10. *Cricket*, 25 August 1904.
11. *Cricket*, 1 September 1904.
12. *Cricket*, 8 September 1904.
13. *Cricket*, 15 September 1904.
14. *Surrey Mirror*, 16 September 1904.
15. *Wisden* 1906, p.135.
16. *Cricket*, 17 August 1905.
17. *Cricket*, 17 August 1905.
18. Cricket Committee Minutes, 29 August 1905.
19. *Cricket*, 24 August 1905.
20. *Cricket*, 31 August 1905.
21. *Wisden* 1906, p.152.
22. *Cricket*, 7 September 1905.
23. *Wisden* 1906, p.154.
24. *Cricket*, 14 September 1905.
25. *Cricket*, 21 September 1905.
26. *Cricket*, 21 September 1905.

4 Quite Exceptional

1. Knowles, *South Africa versus England: A Test Cricket History*, p.46.

2. *Yorkshire Post*, 19 December 1905.
3. *Cricket*, 21 December 1905.
4. *Yorkshire Post*, 26 December 1905.

5. Earlier Vogler had also taken a wicket with his first ball in Test cricket when he caught and bowled Crawford's Surrey colleague and fellow debutant Ernie Hayes. It remains the only instance of two players taking a wicket with their first ball in Test cricket in the same match (there have been only twenty cases in Test history). To complete a trio of peculiarities, Vogler was bowled by Hayes in the second innings, not with Hayes' first ball, but it was to be his only Test wicket.

6. *Yorkshire Post*, 29 January 1906.
7. *Cricket*, 25 January 1906.
8. *Daily Express*, 7 February 1906.
9. *Cricket*, 22 February 1906.
10. *Yorkshire Post*, 12 February & 27 March 1906.
11. *Cricket*, 29 March 1906.
12. *Wisden* 1907, p.464.
13. Leveson Gower, *Off and On the Field*, pp.149 & 150.
14. *Aberdeen Daily Journal*, 23 April 1906.

5 Record Breaker

1. *Cricket*, 10 May 1906.
2. *Cricket*, 10 May 1906.
3. *Manchester Courier*, 17 May 1906 .
4. *Cricket*, 17 May 1906.
5. *Cricket*, 24 May 1906.
6. *Cricket*, 24 May 1906.
7. *Cricket*, 31 May 1906.
8. *Cricket*, 14 June 1906.
9. *Cricket*, 21 June 1906.
10. *Gloucester Citizen*, 20 June 1906.
11. *Cricket*, 5 July 1906.
12. *Cricket*, 19 July 1906.
13. *Cricket*, 2 August 1906.
14. *Cricket*, 9 August 1906.
15. *Cricket*, 16 August 1906.
16. *Cricket*, 16 August 1906.
17. Brodribb, *Hit for Six*, p.101.
18. *Cricket*, 23 August 1906.

19. Brian Close, in his first season in first-class cricket, was eighteen when he achieved the feat in 1949.

20. *Athletic News*, 20 August 1906.
21. *Cricket*, 23 August 1906.
22. *Cricket*, 30 August 1906.
23. *Wisden* 1907, p.49.

24. *Wisden* 1907, p.cxxiv.
25. Sandford, *The Final Over*, p.217.
26. Meredith, *The Demon and the Lobster* p.155.
27. *Cricket*, 9 May 1907.
28. *Cricket*, 16 May 1907.
29. *Cricket*, 23 May 1907.
30. *Derby Daily Telegraph*, 22 May 1907.
31. *Cricket*, 30 May 1907.
32. *Cricket*, 13 June 1907.
33. *Cricket*, 27 June 1907.
34. *Cricket*, 4 July 1907.
35. *Cricket*, 11 July 1907.
36. *Cricket*, 18 July 1907.
37. *Cricket*, 25 July 1907.
38. *Cricket*, 25 July 1907.
39. *Cricket*, 1 August 1907.
40. *Cricket* 22 August 1907
41. *Cricket*, 5 September 1907.
42. *Cricket*, 5 September 1907.
43. *Cricket*, 12 September 1907.
44. Brodribb, *Hit for Six*, p.101.
45. Brodribb, *Hit for Six*, p.102.
46. *Wisden* 1908, pp.103-104.

6 Trip to KangarooLand

1. *Manchester Courier*, 21 September 1907.
2. Hart, *Famous Cricketers: JN Crawford*, pp.15 & 16.
3. *Nelson Evening Mail*, 26 October 1907.
4. *Manchester Courier* 21 September 1907
5. Crawford, *Trip to KangarooLand*, pp. 9 & 10.
6. Hobbs, *My Life Story*, p.83.
7. *Cricket*, 19 December 1907.
8. Crawford, *Trip to KangarooLand*, p.12.
9. Crawford, *Trip to KangarooLand*, p.16.
10. *Cricket*, 19 December 1907.
11. *Cricket*, 28 November 1907.
12. *Adelaide Observer*.
13. *Otago Witness*, 27 November 1907.
14. Crawford, *Trip to KangarooLand*, pp.18-19.
15. *Cricket*, 30 January 1908.
16. Quoted in Crawford, *Trip to KangarooLand*, p.19.
17. Crawford, *Trip to KangarooLand*, p.20.
18. Crawford, *Trip to KangarooLand*, p.20.
19. *Cricket*, 30 January 1908.

20. Crawford, *Trip to KangarooLand*, p.22.
21. *Cricket*, 30 January 1908.
22. *Waihi Daily Telegraph*, 18 December 1907.
23. *Cricket*, 30 January 1908.
24. Crawford, *Trip to KangarooLand*, p.26.
25. *Cricket*, 27 February 1908.
26. *Cricket*, 27 February 1908.
27. Crawford, *Trip to KangarooLand*, p.29.
28. Crawford, *Trip to KangarooLand*, p 29.
29. *Cricket*, 27 February 1908.
30. *Dundee Courier*, 2 January 1908.
31. Crawford, *Trip to KangarooLand*, p.33.
32. *Manchester Courier*, 12 February 1908.
33. *Cricket*, 27 February 1908.
34. *Cricket*, 27 February 1908.
35. *The Register* (Adelaide), 11 February 1908.
36. *Cricket*, 26 March 1908.
37. Crawford, *Trip to KangarooLand*, pp.33 & 35.
38. The timeless Sheffield Shield match had run for seven days from 24 to 31 January, albeit with a rest day on Sunday and no play on day 6.
39. *Cricket*, 26 March 1908.
40. Brodribb, *Hit for Six*, pp.103-104.
41. *Cricket*, 16 April 1908.
42. Quoted in Crawford, *Trip to KangarooLand*, p 39.
43. *Evening Post*, 22 February 1908.
44. Trevor, *With the MCC in Australia*, pp.252-253.
45. Crawford, *Trip to KangarooLand*, p.57.

7 The Practical Cricketer

1. *Cricket*, 27 February 1908.
2. Surrey CCC minutes, 6 March 1903.
3. *On and Off the Field*, p.505.
4. Minutes of Special Meeting of the Committee, 14 March 1907.
5. *Wisden* 1908, p.105.
6. Surrey CCC minutes. 3 May 1906, 2 May & 5 September 1907 & 21 April 1908.
7. Bailey, Thorn & Wynne-Thomas, *Who's Who of Cricketers*, p.262.
8. Surrey CCC minutes, 13 April 1908.
9. Surrey CCC minutes, 2 July 1908.
10. *Cricket*, 16 May 1908.
11. *Cricket*, 23 April 1908.
12. *Cricket*, 23 April 1908.
13. *Cricket*, 7 May 1908.
14. *Cricket*, 14 May 1908.
15. *Cricket*, 14 May 1908.

16. *Cricket*, 14 May 1908.
17. *Cricket*, 21 May 1908.
18. *Cricket*, 28 May 1908.
19. *Cricket*, 11 June 1908.
20. *Dundee Courier*, 15 June 1908.
21. Mark Ramprakash and Azhar Mahmood added 318 for the fifth wicket against Middlesex at The Oval.
22. *Cricket*, 11 June 1908.
23. *Cricket*, 18 June 1908 & 23 July 1908.
24. *Wisden* 1909, pp.46 & 47.
25. Leveson Gower, *Off and On the Field*, pp.84 & 85.
26. *Manchester Courier*, 17 November 1908.
27. *Daily Mirror*, 18 November 1908.
28. Quoted in *Cricket*, 23 May 1907.
29. Crawford, *The Practical Cricketer*, pp.60 & 69.
30. Crawford, *The Practical Cricketer*, pp.72 & 74.
31. 'Special Article No 4: The Art of Bowling – JN Crawford', *Star* (Canterbury), 9 October 1908.
32. Booth, *Walter Read: A Class Act*, p.114.
33. Barlow, *Forty Seasons of First Class Cricket*, p.115.
34. Sewell, *Triangular Cricket*, p.23.
35. Cardus, *JN Crawford: A Most Gifted Cricketer*.
36. Crawford, *The Practical Cricketer*, p.31.
37. Crawford, *The Practical Cricketer*, pp.20 & 22.
38. Crawford, *The Practical Cricketer*, p 31.
39. Shillinglaw, *Bradman Revisited*, p.10.
40. *Derby Daily Telegraph*, 26 June 1909.
41. *Burnley Express*, 26 June 1909.
42. *Cricket*, 27 May 1909.
43. *Cricket*, 25 November 1909.
44. *New Zealand Herald*, 14 August 1909.
45. *Otago Witness*, 10 November 1909.
46. *Cricket* 20 May 1909
47. *Surrey Mirror*, 25 May 1909.
48. *Cricket*, 27 May 1909.
49. *Cricket*, 3 June 1909.
50. *Cricket*, 8 July 1909.

8 Schism

1. *Cricket*, 18 July 1907.
2. There was an additional fixture, played at the same time as the Lancashire match at The Oval, against Oxford University at Reigate (v Keith Walmsley's *Double Headers*) for which John Shuter was brought out of retirement to captain the side. It was lost by an innings and 98 runs.

3. President's Statement, 2 March 1900.
4. *Sporting Life*, 1 July 1909.
5. *Fielding Star*, 17 July 1909.
6. *Cricket*, 22 July 1909.
7. *Cricket*, 29 July 1909
8. *Daily Express*, 20 July 1909.
9. Ferriday, *Before the Lights Went Out*, p.309.
10. *Wisden* 1910, pp.142.
11. *Cricket*, 12 August 1909.
12. *Surrey Mirror*, 20 August 1909.
13. *Hereford Times*, 21 August 1909.
14. *Oamaru Mail*, 12 August 1909.
15. Surrey CCC minutes, 16 September 1909.
16. *Cricket*, 19 August 1909.
17. *Cricket*, 26 August 1909.
18. *Cricket*, 16 September 1909.
19. *Cricket*, 28 October 1909.
20. *Cricket*, 28 October 1909.
21. Surrey CCC minutes, 16 December 1909 & 20 January 1910.
22. *Cricket*, 9 September 1909.
23. Sissons, *The Players*, p.183.
24. *Cricket*, 12 May 1910.
25. Pollard, *The Complete Illustrated History of Australian Cricket*, p.182.
26. Green, *A History of Cricket*, p.152.

9 Return to KangarooLand

1. *Cricket*, 25 November 1909.
2. *Hereford Times*, 6 November 1909.
3. *Sporting Life*, 29 October 1909.
4. *West Australian*, 3 December 1909.
5. Harte, *A History of the South Australian Cricket Association*, p.202.
6. *New Zealand Herald*, 12 November 1909.
7. *Cricket*, 27 January 1910.
8. *Cricket*, 27 January 1910.
9. *Athletic Sports*, 18 November 1909.
10. *Cricket*, 24 February 1910.
11. *Brisbane Courier*, 21 December 1909.
12. *Cricket*, 24 February 1910.
13. *Cricket*, 24 February 1910.
14. In the seventeen seasons from 1907/08 to 1923/24 East Torrens took the premiership on fifteen occasions, including nine consecutive ones.
15. *The Register* (Adelaide), 21 March 1910.
16. *Cricket*, 12 May 1910.
17. *Wisden* 1911, p.24.

18. Surrey CCC minutes, 16 June & 15 September 1910 & *Cricket*, 14 July 1910.
19. *Cricket*, 15 September 1910.
20. *Cricket*, 24 November 1910.
21. *West Australian*, 13 June 1910.
22. Surrey CCC minutes, 21 July 1910.
23. *The Register* (Adelaide), 16 July 1910.

10 Seasons in the Sun

1. *Wisden* 1912, p.511.
2. *Cricket*, 22 December 1910.
3. *Cricket*, 26 January 1911.
4. *Cricket*, 26 January 1911.
5. *Otago Daily Times*, 1 December 1910.
6. *The Register* (Adelaide), 11 March 1911.
7. *Advertiser* (Adelaide), 27 February 1911.
8. *Daily Herald*, 10 September 1911.
9. Moyes, *A Century of Cricketers*, pp.69-72.
10. *Advertiser* (Adelaide), 4 March 1911
11. Hart, *Famous Cricketers: JN Crawford*, p.25.
12. *St Peter's School Magazine*, December 1909, May 1911 and August 1911.
13. *Advertiser* (Adelaide), 1 June 1911.
14. *The Register* (Adelaide), 17 August 1911.
15. *The Register* (Adelaide), 25 April 1911.
16. *Advertiser* (Adelaide), 30 November 1911.
17. *Cricket*, 23 November 1911.
18. *Wisden* 1913, p.566.
19. *The Register* (Adelaide), 7 November 1911.
20. *Daily Herald*, 21 November 1911.
21. Hart, p.26.
22. *Cricket*, 28 December 1911.
23. Hobbs, *My Life Story*, p.137.
24. Harte, *A History of the South Australian Cricket Association*, p.210.
25. *Wairarapa Daily Times*. 12 December 1911.
26. *The Register* (Adelaide), 5 February 1912.
27. *The Register* (Adelaide), 19 February 1912.
28. *Chronicle* (Adelaide), 8 June 1912.
29. *Advertiser* (Adelaide) and *The Register* (Adelaide), 16 July 1912.
30. *New Zealand Truth*, 2 November 1912.
31. *Kalgoorlie Miner*, 26 October 1912.
32. Brodribb, *Hit for Six*, p.10.
33. Moyes, *A Century of Cricketers*, pp 69-72.
34. *Daily Herald*, 4 September 1912.
35. *Referee* (Sydney), 4 December 1912 & 18 December 1912.
36. *Daily Herald*, 3 February 1913.

37. *Sydney Morning Herald*, 17 & 24 February 2013 & *Wanganui Chronicle*, 6 March 1913.
38. *Register* (Adelaide), 10 March 1913.
39. *Barrier Miner*, 2 April 1913.
40. *Register* (Adelaide), 21 April 1913.
41. Thomas, *Glenelg District Cricket Club 1907-2013, Heroes, Memories and Legends.*
42. *Advertiser* (Adelaide), 15 March 1927
43. *Auckland Star*, 26 April 1913.

11 Play Ball

1. *New Zealand Herald*, 23 April 1913.
2. Ferriday, *Before the Lights Went Out*, pp.292-98.
3. *Wairarapa Daily Times*, 18 April 1913 & *The Mail* (Adelaide), 2 August 1913.
4. *New Zealand Herald*, 26 April 1913.
5. *Honolulu Star-Bulletin*, 22 May 1913.
6. *Honolulu Star-Bulletin*, 21May 1913.
7. *Sydney Morning Herald*, 24 June 1913.
8. *The Sun* (New York), 22 June 1913.
9. *New York Tribune*, 5 July 1913
10. *Sydney Morning Herald*, 22 August 1913.
11. *Advertiser* (Adelaide), 22 December 1928.
12. *Advertiser* (Adelaide), 22 December 1928.
13. *Honolulu Star Bulletin*, 8 August 1913.
14. *Advertiser*, 22 December 1928.
15. *The Sun* (New York), 9 August 1913.
16. *Brisbane Courier-Mail*, 27 December 1937. Collins' memory is not quite accurate: the four byes were conceded later in the innings.
17. 13 September 1913.
18. *The Mercury*, 13 September 1913.
19. *Nelson Evening Mail*, 16 September 1913.
20. *New Zealand Herald*, 22 October 1913.

12 Second Schism

1. *Auckland Star*, 3 January 1914.
2. Reese, *New Zealand Cricket 1841-1914*, p.101.
3. *Wairarapa Daily Times*, 3 February 1914.
4. *Auckland Star*, 5 February 1914.
5. *Nelson Evening Mail*, 23 February 1914.
6. *Evening Post* (Wellington), 25 February 1914.
7. *The Sun* (New York), 27 February 1914.
8. *Star* (Canterbury), 2 March 1914.
9. *Wisden* 1964, p.946.
10. *Wisden* 1915, p.513.

11. *Otago Daily Times*, 5 March 1914.
12. *Otago Daily Times*, 6 March 1914.
13. *The Dominion*, 2 April 1914.
14. *The Press* (Christchurch), 6 March 1914.
15. *New Zealand Herald*, 1 April 1914.
16. *Marlborough Express*, 16 March 1914.
17. *Poverty Bay Herald*, 16 March 1914.
18. *Otago Daily Times*, 19 March 1914.
19. *Hawera and Normanby Star*, 28 March 1914.
20. *Oamaru Mail*, 18 April 1914.
21. *Otago Daily Times*, 20 April 1914.
22. *Evening Post* (Wellington), 21 April 1914.
23. *Otago Daily Times*, 22 April 1914.
24. *Otago Daily Times*, 24 April 1914.
25. *Evening Post* (Wellington), 25 April 1914.
26. *Evening Post* (Wellington), 10 June 1914.
27. *New Zealand Free Lance*, 27 June 1914 & *Hawera and Normanby Star*, 11 July 1914.
28. Harte, *The History of the South Australian Cricket Association*, p.216.
29. *Register* (Adelaide), 28 May 1914.
30. They recruited Charlie Macartney, but the advent of war frustrated the appointment.
31. *Register* (Adelaide), 1 October 1914.
32. Millbank, *South Australian Cricket Association 1871-1914*.
33. Millbank, *South Australian Cricket Association 1871-1914*.
34. Harte, *A History of Australian Cricket*, pp.242-243.
35. *Chronicle* (Adelaide), 9 November 1912.
36. *Chronicle* (Adelaide), 23 November 1912, *The Mail* (Adelaide) 24 January 1914 & 14 February 1914.
37. Brooke, *The Fields Were Sudden Bare*, note 44.

13 Frustration

1. *The Press* (Christchurch), 10 June 1914.
2. *The Press* (Christchurch), 5 October 1914.
3. *Otago Daily Times*, 7 October 1914.
4. *Otago Daily Times*, 21 August 1914.
5. *Otago Daily Times*, 22 October 1914.
6. *Otago Daily Times*, 29 October 1914.
7. *Evening Post* (Wellington), 2 November 1914.
8. *Otago Daily Times*, 12 November 1914.
9. *Sporting and Sports*, 3 December 1914.
10. *Otago Daily Times*, 21 December 1914.
11. *Otago Daily Times*, 14 January 1915.
12. *Otago Daily Times*, 18 December 1914.
13. *Auckland Star*, 14 November 1914.
14. *Otago Daily Times*, 7 January 1915.

15. *Otago Daily Times*, 26 November 1914.
16. *Otago Daily Times*, 28 May 1915 & 15 July 1915.
17. *Otago Daily Times*, 13 November 1914 & 14 November 1914.
18. *Otago Daily Times*, 11 March 1915.
19. *Otago Daily Times*, 6 February 1915.
20. *Otago Daily Times*, 9 May & 30 May 1917 & *Observer*, 16 June 1917.
21. *Otago Daily Times*, 29 March 1914.
22. *Chronicle* (Adelaide), 15 May 1915.
23. *Otago Daily Times*, 8 April 1915
24. *Evening Post* (Wellington), 24 April 1915.
25. *Auckland Star*, 12 February 1916.
26. *Otago Daily Times*, 3 March 1916.
27. Sullivan, 'Crawford: the Missing Years', *Wisden Cricket Monthly.*
28. *Auckland Star*, 16 September 1916.
29. *Auckland Star*, 28 October 1916.
30. High Court of Justice minutes, Probate, Divorce and Admiralty Division.
31. *Auckland Star*, 7 October 1916, *Maoriland Worker*, 18 October 1916 & *Auckland Star*, 28 October 1916.
32. *Auckland Star*, 2 December 1916.
33. Army Record.

14 In the Army

1. *Daily Mirror*, 17 April 1919.
2. New Zealand Army Record.
3. *Daily Mirror*, 5 August 1919.
4. 5 October 1916.
5. *New Zealand Free Lance*, 10 November 1916.
6. *New Zealand Free Lance*, 24 November 1916.
7. *Auckland Star*, 20 October 1917.
8. *New Zealand Free Lance*, 16 November 1917.
9. *New Zealand Free Lance*, 30 November 1917.
10. *New Zealand Free Lance*, 15 February 1918.
11. *New Zealand Free Lance*, 14 March 1918.
12. *New Zealand Free Lance*, 21 March 1918.
13. *New Zealand Free Lance*, 28 March 1918 and *The Dominion*, 20 April 1918.
14. *Evening Post* (Wellington), 24 September 1917.
15. New Zealand Army Record.
16. Lawson, *Historic Trentham 1914-1917*, pp.37-38.
17. New Zealand Army Nominal Rolls.
18. Hansen's diary, 10 July 1918.
19. Hansen's diary, 26 August, 2 September & 5 September.
20. *Hawera and Normanby Star*, 11 December 1918.
21. Carbery, *The New Zealand Medical Service in the Great War.*
22. Hart, *Famous Cricketers: JN Crawford*, p.34.

15 Back to Blighty

1. *The Press* (Christchurch), 7 December 1918.
2. Surrey Cricket Committee minutes, 6 January 1919.
3. Surrey Committee minutes, 16 January 1919.
4. *Cricket*, 11 February 1919.
5. *Daily Mirror* 17 April 1919.
6. *Observer*, 13 January 1917.
7. Surrey Committee minutes, 15 May & 5 June 1919.
8. *The Times*, 5 July 1919.
9. *Daily Express*, 2 August 1919.
10. *Brisbane Courier Mail*, 27 December 1937. Collins' memory is less than 100% accurate. The match was in 1919, not 1921 and it was the AIF, not the Australians. He opened the bowling with Gregory and bowled 24 overs against Gregory's 26. They had four wickets each.
11. *Daily Express*, 4 August 1919.
12. *The Times*, 12 August 1919.
13. Lemmon, *'Tich' Freeman and the Decline of the Leg-Break Bowler*, p.27.
14. Palgrave, *The Story of the Oval*, p.38.
15. *Wisden* 1920, p.81.
16. *The Times*, 2 September 1919.
17. Surrey Cricket Committee minutes, 8 January 1920.
18. Surrey Cricket Committee minutes, 11 March 1920.
19. *Referee*, 1 September 1920.
20. *The Times*, 21 May 1921.
21. *The Mail* (Adelaide), 18 June 1921.
22. *The Times*, 1 July 1921.

16 Going Bananas

1. *Lancashire Daily Post*, 7 July 1920.
2. *Lancashire Daily Post*, 14 July 1920.
3. *Burnley Express and Advertiser*, 28 July & 7 August 1920.
4. *Lancashire Evening Post*, 16 July 1920.
5. *Lancashire Evening Post*, 10 July 1920.
6. *Lancashire Evening Post*, 12 July 1920.
7. *Lancashire Daily Post*, 24 May 1920.
8. *Burnley News*, 2 July 1921.
9. *The Times*, 1 July 1921.
10. *Burnley News*, 5 June 1920.
11. He later played a dozen first-class matches for Lancashire as a professional.
12. *Lancashire Evening Post*, 21 September 1920.
13. *The Cricketer*, various issues 1921.
14. *The Times*, 8 May 1922.

15. *Wimbledon Boro' News* 12 May 1922.
16. *The Times*, 15 May 1922.
17. *The Times*, 29 May 1922.
18. *The Times*, 20 August 1923 & 16 August 1926.
19. *The Times*, 24 May 1926 & 25 September 1929.
20. *The Cricketer*, 30 June 1923.
21. *The Cricketer*, 24 May 1924.
22. *The Cricketer*, 26 July 1924.
23. *The Cricketer*, 29 May 1926.
24. *Wimbledon Boro' News*, 20 August 1926.
25. *Wimbledon Boro' News*, 24 September 1926.
26. *Western Daily Press*, 13 July 1929.
27. Possibly the WF Long who later opened the bowling for Moseley in the Birmingham League.
28. Arthur Stockley was the Company's Chief Executive from 1901 to 1931.
29. Hart, *Famous Cricketers: JN Crawford*, p.3 & *The Cricketer*, 23 May 1931.
30. *Fyffes Staff Budget*, December 1952.

17 End of the Road

1. *Chronicle* (Adelaide), 28 July 1923.
2. *Daily Mirror*, 24 July 1923.
3. *Evening Post* (Wellington), 10 September 1923.
4. Her address was changed on Crawford's New Zealand Army Record from 4 Clarke Street, Dunedin to 143 Beulah Road, Norwood, Adelaide.
5. *The Mail* (Adelaide), 16 February 1924.
6. Shipping Passenger Lists.
7. *Barrier Miner* (Broken Hill), 21 February 1924.
8. *Auckland Star*, 11 March 1924.
9. *Western Daily Press*, 29 March 1924.
10. *Auckland Star*, 7 July 1924.
11. *Australian Dictionary of National Biography*.
12. Marriage certificate.
13. *Daily Mirror*, 25 August 1922.
14. *Wimbledon Boro' News*, 25 August 1922.
15. *Medical News Today*, 29 September 2007.
16. *Wimbledon Boro' News*, 4 June 1926.
17. *Nottingham Evening Post*, 11 August 1925.
18. *The Citizen* (Gloucester), 12 August 1925.
19. *The Times*, 19 August 1925.
20. Crawford, *Trip to KangarooLand*, p.10.
21. *Wimbledon Boro' News*, 7 March 1935.
22. Hart, *Famous Cricketers: JN Crawford*, p.3.
23. Simon Barnes, *The Times*, 10 January 2014.

Schism Correspondence

1. Nothing to do with the political scandal later in the century, but correspondence contemporary with that of Alverstone and Crawford between the Duke of Norfolk and a parliamentary candidate alleged to have been a breach of parliamentary privilege. It would have been familiar to *Punch*'s readers at the time.
2. Imre Kiralfy organised spectacles at Olympia, Earl's Court and founded White City in 1908.

REV J.C. CRAWFORD [illegible]
Kent & Surrey
father of V.F.S. & T.H.

LONDON COUNTY ASYLUM,

CANE HILL, PURLEY, R.S.O.

Surrey Sept. 30. 1897.

My dear Sir,

My boy, V.F.S. has this season made over 3100 runs, besides taking 160 wickets. Can you inform me, from your extensive store of knowledge, whether any one has made more runs than this in any sort of cricket in one season? I fancy W. W. Read made 3000 one year, but am not quite sure. [illegible] Walker [illegible] thinks you might be able to enlighten me.

With kind regards, believe me,

Yours faithfully,

John C. Crawford.

I have enclosed you a slip which may interest you as you are fond of "cricket doings". [illegible] told me the other day at Hastings that the [illegible] of the first [illegible] of Between [illegible] the Gentlemen v. Players, in the presence of [illegible]

courtesy of John McKenzie

1897 letter from Rev JC Crawford
about Frank's achievements on the cricket field

BIBLIOGRAPHY

Books

Australian Dictionary of National Biography
Bailey, Philip; Thorn, Philip & Wynne-Thomas, Peter, *Who's Who of Cricketers* (Guild Publishing, 1984).
Barlow, RG, *Forty Seasons of First Class Cricket* (John Heywood, 1908).
Beal, Clifford, *Parkin to Pepper.*
Beaver, Patrick, *Yes! We Have Some: The Story of Fyffes* (Publications for Companies, 1976).
Booth, Keith, *The Father of Modern Sport: The Life and Times of Charles W Alcock* (Parr's Wood, 2002).
—, *Walter Read: A Class Act* (ACS, 2011).
Brodribb, Gerald, *Hit for Six* (Heinemann, 1960).
Burns, Michael, *A Flick of the Fingers: The Chequered Life and Career of Jack Crawford* (Pitch, 2015).
Carbery AD, *The New Zealand Medical Service in the Great War* (Whitcombe and Tombs, 1924).
Cowley, Brian (ed.), *Surrey First-Class Records 1846-2000* (Surrey County Cricket Club, 2001).
Crawford, JN, *Trip to KangarooLand* (Cricket Offices, 1909).
—, *The Practical Cricketer* (Health and Strength, 1909).
Ferriday, Patrick, *Before the Lights Went Out: The 1912 Triangular Tournament* (Von Krumm, 2011).
Frith, David, *The Golden Age of Cricket* (Lutterworth, 1978).
—, *Pageant of Cricket* (Macmillan, 1987).
Green, Benny, *A History of Cricket* (Guild Publishing, 1988).
Hart, Nigel, *Famous Cricketers: JN Crawford*, ed. by Whimpress, Bernard (ACS, 2003).
Harte, Chris, *A History of Australian Cricket* (André Deutsch, 1993).

—, *The History of the South Australian Cricket Association* (Sports Marketing, 1990).
Hobbs, JB, *My Cricket Memories* (Heinemann, 1924).
—, *My Life Story* (The Star, 1935).
Knowles, Ray, *South Africa versus England: A Test Cricket History* (New Holland, 1995).
Lambert, Dennis, *The History of Leicestershire County Cricket Club* (Helm, 1992).
Lawson, Will, *Historic Trentham 1914-1917: The Story of a New Zealand Military Training Camp and Some Account of the Daily Round of the Troops within the Bounds* (Wellington, 1917).
Lemmon, David, *'Tich' Freeman and the Decline of the Leg-Break Bowler* (George Allen & Unwin, 1982).
Leveson Gower, Sir Henry, *On and Off the Field* (Stanley Paul and Co, 1953).
Lodge, Jerry, *100 Surrey Greats* (Tempus, 2003).
Macartney, Charles, *My Cricketing Days* (Heinemann, 1930).
McKinstry, Leo, *Jack Hobbs: England's Greatest Cricketer* (Yellow Jersey, 2011).
Meredith, Antony, *The Demon and the Lobster* (Kingswood, 1987).
Millbank, Susan I, *South Australian Cricket Association, Cricket and South Australia, 1871-1914* (Flinders University, 1981).
Monro, FRD'O, *Repton Cricket 1901-1951* (George Over, 1953).
Moyes, AG, *A Century of Cricketers* (George G Harrap & Co, 1950).
Palgrave, Louis, *The Story of the Oval* (Cornish Brothers, 1949).
Parkin, Cecil, *Cricket Triumphs and Troubles* (C Nicholls & Co, 1936).
Pollard, Jack, *The Complete Illustrated History of Australian Cricket* (Pelham, 1992).
Reese, TW, *New Zealand Cricket 1841-1914* (Simpson and Williams, 1927).
Robertson-Glasgow, RC, *More Cricket Prints* (T Werner Laurie, 1948).
Sandford, Christopher, *The Final Over: The Cricketers of Summer 1914* (Spellmount, 2014).
Sewell, EHD, *Triangular Cricket* (JM Dent, 1912).
Shillinglaw, AL, *Bradman Revisited: The Legacy of Sir Donald Bradman* (Parr's Wood, 2003).
Sinclair, Upton (ed.), *The Cry for Justice: An Anthology of the Literature of Social Protest* (John C Winston Co, 1915).
Sissons, Ric, *The Players: A Social History of the English Professional Cricketer* (Kingswood, 1988).
Surrey County Cricket Club Minutes and Yearbooks
Trevor, Philip, *With the MCC in Australia 1907/08* (Alston Rivers, 1908).
Thomas, Cliff, *Glenelg District Cricket Club 1907 - 2013, Heroes, Memories and Legends* (Openbook Howden, 2014).
Walmsley, Keith, *Double Headers* (ACS, 2013).
Wisden Cricketers' Almanack
Wisden's Cricketers' Note Book

Articles

Cardus, Neville, 'JN Crawford – a Most Gifted Cricketer', *Wisden Cricket Monthly*, July 1963.
Holmes, Norma, 'Cane Hill Hospital', *Bourne Society Local History Records*, Vol 63 May 2010.
Packham, Roger, 'The Crawfords of Cane Hill', *Bourne Society Local History Records*, Vol XIII 1974.
—, 'The Sweet Harmony of the Crawfords', *Bourne Society Local History Records*, Vol XVIII 1979.
Sullivan, Jim, 'Crawford: The Missing Years', *Wisden Cricket Monthly*, March 1992.
Trumble, Robert, 'JN Crawford: A Wasted Talent', *Journal of the Cricket Society*, Autumn 2001.
Whimpress, Bernard, 'JN Crawford: Some Unanswered Questions', *Cricket Lore*, Vol 5.5, December 2003.

Newspapers and Magazines

Aberdeenshire Journal, Aberdeen Daily Journal, Adelaide Observer, Advertiser (Adelaide), Athletic Sports, Auckland Star, Barrier Miner (Broken Hill), *Brisbane Courier, Burnley Express, Burnley Express and Advertiser, Chronicle (Adelaide), The Citizen* (Gloucester), *Cricket, a Weekly Record of the Game, The Cricketer, Daily Citizen, Daily Express, Daily Mail, Daily Mirror, Daily News* (Perth), *Daily Telegraph, Derby Daily Telegraph, The Dominion, Dundee Courier, Evening Post* (Angus), *Evening Post* (Wellington), *Fielding Star, Hawera and Normandy Star, Hereford Times, Honolulu Star-Bulletin, Indian Pioneer, Journal of the Cricket Society, Kalgoorlie Miner, The Mail* (Adelaide), *Manchester Courier, Manchester Daily Post, Manchester Evening News, Manchester Evening Post, Maoriland Worker, Marlborough Express, Merton Parish Magazine, The Mercury, Nelson Evening Mail, Newcastle Mining Herald, New York Tribune, New Zealand Herald, New Zealand Free Lance, Northern Miner, Nottingham Evening Post, Oamaru Mail, Otago Daily Times, Otago Witness, Queensland Times, Philadelphia American, Poverty Bay Herald, The Press* (Christchurch), *Referee* (Sydney), *The Register* (Adelaide), *Repton Register, Reynold's News, Sporting Life, Sporting Times, Star* (Canterbury), *The Sun* (New York), *Sunday Times* (Perth), *Surrey Mirror and Advertiser, Sutton Advertiser, Sydney Morning Herald, The Sportsman, The Times* (London), *Waihi Daily Telegraph, Wairarapa Daily Times, West Australian, Western Daily Press, Wimbledon Boro News and Merton and District Advertiser, Wisden Cricket Monthly, Yorkshire Post.*

Websites

Ancestry, Australian Newspapers online, British Newspaper Archive, Cricket Archive, Cricket Canada, Papers Past, United States Newspapers Online.

Index

Abel, William 228
Adelaide Oval 68-69, 127, 135, 139-143, 164, 168, 180, 184
Alcock, Charles 45, 53, 82-83, 285
Alverstone, Lord Richard 83, 86, 103, 106-107, 112, 114-116, 129, 137, 210
Armstrong, Warwick 31, 72-73, 139, 168, 170, 172, 218, 227
Arnold, EG 42
Arnott, PS 150, 152, 157, 162

Bardsley, W 122, 152, 156-157, 160, 162
Barnes, Sydney 63, 66, 71, 78, 138, 141, 225, 240
Bird, Morice 101, 104, 114, 137
Blythe, Colin 36, 39, 42, 49, 56, 58, 63, 66, 74
Bonnor, George 214
Braund, Len 25, 42, 66, 69, 71

Campbell, GC 152, 157, 160, 162
Cane Hill Asylum 1-4, 6-7, 86, 88, 129, 209, 237
Carisbrook 184-185, 187, 189, 191-192, 194, 196
Chinnery, Harry 85, 210
Collins, Herbie 73, 152, 161-162, 169-170, 213, 241-242
Cotter, Albert 72-73, 138
County Championship 14, 30, 43, 46-48, 51, 54, 86, 89, 103, 113, 215, 286
Crawford, Alice (mother) 3-4, 120-121, 238
Crawford, Andrew (grandfather) 2, 236-237
Crawford, Anita (first wife) 181-182, 192-193, 205, 231-234, 243
Crawford, Audrey (sister) 2, 6, 9, 160, 209, 238
Crawford, Beatrice Lesley (sister) 2, 4
Crawford, Edith (sister) 2-3, 7-8, 120, 209, 238, 244
Crawford, Hilda (second wife) 235, 238, 239, 240

Crawford, Jack
- birth 2
- bowling technique 91-93, 188
- death 240
- divorce 196, 231-232, 243-244
- marriage 192-193
- military enlistment 196-197, 198-200
- singing 130, 143, 180, 191
- split with South Australia 175-179, 244
- split with Surrey 105-110, 242
- Test debut 36

Wisden Cricketer of the Year 52
youngest Surrey centurion 29
youngest Surrey double centurion 88

Crawford, Marjorie (sister) 2, 8, 238
Crawford, Reginald (brother) 2, 4-5, 7-9, 12, 14-15, 24, 85-86, 89, 91, 111, 120-121, 129, 200, 209, 237-238
Crawford, Rev John Charles (father) 2-9, 24, 47, 55, 65, 84, 114-115, 120-121, 129, 143, 171, 216, 228, 237-239
Crawford's Colts 89, 172, 186-189, 191-193
Crawford, Vivian Frank (brother) 2, 4-7, 9, 12, 14-15, 21-22, 24, 26-27, 48, 50, 53, 64, 77, 85, 89-90, 110, 120-121, 129, 199, 201, 209, 214, 235, 237-240

Dalmeny, Lord Harry 20, 23, 28-31, 43-46, 48-49, 52, 54-55, 59, 81-84, 86-87, 242
Darling, Joe 31
Davis, William 27-28, 102, 104
Denton, David 34-36, 39, 51
Derbyshire 47, 51-52, 54, 57, 87, 89, 99, 103-104
Dolling, Charles 172
Ducat, Andrew 99, 104, 213
Dunedin 172-174, 176, 186, 192-197, 201, 205, 211, 231-232
Dunlop Rubber 216, 221

East Torrens 123-124, 127-128, 135-136, 142, 146, 148
Elders and Fyffes 220, 225-229, 242
Essex 39, 44, 54, 58-99, 120

Fane, Frederick 38-39, 66-67, 71-72, 75, 77, 120, 242
Fielder, Arthur 53, 63, 66, 75-76, 78
Findlay, William 53, 55, 60, 82-83, 85, 107, 113
First World War 1, 182, 185, 189, 193, 242
Fishwick, Tom 24
Foster, Reginald 42, 56, 60, 137-138
Fry, CB 12, 19, 42, 98

Gehrs, Algy 132, 144, 167
Gentlemen v Players 48, 57, 217-218, 221, 224
Gilligan, Arthur 224
Glenelg 128, 142, 146-148, 167, 180
Glengorse Preparatory School 4
Gloucestershire 13, 23, 26, 46-47, 55, 87, 89
Goatly, Edward 28, 49, 57, 104
Gooder, Leonard 28
Gordon, John 48
Graburn, WT 15, 82
Grace, WG 3, 48, 52, 54, 70, 85, 241
Gunn, George 66, 75
Gunn, John 6, 51, 57, 60, 138

Haigh, Schofield 33, 35, 36, 37, 39, 51
Hampshire 44, 54, 87, 89, 98
Hardstaff, Joe 66, 69
Harrison, HS 104
Hawke, Lord Martin 8, 33, 98
Hayes, Ernie 31, 45, 47-49, 51-52, 55, 65-66, 78, 89, 104, 108, 210
Hayward, Tom 25, 31, 42, 44, 46-47, 49, 51-52, 54, 56-57, 89, 98-99, 104-105, 120
Hill, Clem 19, 123-127, 132, 134, 137, 141, 144-145, 167, 177, 242
Hirst, George 29, 42-43, 50-51, 92, 97, 224
Hitch, Bill 57, 104-105, 128, 138, 215
Hobbs, Jack 22-23, 29, 44, 48-49, 52, 65, 73, 89-90, 96-97, 99, 103-105, 137, 141, 212-213, 215-216, 228, 239-240
hockey 12, 90, 175, 191, 229
Holland, Fred 45, 49, 58-59, 85, 88
Hordern, HV 137-138
Hornby, AH 31
Humphries, Joe 66, 75-76

Hutchings, Ken 53, 66, 69, 242

Jackson, FS 17, 40, 97
Jephson, Digby 22, 53, 81-82, 213, 242
Jessop, Gilbert 26, 42, 68, 171, 214
Jones, Arthur 65-66, 75, 96, 110, 138

Kelly, James 31
Kensington Wanderers 15
Kent 3-5, 13, 23-24, 26, 30, 39, 48, 53, 57, 59-61, 111, 120, 215-216, 237
Kinneir, Sep 138
Kirk, EC 104-105, 128
Knight, Donald 110, 212-214, 216
Knox, Neville 22, 29, 31, 44, 46, 49, 52, 56, 58, 61, 79, 86, 91

Lancashire 43, 50, 57, 83, 99, 112, 129
Laver, Frank 77, 168
Lees, Walter 25, 29, 31, 35-36, 39, 44, 46-49, 51-52, 54, 56, 58, 61, 85, 99, 102, 104-105, 129
Leicestershire 4, 21-22, 24, 26-28, 30, 44, 46, 55, 89, 91, 129, 148
Leveson Gower, Henry 31, 39, 81-85, 98-102, 104-108, 112, 114, 116, 137, 243
Lilley, Arthur 25, 42, 97
Lohmann, George 23, 26, 33, 50, 78, 113, 214
Lusk, HB 200-202

Macartney, Charles 145, 152, 155, 157-162
MacLaren, Archie 60, 96, 98
Mailey, Arthur 152, 155-158, 162, 170
Malvern College 13-14, 16-18
Marshal, Alan 54, 87, 89, 102-105, 114, 129, 210
Mayne, Edgar 141, 150-153, 157, 161-163
McAlister, PA 73, 99, 133
MCC 3, 6-7, 15, 31, 33-34, 37-40, 51, 59, 63, 67, 70, 77, 107, 119-120, 126, 135, 137, 139-142, 148, 223, 242
McDonell, HC 13, 26
Merton 3, 226-228, 235-236, 238-239
Middlesex 13, 25, 49, 51, 86, 105, 113

New South Wales 71, 76-77, 123-127, 133, 137, 140-141, 144-145, 167-168
Nice, Ernest 27-28
Noble, Monty 31, 97-98, 122, 168, 170
Northamptonshire 29-30, 44, 51, 54, 87, 98
Nottinghamshire 46, 49, 55, 60, 201
Nourse, AD 33, 36-37

Otago 172-176, 178, 185-186, 189-192, 194-195, 200-201, 225, 242, 244
Oval (Kennington) 21, 24, 26, 29-30, 44-50, 54-60, 65, 83-85, 87, 95-96, 99, 105, 110, 112-113, 184, 211-212, 214, 216, 221

Palairet, Lionel 25
Parkin, Cecil 212, 217, 221-225, 240
Pellew, 'Nip' 212-213

Quaife, William 25
Queensland 71-72, 124-125, 182

Ransford, Vernon 122, 133, 168, 170
Raphael, John 23, 26-27, 45-46, 210
Read, Walter 22-23, 33, 53, 92, 113, 241
Repton School 5, 10-19, 21-24, 31, 39, 65, 88, 95, 113, 120, 207, 212, 239
Rhodes, Wilfred 29, 58, 63, 66-67, 96-97, 224, 240
Richardson, Tom 6, 23, 70, 113, 138
Rochdale 216-217, 221-225
Rushby, Tom 51, 55, 99, 102, 104-105, 108, 111-112, 128-129, 210, 212-213

Shacklock, Frank 201
Sharp, Jack 225

Sheffield Shield 123-125, 127, 133, 143-144, 167, 168-169
Sims, Arthur 166, 168-170, 195
Sinclair, James 33, 37
Smith, Sir Keith 232-235, 241
Smith, WC 27, 29, 30, 33, 57, 73, 94, 104, 128, 129, 133
Somerset 25, 88
South Australia 67-69, 119-120, 123-125, 127-129, 132-141, 143-144, 147, 167, 175, 177-182, 189, 193, 213, 225, 234
Spooner, RH 225
Spring, William 104
Steel, AG 17, 52, 69, 111, 148
St Peter's College 111, 121-124, 128, 130, 135-137, 141, 143, 180-181, 212
Strudwick, Herbert 104, 138, 141
St Winifred's School 4-5, 7
Surrey 2-7, 13, 15, 17, 21-29, 31, 39-40, 43-45, 47-55, 57-61, 63-65, 67-68, 73, 78, 81-85, 87-90, 95, 98-117, 119-121, 123, 126-129, 135, 137-138, 168-169, 172, 179, 186, 189, 194, 207, 209-213, 215-216, 218-219, 225-228, 235, 237, 240-243

The Practical Cricketer 64, 81, 91, 95-96
Trentham Camp 200-205
Trip to KangarooLand 34, 63-64, 68, 72, 87, 96, 238
Trumper, Victor 98, 104, 123-124, 137, 145, 153, 155, 166, 168, 170-171, 242
Tyldesley, JT 42

Uppingham School 13-18

Victoria 70, 77, 114, 123-125, 127, 133, 139, 140-142, 144, 168, 201
Vine, Joseph 138
Vogler, Ernie 36

Warner, Pelham 'Plum' 32, 34-40, 50-51, 71, 138, 141, 148, 239
Warwickshire 24, 29, 47, 55-56, 98
Western Australia 66, 144
Whitty, WJ 99, 126, 133, 152, 167
Woods, Sammy 25, 214
Woolley, Frank 48, 59, 137, 240
Worcestershire 48
Wynyard, Teddy 39

Yorkshire 29-31, 34, 36, 39, 43, 48, 50, 58, 97, 115-116, 214-216, 224
Young Amateurs 15, 22, 28, 89
Young, Richard 12, 15, 17, 65-66, 242

Also from Chequered Flag Publishing:

THE FATHER OF MODERN SPORT

THE LIFE AND TIMES OF CHARLES W. ALCOCK

by Keith Booth
Foreword by Sir John Major

SHORTLISTED FOR CRICKET SOCIETY BOOK OF THE YEAR 2002

A model Victorian sporting all-rounder, Charles Alcock was a prime mover in the development of both football and cricket as the world's biggest sports.

As a player, he was the first ever footballer to be ruled offside, the captain of the first FA Cup winners and played club cricket to a high standard.

As Secretary of the FA, Alcock was one of the men responsible for the first ever football international and was the driving force behind the creation of the FA Cup in 1871. In cricket, he arranged the first Test match in Britain, between England and Australia at The Oval in 1880.

Close attention to detail combined with a breadth of vision to change the sporting world - this is the definitive biography of the nineteenth century's most important sports administrator.

Also from Chequered Flag Publishing:

Lahore To London

by Younis Ahmed

Younis Ahmed was a talented middle-order batsman who left his native Pakistan to forge a successful career in cricket around the globe. But he is not remembered for his vibrant batting. Instead it is for moments of controversy: an international ban for touring apartheid-era South Africa, taking Surrey to a tribunal, leaving Worcestershire under a cloud. Now Younis tells his side of the story.

Younis also describes winning the County Championship and Quaid-e-Azam Trophy, replacing Garry Sobers at South Australia at the invitation of Don Bradman, pioneering professionalism and sponsorship in cricket, taking the sport to the Middle East and playing alongside legends including Javed Miandad and Imran Khan.

This is the colourful and chequered story of how one cricketer's journey from Lahore to London took him to the top of the game, but also to the depths rejection and despair.

Also from Chequered Flag Publishing:

THE CHAMPION BAND

The First English Cricket Tour

by Scott Reeves

CRICKET WEB BEST NEW WRITER 2014

In 1859, twelve cricketers left Liverpool to embark on the first overseas tour by a representative England side. Their destination was the place where cricket looked most likely to flourish: Canada and the United States.

It was not an easy trip - the English players experienced death on the high seas, were threatened at gunpoint and sensed unrest in the pre-Civil War USA.

Led by George Parr, the English tourists came up against the best of the New World cricketers. Some of the locals would go on to pioneer the sport that ultimately caused the death of North American cricket: baseball.

A gripping account featuring original research, THE CHAMPION BAND tells the fascinating story of the first English cricket tour.

Printed in Great Britain
by Amazon